Management Control and
Union Power

Management Control and Union Power

A Study of Labour Relations in Coal-mining

CHRISTINE EDWARDS

and

EDMUND HEERY

WITH MARGARET BIRD

CLARENDON PRESS · OXFORD
1989

Oxford University Press, Walton Street, Oxford OX2 6DP
Oxford   New York   Toronto
Delhi   Bombay   Calcutta   Madras   Karachi
Petaling Jaya   Singapore   Hong Kong   Tokyo
Nairobi   Dar es Salaam   Cape Town
Melbourne   Auckland
and associated companies in
Berlin   Ibadan

Oxford is a trade mark of Oxford University Press

Published in the United States
by Oxford University Press, New York

British Library Cataloguing in Publication Data
Edwards, Christine
Management control and union power: a study of
labour relations in coal mining.
1. Great Britain. Coal industries. Industrial
relations, 1974–1987
I. Title II. Heery, Edmund III. Bird, Margaret
331'.0422334'0941
ISBN 0-19-827267-7

Library of Congress Cataloging in Publication Data
Edwards, Christine.
Management control and union power: a study of labor relations in
coal mining/Christine Edwards and Edmund Heery.
p.   cm.
Bibliography: p.   Includes index.
1. Coal miners—Great Britain. 2. Industrial relations—Great
Britain. 3. National Union of Mineworkers. 4. Coal trade—Great
Britain—Management. I. Heery, Edmund. II. Title.
HD6976.M6152G74 1989   331'.0422334'0941—dc 19   88-38708
ISBN 0-19-827267-7

Phototypeset by Dobbie Typesetting Limited,
Plymouth, Devon

Printed in Great Britain
by Biddles Ltd,
Guildford & King's Lynn

For Jeff, Alex, and Dom
and
For Janet and Patrick

Preface

This book represents the culmination of over sixteen years of study of the coal industry, spanning a period starting with the first national victories of the NUM in the early 1970s and finishing with the miners' defeat and the contraction of the industry in the 1980s. The long-term and extensive empirical research which took place over these years was both time-consuming and expensive and was only achieved through considerable financial support. Our first thanks therefore must go to the Economic and Social Research Council (then the SSRC) who supported the first stages of the research and to the National Coal Board who made a generous grant available to replicate and extend the study. Apart from being set some very broad parameters, Christine Edwards was allowed a completely free hand in designing and implementing the research and British Coal has not commented on this text. Consequently, the accuracy of the information presented and the views expressed are the responsibility of the authors alone.

An under-manager interviewed in the course of the research described coalmining as a 'violent and rough-tongued industry'. There is much truth in this description as the events of the 1984/5 strike and the continued tradition of militancy demonstrated. None the less, there is another side, one which is overwhelmingly friendly and which often transcends the underlying conflicts. It is this latter fact, combined with the dedication and interest of all those engaged in coal-mining which made the research both easy and fascinating. Mining people have a strong sense of the drama, history, and resonance of their industry in the life of the nation. This means that the presence of academic researchers is treated almost as natural, and people are willing to relate their experiences and usually strongly held opinions to them. We would like to express our gratitude to all those miners, managers, and trade-unionists who made us so welcome at their pits, areas, and national headquarters and who answered our interminable questions with such patience and good humour. Our thanks also to the administrative staff who assisted our interview programmes, made sure we always had the right size pit-boots and provided a wealth of statistical material; to John Charlton and Roy Harrison for their support and Professor Alan Griffin, Dick Bodley, and the many local and area NUM and NACODS officials and British

Coal managers who, in their private capacities, have commented on our work.

We would also like to thank our friends and colleagues in academic life. Our first debt of gratitude is to Margaret Bird who worked on the 1980–2 study and whose research skills, appetite for work, and enthusiasm were vital to the success of the project. We are most grateful to Rod Martin and John Kelly for their helpful comments on the text. We would also like to express our warm appreciation to Diane Ball for her superb administration and typing and most of all for keeping cheerful despite a less than perfect word-processing system. Finally we would like to thank our partners and children for their tolerance, interest, and support.

C.E. and E.H.

Contents

Abbreviations

BACM	British Association of Colliery Management
BC	British Coal
COSA	Colliery Staff and Officials Area
EFL	External Financing Limit
FIDO	Face Information Digested Online
JSSC	Joint Shop Stewards Committee
MINOS	Mine Operating System
NACODS	National Association of Colliery Overmen, Deputies and Shotfirers
NCB	National Coal Board
NPLA	National Power Loading Agreement
NUM	National Union of Mineworkers
TUC	Trade Unions Congress
UDM	Union of Democratic Mineworkers
WIPS	Weekly Paid Industrial Staff

Introduction

This book is about the process of management control and how it is achieved in coal-mining. In selecting management control and union power as its central themes it acknowledges conflict to be at the heart of the employment relationship. At its starting-point therefore is the view that the interests of management and work-force, although overlapping, are not the same and that securing the co-operation of labour in the process of production will inevitably present problems for management. Thus, although the two parties to the employment contract are interdependent in that management depends on labour for its labour-power and labour on management for its means of subsistence, the exact nature of the exchange is open to conflicting interpretations. For example, the amount of effort or care workers expend in return for their wages, the conditions under which they work, and the obligations they owe to an employer and the employer to them, may all be the subject of disagreement. It is this fact which leads us to a consideration of two core aspects of industrial relations—the processes of control used by management to secure the co-operation or compliance of labour in pursuit of its goals, and the ability of labour to resist management and impose its own terms of exchange on the employment relationship.

The British coal-mining industry provides a fertile testing ground for those who wish to study the problem of managerial control and union power. The nature of coal extraction is such that, despite technological developments, management remains singularly dependent upon the co-operation of the work-force in achieving its goals. Thus, the strategic position of the work-force has favoured the development of strong union power and provides the potential for considerable opposition to management's will. Over most of the period covered in our study, the coalminers' union, the National Union of Mineworkers (NUM) was reputed to be one of the most powerful in Britain. At the inception of the research it had recently emerged victorious from two major confrontations with management in the national strikes of 1972 and 1974. The defeat of the Conservatives under Edward Heath in February 1974 was widely attributed to the miners twice forcing the government into major political retreat. For many, the miners at this time were at the vanguard of the labour movement, symbolizing the victory of the traditional working class against capitalism personified by the Tory Government. This reputation remained with the mineworkers until their devastating defeat in 1985. One of the aims of the book is to analyse systematically the power of the NUM and examine its consequences for the management of labour. Suffice to say here that the presence of this powerful union poses particular problems for management which have stimulated the development and use of a variety of control strategies in the industry and tested their efficacy to the full.

The approach of coal-mining management to the problem of control has been both innovative and thorough, embracing many of the most recent trends in industrial relations management. For example, in 1977 it introduced a carefully regulated group incentive scheme, which had distilled within its rules virtually all the scholarly and received wisdom said to ensure maximum performance while at the same time avoiding many of the dysfunctional consequences associated with systems of payment by results. It has a highly sophisticated computer-based management information system which allows management access to colliery data on a nation-wide basis. It has also applied a variety of control techniques—such as job evaluation and work study and experimented with many motivational devices such as briefing groups, team meetings, and joint consultation. More recently, it has been at the forefront of the attempts to develop more flexible working practices and a more decentralized pattern of public-sector industrial relations. Thus, there is a wealth of experience of most modern management control techniques and strategies within the industry. As we will demonstrate in the chapters which follow there is much to be learned from the coal-mining management's use of these strategies to achieve management control in the face of a well-organized and powerfully placed work-force.

Levels of Analysis

This book describes and analyses the processes involved in the management of British coal-miners. It examines the processes of labour management employed at different levels of the mining industry and attempts to explain why management has selected particular techniques and methods. There is also an attempt to evaluate the success or failure of these methods in management's terms and to review the wider, frequently unanticipated consequences of their adoption. This in turn involves tracing the responses of the work-force and its trade-union representatives to these management initiatives.

The book is divided into five parts, each one devoted to a separate facet of labour management within the industry.

Part I examines management strategy for the control of work from the mid 1960s to the present day. It is argued that the National Coal Board (NCB) used the dissemination of semi-continuous mining techniques throughout the industry in the 1960s, known as powerloading, to develop a new approach to the management of mining labour. The earlier piece-work system was replaced by measured day-work under the National Powerloading Agreement (NPLA), and management sought much greater direction over work and workers at the point of production through the mechanization of operations, through increased supervision, and through greater reliance on work study. Evidence is presented which indicates that this ambition was disappointed in very large degree, prompting management to search for a new means of galvanizing the direct labour-force, for a means of tapping its capacity to work at a higher rate of productivity than that being achieved under the day-wage system. This search eventually found fruition with the introduction of Area Incentive Schemes in 1977/8. These proved effective in halting the downward spiral of the industry's productivity and since then reliance on payment by results, to align management and work-force objectives, has been at the heart of management's strategy for the control of work. Indeed, following the miners' strike of 1984/5 British Coal has successfully attempted to refashion the industry's system of payment by results in order to further accentuate the work-force's financial dependence on the achievement of management's objectives.

Part II considers the Coal Board's attempts to deal with a new problem which emerged with the reintroduction of incentives in the late 1970s. The Area Incentive Schemes, which all conformed to a national blueprint, provided for local bargaining with the NUM over incentive targets. If the schemes were to be effective management instruments it was necessary, not only that they should galvanize work groups, but also that they should not produce a relentless inflation of wage costs. Part II, therefore, describes the techniques used by the Board to control local incentive-scheme bargaining and reviews their effectiveness. A substantial part of this discussion is concerned with the role of the industry's industrial relations managers, who were given responsibility for monitoring local bargaining and for ensuring that the negotiations conducted by their colleagues in line management did not have adverse consequences. It concludes with a description of how British Coal has altered the controls over local wage-bargaining in the wake of the 1984/5 miners' strike.

Part III continues with the focus on colliery-level industrial relations. In this case, though, the object of concern is the workplace union and the extent to which its representative and disciplinary powers can be used by colliery management to facilitate control of the labour-force. It is argued that workplace industrial relations in mining have been characterized by the existence of fairly co-operative bargaining relationships between colliery managers and local branch or lodge representatives, the equivalents of senior shop stewards in other industries. However, the main thrust of the argument developed is that workplace trade-unionism in mining has constituted a rather problematic management resource and that theories of the 'incorporation' or 'bureaucratization' of workplace trade-unionism do not match the situation prevailing in the majority of the industry's pits.

Part IV differs slightly in form from those which precede it. In this case there is no discussion of particular techniques or instruments of labour management. The concern is solely with the extent of the power of the NUM in collieries, its determinants and its consequences for labour management in the industry. Chapters 7 and 8 report the results of two surveys which systematically measured union power over colliery level decision-making, one conducted in the mid 1970s, when the NPLA strategy remained in force, and the other in the early 1980s, when it had been supplanted by reliance on incentives. They present a picture of the 'frontier of control' in mining as it existed at these two points in time. It is concerned, therefore, with the end-product of the various processes described in Parts I, II, and III. The analysis of union power, however, goes beyond the usual examination of the outcomes of management–union bargaining to assess the role of the union in the initial decision-making process, its priorities in relation to decision-making and its influence on colliery decisions which are not the subject of bargaining.

Part IV serves as a summary for the discussion of workplace employment relations in mining which forms the bulk of the book. In Part V the focus of attention is shifted upwards onto the dynamics of employment relations at the national, industrial level. Here, the actors are not union branch secretaries, colliery managers or area industrial relations officials, but government ministers, the chairman of the National Coal Board, and the national officers of the NUM and, latterly, the Union of Democratic Mineworkers (UDM). Part V offers an analytical account of the changing relationships between government, management, and unions in the industry from the waxing of national union strength in the aftermath of the successful 1972 and 1974 strikes to the waning of that strength in the mid 1980s. The discussion contrasts two national industrial relations 'settlements' in mining; that achieved in 1974 when the NUM had sufficient power to develop a wide-ranging 'political exchange' with the state, and that imposed on a gravely weakened NUM in the months after the miners' return to work in March 1985. Linking the description of these settlements is an account of the complex event which permitted the transition from one to the other, the great strike of 1984/5. The purpose of this account is to explain how and why the union lost the capacity to insist that its own interests be incorporated within the basic objectives of the industry.

Theoretical Perspectives

Because each of the parts of the book discusses a different aspect of labour management, each is informed by a different theoretical literature. One of the oddities of contemporary writing on employment relations is that writers from different theoretical traditions tend to select different objects of study. Sociologists who have explored this area, for instance, have tended to concentrate on the organization of work in contributions to what has come to be known as the 'labour-process debate'. Industrial relations scholars, in contrast, have tended to select as their object of study collective bargaining between employers and trade unions, though recently there has been a tendency to concentrate on management policies which determine the structure and dynamics of collective bargaining. Finally, the interfaces between employers, trade unions, and the state have principally been the concern of political scientists, particularly those concerned with the development of 'corporatist' and 'labour movement' theory.

The account of the 'control of work' presented in our first section is informed, in part, by 'labour-process' literature. The NPLA strategy implemented by the NCB in the mid 1960s, for instance, is described in terms of Friedman's (1977) notion of 'direct control'. Management at that time, in its strategy for the organization of work, was committed to reducing its dependence on work-force co-operation for the achievement of its production objectives. This was to be done by replacing workers with machinery (which also reduced management's reliance on traditional mining skills), by specifying the responsibilities of workers with greater clarity in tighter job descriptions, by setting performance standards through work study, and by ensuring the achievement of those standards through increased supervision.

However, our emphasis on the use of payment by results and on the significance of payment-system reform as a means through which management can control work is not shared by labour-process writing. In this body of work there is a tendency to neglect these more 'traditional' labour management techniques in favour of an emphasis on processes of job design; on the detection of 'deskilling' or the emergence of 'flexible specialization'. Part I concludes, in fact, with an attempt to defend our interpretation of developments in work organization in mining, with its emphasis on payment-system reform, from an alternative developed from a position much more securely within the labour-process tradition by writers from the University of Bradford (Burns et al., 1985). The Bradford Group argue that new technology, which is currently being deployed in the mines, is being used to deskill the work-force and achieve a much closer control of the production process. Essentially, their view is that new technology is being used by management in coal-mining to achieve the 'real subordination' of mining labour. In our view, while the introduction of new technology in mining clearly has serious implications, particularly for the numbers of miners to be employed in the future, the Bradford Group has overestimated its capacity for control. Management in mining in the 1980s is committed to continued reliance on incentives and has attempted to reform the remuneration package in order to increase its potential for motivating the workforce. There has also been a growth of management interest in methods of communicating with the work-force and in techniques for stimulating worker 'involvement'. Innovations such as these, we suggest, betoken not so much an anticipation of the 'real subordination' of labour but a conviction that management remains critically dependent on the co-operation of the direct work-force if the productive potential of new microprocessor controlled machinery is to be fully realized.

In Part II the discussion of the other side of incentives in mining, the process of collective bargaining over performance standards at the workplace, is informed by industrial relations theory. A central theme in this body of literature is the variable capacity of industrial relations institutions to regulate successfully conflicts issuing from the employment relation. The structure and character of these institutions have been isolated as crucial variables influencing the level and form of industrial conflict and the relative success of different national economies. Applied to the case of Britain, this argument has tended to produce statements as to the relative incapacity of British industrial relations institutions successfully to regulate conflict. Repeatedly the inadequacy of Britain's industrial relations institutions has been adduced as a major contributory factor to the country's poor economic performance. This was a central message of the Donovan Report, which was published in 1968, with its complaint about the 'disorderly' nature of British industrial relations, particularly at the workplace. More recently, Fogarty, in a conscious attempt to update Donovan's analysis, has referred to the 'failure of managements, unions and the government to follow the lead of a number of other countries towards creating a better "climate of predictability" in industrial relations at enterprise level' (1986, p 24). This is a clear echo of Donovan's diagnosis of 'disorder', and like Donovan, Fogarty claims the consequence of inadequate industrial relations institutions is poor economic performance.

Writers who have shared this diagnosis have tended to propose a number of palliatives for the British industrial relations malaise. Since Donovan a series of prescriptions have been issued for the reform of British industrial relations institutions, particularly at the workplace and enterprise levels. Common to most of these has been an attempt to foster a better 'climate of predictability'. It has been argued that this can be achieved by adopting more formalized and standardized procedures at the workplace, which will clearly specify both the rights of the parties and the negotiating agenda and which will channel conflict along predetermined lines towards non-disruptive solutions. It has also been argued that the same result can be achieved by centralizing industrial relations within the plant or company, so that the power to make agreements is invested in senior workplace trade-union representatives and relatively senior managers. Finally, reform, particularly on the management side, has been said to require greater reliance on specialist labour management techniques, such as job evaluation and work study, and greater reliance on specialist industrial relations managers, equipped with the skills necessary to guide British industry in the direction of reform.

In the late 1970s and early 1980s a number of surveys of British industrial relations institutions indicated that reform on these lines had taken place in many organizations since the Donovan Report was published (Batstone, 1984; Brown, 1981; Daniel and Millward, 1983). Opinion differed, however, as to the effectiveness of reform in furthering the regulation of industrial conflict and producing a better 'climate of predictability' in industrial relations. Some claimed that 'disorder' had been reduced (Brown, 1980); others that it remained a defining characteristic of the British industrial scene (Batstone, 1984). The relevance of this debate to the study of workplace pay-bargaining in the mining industry is that many features of the incentive scheme introduced by the NCB in 1977/8 conform closely to the principles of industrial relations reform adumbrated by scholars in the post-Donovan era. For example, the scheme was based on a strict framework of rules intended to guide and constrain the collective bargaining process at pit level; it was work-study based; deliberate attempts were made to restrict the capacity of supervisors to yield off-the-cuff concessions to work groups; negotiating rights were concentrated in the hands of senior branch officials and colliery managers and the scheme was to be monitored for symptoms of incipient decay by industrial relations staff situated at area headquarters. The value of the research on the coal industry, we feel, is that it provides detailed material on how each of these components of 'reformed', more formalized, industrial relations operates in practice in a major British industry with a tradition of strong workplace trade-unionism. It thus provides a counterweight to the survey-based and necessarily more superficial discussions of the consequences of industrial relations reform which have been published elsewhere.

In Part III the main body of theoretical work used to organize our empirical material is drawn from the vigorous British tradition of 'radical' industrial relations writing. A primary concern of writers within this tradition in recent years has been the impact of industrial relations 'reform' on the organization and functioning of workplace trade-unionism. It is argued that government and employer initiatives in the 1960s and 1970s, which were intended to foster more predictable, less disorderly industrial relations in the workplace, had major consequences for both the form and effectiveness of workplace trade-unionism in British industry. They produced a more centralized and hierarchical form of workplace trade-unionism which was dependent on a 'lay élite' of senior shop stewards and convenors. This change, in its turn, was said to be associated with a downturn in trade-union militancy and the growth of more co-operative relations with employers. In Hyman's phrase the 1970s witnessed a 'bureaucratization of the rank and file' (1979). In his view this was the essential base upon which the Labour Government's experiment in corporatism was constructed and its enfeebling consequences are also said to have muted trade-union opposition to the restructuring of British industry in the 1980s (Terry, 1983b).

At the core of this argument is an attempt to apply the classical Marxist theory of trade-union bureaucracy to workplace trade-unionism. The classical theory rests on the hypothesis that the development of a specialist corps of full-time trade-union officers produces a divergence of interests between 'the bureaucracy', who are removed from the point of production, and the rank-and-file trade-union membership who remain exposed to alienating and exploitative conditions of labour. The function of the bureaucracy in this view is to contain worker discontent arising from the condition of wage labour and to channel its expression into the complex of procedures and institutions which compose the industrial relations system.

In Marxist analyses of British trade-unionism it is frequently argued that the strong tradition of shop steward organization served as a valuable counter to the 'incorporation' practised by the bureaucracy situated beyond the workplace. For writers like Hyman, however, the same divergence of interests between members and representatives which has long been characteristic of the relationship between full-time officials and the rank and file now characterizes many workplace trade union organizations. Senior workplace representatives are said to have developed a particular set of interests arising from their dependence on management support for their position and role. This relation of dependence, it is said, encourages moderation on the part of such representatives and ready co-operation in management's pursuit of more orderly industrial relations at the workplace.

One of the purposes of our research was to test this argument. A 'lay élite' of senior workplace representatives is readily identifiable in mining, and its position has been sponsored by management at least until the 1984 pit strike, through the granting of relatively generous time off work for the performance of union duties and through the provision of office and other facilities. The empirical material presented in the two chapters is used to examine the extent of the workplace leadership's independence from the membership and to establish the nature of its objectives and interests. It is concluded on the basis of our evidence that the 'bureaucratization' thesis cannot satisfactorily account for the activities of the 'lay élite' or the dynamics of workplace trade-unionism in coal-mining.

The theoretical literature which informs our fourth section is that concerned with trade-union power. This literature addresses three main issues. In the first case it is concerned with the conceptualization of trade-union power, and with establishing a standard for its measurement. Debate on these questions has been structured by more abstract controversies over the general nature of power in social relationships (Lukes, 1974; Baratz and Bacharach, 1962, 1970; Hindess, 1982). Studies of trade-union power have typically employed a conflict model of power, assessing the ability of each party to get their own way in the face of opposition. Assessments which focus solely on the outcomes of conflict, however, have been subject to considerable criticism on the grounds that they ignore the wider institutional and ideological structures within which bargaining takes place. Thus, writers such as Fox (1974) and Hyman (1979) argue that the outcomes of management–union bargaining merely represent marginal adjustments in an overall structure of inequality in which management dominates. These arguments often appear to deny the validity of empirical power research (see especially Hyman, 1979). Nevertheless, we would reject this view, arguing that while any claims to measurement of the overall balance of power between management and unions on the basis of empirical data may be invalid, it is none the less possible to assess aspects of union power in respect to specific decisions (see also Lukes, 1974; Edwards, 1983). A methodology for power measurement and analysis is proposed, therefore, which attempts to take into account at least some of the processes which constrain union power in the workplace. The data are also used to illustrate the significance of the way in which power is conceptualized and measured for the interpretation of management–union relations.

A second preoccupation of the literature on trade-union power lies with the determinants of the capacities of unions to realize their objectives. This involves accounting for variations in power between different union organizations. Some research has focused on the initial structural characteristics of the union itself (as in the case of theories of trade-union bureaucracy) or on factors such as leadership style and the bargaining relationship with management (Batstone et al., 1977). Others have considered such matters as membership size, union density, or the product market (Poole, 1976, Batstone and Gourlay, 1986). The tendency has been to select a narrow range of potential factors for study rather than to attempt a comprehensive explanation of differences in power capacities. In this study, however, we cast our net wider drawing on the work of organization theorists and political scientists as well as industrial relations scholars in our attempts to explain variation in union power in the workplace. In doing so we investigate a considerable number of organizational and environmental factors to ascertain which are the most important.

The final issue which is addressed in the literature on trade-union power, and which is discussed in Part IV, is the power of trade unions in the context of high unemployment. Here discussion has focused on the extent to which the lengthening of the dole queues has sapped union strength. A major concern of this debate has been with the impact of recession on the power of workplace trade union representatives (Batstone and Gourlay, 1986; Kelly, et al. 1987; Terry, 1986). We conclude our discussions therefore by using our power analysis to assess the vulnerability of the power of the NUM in the workplace to erosion through a slackening of the labour market.

Considerations of the determinants of trade-union power also influence the account of developments in national industrial relations in mining in the fifth and final section of the book. An important element in this account is an attempt to explain why the NUM was unable to maintain the relatively favourable exchange it achieved with government in the 1970s in the harsher environment of the 1980s. The strike of 1984/5 revealed that there had been a significant reduction in the capacity of the national union to force government to treat with it and accept its priorities. In analysing this change use is made of a framework for examining trade-union power developed by Erik Olin Wright (1984). Wright argues that there are two components of trade-union power. On the one hand there is 'positional power', the ability of unions to inflict disruption through industrial action, while on the other there is 'organizational power', the capacity of trade union leaders actually to deploy the disruptive potential of their members.

In Part V this framework is used to analyse the process of transition from the 1974 settlement in mining, when the NUM achieved a favourable political exchange with government, to the 1985 settlement, when the union was largely excluded from strategic influence over the industry's development. It is argued that the course of the 1984/5 strike revealed significant reductions in both the 'positional' and the 'organizational' power of the NUM. Compared to many other unions the NUM remained well-endowed with both elements of power in 1984 and was able to call the majority of its membership out on a year-long strike which inflicted serious damage on the economy. Compared with the situation in 1972 and 1974, however, there had been significant changes. Despite the length of the dispute British industry remained virtually unaffected by power-cuts, indicating reduction in the 'positional power' of the miners. And the union itself was divided, with substantial numbers of miners continuing to work throughout the strike, indicating a reduction in its 'organizational power'.

Wright's framework for analysing trade-union power is used to guide the description of the 1984/5 strike, the passage of transition from the 1974 settlement to that of the late 1980s. In attempting to typify each of these settlements we make use of the literature on state–trade union relations. The period from 1974 to the early 1980s is described as one of 'sectional corporatism' in mining. It was distinguished by a fairly extensive exchange between government and union in which the latter was given access to strategic decision-making in return for co-operation with the Social Contract incomes policy and with management's attempts to raise productivity through the reintroduction of incentives. The main threat to the continuation of this exchange in the 1970s came from the NUM's powerful left wing which was committed to a policy of 'militant independence'. At the core of this was a rejection of compromise with either government or the National Coal Board in favour of the continual deployment of the miners' disruptive strength to extract a widening range of concessions. The NUM left, however, never succeeded in breaking or transcending the political exchange established in 1974. Instead, this was eventually done by Mrs Thatcher's Conservative Government. The Conservative's entered government in 1979 with a deep antipathy to public sector trade-unionism in general and to the National Union of Mineworkers in particular. In their eyes the exchange with the NUM required the state to incur costs out of all proportion to the benefits. Permitting the union to exercise influence over the industry's strategic management, they felt, had led to an escalating public subsidy of coal-mining and an inefficient use of resources. In order to reduce the burden of the industry on the economy at large and in order to rationalize its operations, therefore, the Conservative Government resolved that the exchange with the NUM must be repudiated and the union's influence sharply reduced. The defeat of the NUM in the 1984/5 strike permitted both of these objectives to be very largely achieved.

The post-strike settlement in mining is described as approximating to Crouch's notion of 'labour exclusion' (1985). Although trade-union organization remains firmly embedded in the industry and though management remains committed to the joint regulation of miners' wages and conditions, there has been a successful attempt to push back the scope of union influence. At the industry's core, trade-union priorities, such as the provision of employment, have been displaced by a new set of strict financial guides for management action. The government and British Coal have insisted that henceforward the role of the NUM will be confined to the lower levels of the industry and to a relatively narrow range of 'personnel' issues. The management prerogative must be left untrammelled to pursue the new commercial objectives set by government and, ultimately, to fashion a coal industry capable of standing free of state support.

The book concludes with a discussion of the concept of managerial strategy and its usefulness as a tool for analysing the processes of labour management. In doing so it relates the findings from our study in the mining industry to some of the major debates which have coalesced around the concept of managerial strategy in recent years.

The Organization of the Coal-mining Industry

Coal-mining was nationalized in 1947 and British Coal now controls the publicly owned coal mines (often referred to as collieries or pits) in operation in England, Scotland, and Wales. This controlling body was called the National Coal Board (NCB) until the introduction of the 1986 Coal Industry Act, when the name was changed to 'the British Coal Corporation' in order to present a more businesslike or commercial image of the industry. Most of the research was completed under the auspices of the NCB, but we also are concerned with the current situation. Therefore, in order to avoid confusion we have adopted the following rules on nomenclature. The term 'National Coal Board' has been used in the book when discussing the industry prior to the decision to trade under the new name in 1986. When discussing the industry after that date we have used the term 'British Coal'. Throughout the book we have also used the terms 'the Board' and 'the Coal Board'. These are the terms used most frequently in the industry itself by work-force, trade unions, and management and they continue to be used despite the official change in name.

This book is concerned with the relationships between the NCB and its management, and the mineworkers represented by the industry's largest and most influential union, the National Union of Mineworkers (NUM). Although the NUM's near monopoly was broken by the emergence of the Union of Democratic Mineworkers (UDM) during the 1984/5 strike, at the time of our study the NUM represented the vast majority of manual workers employed in the industry. The organization of both the NCB and the NUM is based on a regional grouping of units with three levels—national, area, and local. At the colliery level the local NUM branch committee usually consists of a secretary, a president, a treasurer, and a delegate (the contact with the area union) and up to twenty-five ordinary members. These are elected by the membership in a secret ballot on an annual or sometimes a triannual basis. Branches are usually based on a single colliery. The local officials are equivalent to shop stewards in other industries and are allowed varying amounts of time off by management in order to fulfil their duties. On the management side, the colliery manager heads a management team usually consisting of a deputy manager (in larger collieries) and a number of functional assistants and face managers. At the time of the research, management and unions met frequently at all levels to negotiate or consult in various capacities. At the local level there were usually formal meetings on a weekly or fortnightly basis and most colliery managers had an 'open door' policy with regard to the NUM officials. Area NUM and NCB managements were rarely directly involved in colliery affairs except in the relatively unusual case of total deadlock between the two local parties.

In a very few collieries the winding enginemen and craftsmen (electrical and mechanical engineers), although part of the NUM, have separate organizations at the local and area level (known as the Enginemen and Mechanics respectively). Colliery white-collar workers also have their own organization, affiliated to the NUM, the Colliery Staff and Officials Area (COSA). Supervisors belong to a separate union, the National Association of Colliery Overmen Deputies and Shotfirers (NACODS). Colliery management is represented by the British Association of Colliery Management (BACM).

The Research

The empirical material on the processes of labour management in mining was obtained over a prolonged period of involvement. One of us began researching in mining in the early 1970s, while the other has clocked up nearly a decade of interest in mining and the people within it. The earlier work was supported by the then Social Science Research Council (now the Economic and Social Research Council) and in 1980 the Coal Board made a grant to Christine Edwards to continue the research.

Our data were obtained through a variety of means. Qualitative and historical material was provided by intensive investigations at twelve collieries prior to the 1976/7 study and five collieries in preparation for the study in 1980/1. These involved visits underground, observation of work, attendance at union meetings, and unstructured interviews with the full range of colliery personnel including management, union officials, supervisors, and mineworkers.

The main sources of quantitative data were two national surveys of local industrial relations carried out in 1976/7 and 1980/1 before and after the introduction of the incentive scheme. In each, personal interviews were held with colliery managers and NUM officials at thirty-five collieries distributed through seven of the twelve NCB administrative areas (about 16 per cent of the total number of pits at that time). These provided systematic measurements of the power of workplace trade-unionism in mining. Questions covered the areas of management decision-making subject to union influence and whether union influence was exerted against the wishes of colliery management as well as more general information on the management–union relationship. (The methodology is described in more detail in Chapter 7 and in Edwards, 1978, 1983). There were some differences in the scope of the two surveys. In 1976/7 the results of an attitude survey of over 1,000 workmen in the industry were available (Edwards and Harper, 1976). In 1980/2 self-report questionnaires were left with each of the colliery managers and NUM branch officials who took part in the main survey. These contained a range of questions on the effects of the return to incentives on performance and labour relations.

In both studies, personal interviews were held with the NCB area industrial relations officers and NUM area full-time officers responsible for the collieries in the sample. The theme of the interview was their role in industrial relations, most particularly in relation to colliery affairs.

Finally, a wealth of statistics on area and colliery structure, performance, manpower, and disputes was collected from collieries and from the NCB headquarters at Hobart House.

Given the sensitive nature of our research topic we might have expected some difficulties in eliciting frank responses to our enquiries, or in gaining access to information. In both 1976 and 1980, management denied us complete access to collieries in the Yorkshire coalfield for systematic data-collection because of internal problems with management in the area, although we were able to collect statistical data and conduct some personal interviews. Otherwise, however, we received a 100 per cent response rate and enthusiastic assistance.

The ease with which we were able to study the industry is partly accounted for by the climate of local industrial relations at that time. Despite a tradition of militant opposition to management's will and despite the underlying conflicts of interests, the interpersonal relations between managers and union officials were generally open and congenial. Coal-mining remains among the most hazardous of all occupations and close co-operation between management and men is vital to the safety of everyone in the pit. Furthermore, there is less 'social' distance between local management and work-force than is usual in other industries. Colliery managers often come from the same social background and community as their workmen, and a fair number have worked their way up through the ranks. Even graduate entrants often come from mining families, have a two-year period of face-work as part of their training and most expect to dedicate their life to the industry. Most colliery managers, moreover, make regular visits underground and are important contributors to the social life of the local community. Any antagonism towards management expressed in the course of our research, therefore, was more often than not directed towards the 'remote' area management of the NCB, and cases of collusion between the local management and NUM officials in contravention of the policies of area management were frequently encountered in the research.

A strong feeling of camaraderie embraced everyone who worked in the industry at that time, even including senior management at Hobart House. Such was its strength that the Thatcher Government brought in as chairman an outsider, Ian McGregor, in September 1983 to carry out their 'rationalization' of the industry. He in turn felt it necessary to rid the industry of a number of area and national managers who were considered to be too close to the unions and to replace them with his own men in order to implement his policies.

The climate in which the research was conducted, therefore, was very different from that which prevails today. Consequently we have in various ways attempted to 'update' our knowledge. It is clear that the 1984/5 miners' strike represents an important turning-point in the development of the coal industry and we felt it was vital that we obtain information on how the processes of labour management have been altered as a result of the NUM's defeat and the imposition of a much tighter financial discipline on the industry. In each of the five parts of the book, therefore, there is a discussion of how employment relations have changed or are being changed in the wake of the miners' strike by a more assertive management. The main source of data which informs this discussion of the new context in coal is a series of in-depth interviews conducted with senior industrial relations staff at Hobart House in the spring of 1987. These covered the main elements of management's post-strike strategy and its rationale and were supplemented by examination of internal British Coal documents on issues such as the reform of the industry's system of payment by results. Unfortunately it was not possible to extend this research by directly examining the impact of new management initiatives at workplace level. A further and valuable source of information which does inform our discussion of developments since the miners' strike is the wealth of material on the industry which has appeared in academic publications and in the press. The strike focused media attention on the coal industry and a consequence of this has been much excellent and detailed reporting of its aftermath. Like many other students of employment relations in Britain, we owe a particular debt to the skills of the Labour staff of the *Financial Times*.

PART I The Control of Work

1
The Day-wage System

Introduction

Our aim in this chapter and the one that follows is to examine the development of work organization in mining over the past two decades. More specifically, we are concerned with describing, analysing, and evaluating the various techniques that managers in coal-mining have used to raise and maintain the work performance of British miners. A central theme in our discussion is the contrast between two distinct strategies of labour management which have been employed by the National Coal Board in the period we have chosen to examine. The first of these was measured day-work, which was formally adopted by the industry with the signing of the National Powerloading Agreement (NPLA) with the NUM in 1966. This was a distinctly managerialist strategy, which emphasized managerial responsibility for levels of work performance and sought to institute relatively close managerial direction of workers at the coal-face. Under NPLA the practice of labour management in coal-mining approximated towards Friedman's notion of 'direct control' (Friedman, 1977, p. 78).

The key feature of the second strategy which was introduced in the late 1970s was reliance on group incentive payments. Such payments were deemed necessary to raise the disappointing levels of productivity achieved under NPLA. Management withdrew somewhat from its attempt to deliver labour towards consistent high performance, and chose, instead, to rely on payment by results as a means of galvanizing work-groups. Incentives were seized upon as a means of securing congruence in management and worker goals at the point of production.

In addition to describing the rise and fall of measured day-work in mining and the retreat back to payment by results, we are concerned with two additional issues. The first of these is the extent to which management has capitalized on the defeat of the NUM in the 1984/5 strike and has introduced new forms of labour control. The second issue is related to the first. We are concerned with the debate over the impact of new technology in mining and the extent to which it is likely to usher in completely novel forms of work organization.

The Task of Labour Management

Before embarking on our treatment of concrete developments in mining we want to advance an analytical framework which will serve to guide the empirical discussion. Our starting-point, here, is the interdependence of the two parties to the employment contract. Formally free labour is dependent on securing paid employment to obtain the means of subsistence, while employers are dependent on securing appropriately qualified labour-power in order to set the means of production in motion. The dependence of employers on labour, however, does not conclude with the recruitment of labour. As has frequently been noted, the employment contract is peculiarly open-ended and once labour-power has been acquired it must be realized in actual labour. Managers are therefore faced with the task of ensuring a more rather than less efficient use of the labour purchased on the market. They are concerned with achieving an economic transformation of labour-power into actual labour, in which the optimum amount of work of sufficient quality is secured in return for each unit of labour costs.

Management's difficulty in achieving this transformation is compounded by the fact that there is an antagonism of interests at the heart of the employment contract. Despite their interdependence the interests of employers and of the workers they employ are not identical. Though both are dependent on the continued survival of the employing organization, conflict is likely over the distribution of the economic surplus between wages and profits and over the amount of effort or care workers are expected to invest in their tasks in return for their wages. Such conflicts, moreover, are likely to be exacerbated by the fact that individuals or small groups of workers may choose to free-ride. That is, they may pursue their own goals of wage maximization or effort minimization without regard to the effects this has on the overall health of the enterprise. The effects of particular sectional actions on overall efficiency may not be readily apparent to those who engage in them, thus widening the divergence in interests between workers and managers, who must perforce (at least at the highest levels) adopt a general view.

The initial point in our analysis, therefore, is that labour and management are interdependent but that this interdependence is not such as to purge all traces of conflict and antagonism from the employment relation. Management requires the co-operation or compliance of labour in the pursuit of its goal but there is no guarantee that this co-operation will be given to the extent that management need or desire. Given this, we believe management is faced with two broad options. It can take actions to reduce its own dependence on labour, to permit it to produce goods or services without having to pay excessive concern to the problem of obtaining labour's co-operation. It can also take actions to increase labour's

Means of Reducing Management's Dependence on Labour

SUBSTITUTION	Duplication of work-forces Replacement by 'dependable' workers Replacement by machinery/new technology
CONTROL	Job design–deskilling Bureaucratization of work–setting of work rules and performance targets Monitoring of performance Disciplinary sanctions

Means of Increasing Dependence on Management

INCENTIVES	Linking rewards to performance—merit and bonus schemes and profit related pay
INTERNAL LABOUR MARKETS	Linking promotion and career progression to performance
PATERNALISM	Broadening the employment contract—provision of welfare and other benefits
WORKER PARTICIPATION	Job enrichment Direct participation—briefing groups, quality circles, indirect participation—joint consultation, collective bargaining

Figure 1.1. The task of labour management

dependence on management and on the employing organization in the expectation that this will increase the propensity of workers to co-operate.

Both of these courses of action can be pursued in a number of ways (see Figure 1.1). Management's dependence on labour can be reduced, for example, either by rendering workers substitutable or by developing means of directing or controlling workers' behaviour at work. Measures of the first kind increase the organization's ability to fulfil its operations without labour or without specific groups of workers, while measures of the second kind reduce the 'risks' inherent in the use of labour.

Means of Reducing Management Dependence on Labour: Substitution

Three examples of managerial actions which attempt to render workers substitutable are as follows:

1. The duplication of work-forces. A good example of this is the use of what Massey (1984, pp. 74–7) has termed a 'cloning branch-plant' structure, in which identical production units are dispersed throughout the country and controlled from a separate corporate headquarters. The principal reason why firms adopt such structures is to obtain easy access to

local markets (Massey, 1984, p. 75). An additional advantage, however, is that the duplication of production resources permits management to withstand sanctions imposed by any particular branch-plant work-force, and thus can shift the balance of power in the employment relation decisively in management's favour (Purcell and Sisson, 1983, p. 102).

Within mining the most notable example of the use of the duplication of work-forces to reduce employer dependence on labour was seen during the miners' strike. The government, rather than the National Coal Board itself, activated contingency plans which permitted British mined coal to be partially replaced by imported coal and by oil. The preservation of spare oil-fired capacity in the electricity supply industry was of particular importance in neutralizing the miners' industrial action (see Chapter 5).

2. The replacement of work-forces with more 'dependable' workers. Two examples of management action of this kind are the relocation of production either in green-field sites (Nichols and Beynon, 1977) or in countries where the labour movement is subject to repression. Again, although such locational decisions are unlikely to arise solely from labour management considerations, companies which do move their operations in either of these two directions could well gain substantially from reduced dependence on well-paid and possibly militant workers.

For the National Coal Board replacement of work-forces in this way has not been possible. Even where new coalfields have been developed, as at Selby, technical and political considerations (the need to guarantee the job prospects of NUM members) have necessitated the relocation of existing workers to operate the new mines. The result of this has been the transfer of the custom and practice and strong bargaining awareness of the Yorkshire miners into the Selby complex (Thomas, 1983).

However, although the Board has not been able to relocate operations to secure more 'dependable' workers, the rationalization of the industry does permit management to achieve a similar effect. It could be that the relative militancy of miners in different pits and areas could be a factor influencing closure and investment decisions. Put bluntly, management may choose to favour Nottinghamshire at the expense of South Wales, Kent, and Scotland, because workers in the former broke the 1984/5 strike while those in the latter did not. Since the dispute it has been made clear by British Coal that new investment will be dependent on prior commitments to co-operation from the work-force. The development of Margam Colliery in South Wales and of several other new pits, for instance, has been linked to the acceptance by the unions of new shift patterns.

3. The replacement of workers with machinery. The elimination of direct labour through the use of machinery has been a persistent trend in the history of industrialization. The new microprocessor technology is believed by many to be intensifying this trend, and to enable managers to dispense with direct labour in many fields of activity hitherto little affected

by mechanization (Gill, 1985). In mining, the replacement of labour with machinery has been a dominant theme in the development of work organization since nationalization, and in the not too distant future the first fully automated coal-faces may be developed in the British coalfields.

Management's motives for introducing new technologies which displace labour are likely to be complex (Batstone and Gourlay, 1986, pp. 153–9). Machinery, most obviously, can raise output and permit savings in labour costs. It may also be valued because it improves product or service quality or permits the development of new products and services. From the perspective of labour management, however, its value resides in the fact that it reduces the uncertainty inherent in the use of labour. By permitting the removal of workers who *intervene* between management and the production process, it enhances direct managerial control over the production of goods and services (Child, 1985, pp. 120–1).[1] In the coal industry, for example, a major problem facing engineers has been how to increase the proportion of shift-time during which coal-cutting machinery is in operation. In part, this has been viewed as a labour relations problem and various techniques have been used to motivate workers towards better machine utilization. An additional response, however, has been to further mechanize mining operations in order to increase management's ability to direct operations at the face. British Coal, for example, is currently developing an automated system to control the advance of the coal-face conveyor and roof supports, an automatic coal-face surveyor, and the automation of coal-shearing equipment (Winterton, 1985, p. 234). All of these innovations threaten coal-face jobs.

Reducing Management Dependence: Controls

It was stated above that the second means by which managers can reduce their dependence on labour is through instituting controls over the activities of labour at work. In our view, such controls can be classified in four ways:

1. Designing jobs which minimize the discretion of workers. The first method through which managers can control worker performance is job design, the creation of jobs which allow for limited discretion and which thus reduce the ability of the worker to act in opposition to management's objectives. Changes in technology are frequently used by managers to design the discretion out of jobs in this way. According to Child (1985, p. 130), 'Managers are able today to use new technology in an attempt to

---

[1] This is not to say, however, that the removal of one strategic group by the introduction of machinery will not prevent the emergence of another. In the pits the displacement of direct labour by the mechanization of mining operations has been accompanied by a rise in the numbers and influence of skilled maintenance workers.

avoid reliance on the skills and judgement of workers, and to regulate their performance more precisely.'

The principles of such job design have been analysed in detail many times (e.g. Braverman, 1974). Most fundamental is the separation of conception from execution, so that the objectives and methods of work are devised by management while workers are left with prescribed and routine tasks. A second principle is the fragmentation of tasks so that each job is limited to a small number of core activities. This process, however, need not necessarily result in worker specialization. In mining, the production task has been broken down into a number of discrete activities but it is expected that the members of the production team will be interchangeable and able to fit into any of the 'slots' designed by management.

2. The 'bureaucratization' of work. Closely associated with the design of simple tasks which demand relatively little exercise of discretion, is the specification of effort levels and methods of working in formal rules and instructions. Once management has isolated a relatively routine task it is normal for the task to be further analysed, usually by work study, and for rates and methods of performance to be set. Scientific management of this kind can be viewed as a supplement or extension of job design, its purpose is to impose further regulation and to minimize whatever discretion remains within already routine tasks.

3. The development of information systems to monitor worker performance. The task of monitoring worker performance in order to ensure that work is performed at a level and in a manner that is satisfactory to management, is facilitated by the design of relatively simple jobs and by the regulation of worker activity within those jobs. Where responsibilities are kept to a minimum then failings in performance are easier to identify, while the setting of targets and methods of operation itself permits the identification of 'rule divergence'; the failure of workers to abide by management prescriptions.

The monitoring of worker performance can be performed in two broad ways. The first of these is through direct supervision. Workers are watched at work by representatives of management who are supposed immediately to correct any failings in worker performance. The second way is through the development by management of written or statistical indicators of worker performance and the compilation and analysis of information relating to the work task. Monitoring of this kind is designed to render the process of work visible to management at a higher level than the supervisor and also permits the evaluation of longer-term trends in worker performance. The collection of records of this kind has been an important feature of scientific management since the turn of the century. In recent years, however, micro-electronic devices with their capacity to capture, store, and analyse information have greatly increased management's ability to 'watch' work at a distance. In coal-mining, for example, management has developed FIDO (Face Information Digested Online), which one manager described to us as 'the spy in the cab'. This information system automatically relays the cause and duration of any breaks in coal-cutting activity to a control room located on the pit-top (Winterton, 1985, p. 234).

4. Disciplinary sanctions for failings in work performance. The purpose of monitoring worker performance is to provide information to correct any divergence from the set of activities prescribed by management. The authority of the supervisor is one sanction that can be used to correct worker performance, though certainly in mining the overman has largely lost his terrors. Another means is the formal disciplinary system. This, however, is a cumbersome means of controlling work performance, though it is certainly invoked in mining to punish such things as leaving the pit before the end of a shift or disobeying instructions. In 1987 British Coal took action to strengthen the disciplinary sanctions at the disposal of its managers. A new disciplinary code was imposed on the unions, which increases the range of offences for which men can be disciplined, permits managers to discipline men for offences committed away from the pit, gives the Board the right to decide which union official should represent a miner at disciplinary hearings, and permits management to dismiss instantly any miner who has received a formal written warning in the previous three years for any disciplinary offence. Although the new code is largely based on the recommendations of the Advisory, Concilation, and Arbitration Service the NUM's national conference voted to reject it and initiate industrial action against it in July 1987. This decision was followed by a large unofficial strike by Yorkshire miners against the use of the new code at Frickley Colliery to discipline six miners who management claimed had left work before the end of their shift.

The sanctions which can be deployed to control work performance are limited and regulated by both the law and the trade union. Management in mining has sought to develop other means of inducing worker co-operation. Rather than trying to direct and punish workers for failings in compliance, management has tried to align worker, trade-union, and managerial interests so that, if co-operation is not forthcoming, workers effectively 'punish' themselves.

Increasing Worker Dependence on Management

This brings us to our second class of responses managers can make to the problematic nature of the employment relation. These are actions which seek to increase the dependence of labour on management. The major types are as follows:

1. Linking rewards to performance. Labour's dependence on the employer derives ultimately from the need for workers to seek paid

employment to obtain the means of subsistence. Employers can accentuate this fundamental relation of dependence either by locating work in areas of high unemployment or by paying wages above the market rate in order to attract good quality labour with a long-term commitment to the organization. Over and above steps such as these, however, employers can further exploit labour's dependence by linking levels of reward directly to level and quality of performance.

In British industry incentive payments remain a major form of labour control for manual workers and there is growing interest in merit and bonus schemes for white-collar staff (Batstone and Gourlay, 1986, p. 121). Examples of payment systems which attempt to align worker and employer interests range from payment by results and attendance bonuses which attempt to influence directly the behaviour of individuals or work groups, through to company bonus schemes, profit-sharing and employee share ownership, which attempt to evoke a more diffuse commitment to organizational objectives. In mining management has tended to rely on the former, more specific controls.

2. Internal labour markets. A further means of linking performance and reward is through a career and promotion system. This serves to increase worker dependence on the employer by making upward mobility through the organizational job hierarchy dependent on current performance. Commitment and co-operation become the price of future advance. In Britain, managers have tended not to develop very elaborate job hierarchies for manual workers. In mining, for example, though the industry's supervisors are recruited from the ranks of face-workers, giving some opportunity for upward movement, most miners remain at the same grade once they have qualified for coal-face work.

3. Broadening the employment contract. In addition to seeking to bind workers through the prospect of future promotion, employers may also seek to build supplements into the employment contract in order to expand the range of requirements which workers must satisfy through their employment. Fringe benefits and company welfare schemes are the most obvious examples of this technique. The intention, as with the development of internal labour markets, is to increase employee dependence on the organization with the aim of eliciting greater co-operation.

Broadening the employment relation in this way may also be associated with the adoption of a 'diffuse' commitment to employees on the part of the employing organization. Managers may cultivate a reputation for their organization as a 'good employer', through displaying a concern with the welfare and interests of employees. At the core of such action is the belief that if management moves beyond purely contractual relations, then labour will do likewise and adopt a 'diffuse' commitment to the firm.

Paternalism of this kind has been and continues to be a feature of the

British mining industry. In east Nottinghamshire in the 1920s, for example, the Bolsover and Barber-Walker companies developed 'new model' villages where virtually all elements of communal life were regulated by the employer (Waller, 1983). Their pits were strongholds of the breakaway Spencer union in the years after the 1926 strike. In the industry generally, nationalization was the occasion for a broadening of employer commitment to the work-force, seen, for instance, in the building of colliery baths and canteens. There was also the establishment of the Colliery Welfare System which continues to provide extensive sporting and social facilities within many pit villages, and which is operated jointly by management and unions. Concessions such as these, however, have long since ceased to evoke 'diffuse' commitments from British miners. They have come to be viewed as entitlements which impose no obligation. Indeed, to the extent that Colliery Welfare and other facilities sustain mineworkers' commitment to their community and their pit, they can generate problems for the industry's management. The intense loyalty of many miners to their communities was an important factor in the outbreak, length and bitterness of the 1984/5 strike.

4. Workers' participation. In addition to offering workers a broader set of economic rewards in order to induce greater commitment, managers may offer the opportunity to participate in the running of the enterprise. Such participation can be offered at two levels. At the level of the individual or the work-group management may ask workers to assume greater responsibility for the planning and execution of work. This may involve the reversal of earlier attempts to minimize worker discretion. Above this level managers may seek to draw the representatives of workers, who may or may not be the holders of trade-union office, into a co-operative discussion on matters pertaining to the workplace or enterprise. To the extent that measures of both kinds serve the interests of workers and their representatives they can be seen as attempts to increase the dependence of labour on a particular employer. Individual workers may find the opportunity to participate increases job satisfaction and fulfils their need for involvement in the work task. Representatives, on the other hand, may become committed to participation because it gives them access to management decision-making and so can raise the 'institutional centrality' of the union or other representative body to which they belong. In the first case, it is anticipated that greater involvement will lead to a stronger employee attachment to the employer's objectives, while in the latter it is anticipated that employer support for the representative function will lead to a readiness on the part of representatives to ensure the co-operation of their constituency.

In the mining industry there has been intermittent managerial support for participation of the first type. In the 1970s, for example, there were experiments with coal-face production meetings, which were intended to resolve technical and organizational problems and develop teamwork (Brown, 1977, p. 349). This occurred at a time when management was increasingly alarmed at diminishing productivity and could fit Ramsay's (1977) contention that participation is used by management in periods of worker strength. The main form of participation used by the NCB, however, has been the attempt to develop a co-operative approach to managerial problems with the NUM. The industry has had a well-developed system of joint consultation since nationalization and for most of that period a fairly close relationship has existed between the leaderships of the NCB and the NUM (Allen, 1981, pp. 63–5). Supplementary to co-operation at national level have been attempts to use the union to discipline the work-force within the pits. Although, in our experience, joint consultation has not been valued greatly by either NUM branch officials or local managers, there has been widespread reliance on 'strong bargaining relations' to solve management problems. Managerial support for the local union and assistance in its representative task has been frequently exchanged for assistance in resolving difficulties relating to work organization and worker motivation.

In this section we have attempted to categorize the tasks management faces in managing labour and have emphasized the uncertainty of labour's co-operation or compliance. We have then argued that management can respond to this situation by attempting either to reduce its own dependence on labour or to increase labour's dependence on the employing organization. Actual managerial practice is likely to involve a combination of both kinds of response. This is certainly the case in mining. What we want to do now is show how the National Coal Board has made selections from the list of practices set out above and combined them in particular labour management strategies. In turn, we want to examine the 'selections' which composed measured daywork, from 1966 to 1977, the strategy of incentives, from 1977 to 1984, and the new phase of labour management which has followed in the wake of the 1984/5 strike.

Measured Day-work: The National Powerloading Agreement

The basis and justification for the adoption of measured day-work by the National Coal Board in 1966 was the mechanization of the industry in the previous ten years. Between 1957 and 1968 the proportion of mechanized output increased from 23 to 93 per cent. In this period powerloading, in which coal was mechanically sheared from the face and deposited on an armoured flexible conveyor for transport out of the pit, replaced 'conventional' mining as the predominant method of production. Under the latter system the coal was undercut and blasted on one shift, 'filled' by hand, on another, onto a conveyor, which was dismantled and advanced, along with the roof supports, on a third (Trist and Bamforth, 1969). 'Conventional' mining was both cyclical and labour-intensive. Powerloading was a 'semi-continuous' form of production. The processes of cutting coal, loading it onto a conveyor, and advancing the face could be completed within the span of single shift, and also required far less manpower. Powerloading permitted a reduction in labour costs (from 65 per cent of total costs in 1947 to 49 per cent in 1975/6), and an increase in labour productivity (from 262 tons per man-year in 1947 when 2.4 per cent of production was powerloaded, to 373 tons in 1965 when 75 per cent of output was powerloaded, and to 455 tons in 1976 when powerloading accounted for 93.6 per cent of total output).

Viewed from the perspective of labour management the significance of the development of powerloading was that it reduced dependence on worker effort. Machinery displaced muscle-power, most obviously in the filling of coal, and for this reason the NCB believed incentives would be increasingly redundant in the powerloading era. The mechanization of mining also resulted in the simplification of certain tasks. At the coal-face, for example, the task of guiding the powerloading shearer 'required less effort and skill than did steering the old coal cutter' (Handy, 1981, p. 193) and where powered roof supports were introduced the task of support setting became much lighter and less skilled. Away from the coal-face the mechanization of haulage and coal handling, developments which occurred in tandem with powerloading, tended to produce 'button-pushing' jobs for workers elsewhere below ground. However, as Handy (1981, pp. 193–4) has pointed out, the extent of deskilling occasioned by the spread of powerloading was limited. In the 1960s the important tasks of stable-holing and face-ripping, which effectively determined the pace of face advance, remained as arduous and as skilful as they had been under the 'conventional' system. In addition, powerloading and associated forms of mechanization increased the numbers of skilled maintenance workers employed underground.[2]

In developing powerloading, therefore, the NCB reduced its dependence on work-force co-operation both by displacing labour and by simplifying certain tasks. However, considerable space for work-force discretion remained at the coal-face. Powerloading did not provide for the machine-pacing of labour as production was dependent on the work-force

---

[2] Although powerloading represented a process of deskilling through the supersession of traditional mining tasks, we would not wish to evaluate this process in a wholly negative way, as writers such as Braverman have done. Work under the 'conventional' system, and under hand-got mining which preceded it, was dangerous and arduous. Many men were broken by it by middle age. In the words of one deputy who we interviewed who had experienced piece-work on conventional faces, 'Men worked like animals then.' Powerloading has produced safer and less sapping work. It should not be presented one sidedly as a fall from skilled grace.

TABLE 1.1   Coal industry productivity in tonnes per manshift, 1971–1977

	1971	1972[a]	1973	1974[a]	1975	1976	1977
Output per manshift	2.24	2.13	2.33	2.15	2.29	2.28	2.21
Output per manshift (all underground)	2.92	2.76	3.00	2.77	2.94	2.91	2.83
Output per manshift (coal-face)	7.30	7.05	7.56	7.30	7.89	7.89	7.75

[a] Figures influenced by national strike.

Source: NCB Report and Accounts.

activating the machinery. Mechanization, therefore, presented the NCB with the problem of ensuring the full utilization of powerloading equipment; of ensuring that production continued for the maximum amount of time possible in each shift. Management's response to this problem was to rely on two methods of directing labour—work study and supervision. It was envisaged that work study would play a much fuller role in labour management in the powerloading era, setting manning levels and production targets for each coal-face. It was also decided to increase the level of supervision, to ensure that work-teams at the coal-face performed in accordance with work-study standards. A further important function envisaged for supervision was to guarantee flexibility in the use of labour. Supervisors were to redeploy men at the coal-face in response to the many contingencies which unavoidably bedevil the coal extraction process.

The combination of mechanization, work study, and supervision which lay at the heart or the NCB's measured day-work strategy did not prove adequate for the control of mining labour. Together, it was believed, these measures would enable management to maintain production without the galvanizing stimulus of payment by results. In the years after the signing of the NPLA, though, it became apparent that the industry faced a serious problem of worker motivation and consequent low productivity (Handy, 1981; Searle-Barnes, 1969). This was disguised at first by the continuing programme of coal-face mechanization. As the introduction of powerloading was completed in the early 1970s, however, the full extent of management's problem was exposed.

Table 1.1 shows the industry's disappointing productivity record in the day-wage era. Although investment continued in the seven-year period for which figures are shown, productivity remained fairly stable according to the first two indices and increased only marginally according to the third. Overall output per manshift was lower in 1977 than it had been in 1971. At the end of 1976 the NCB's management journal stated that; 'An analysis of recent trends considered by the Board reveals that productivity has shown no net advance since 1970. Output per machine shift has remained virtually static and the number of machine shifts fell from 9,989 a week in 1967/8 to 7,331 last year.' Particular concern was voiced in this period over the disappointing levels of performance achieved by rippers working at the face-ends and by development workers (Griffin, 1972; Handy, 1981 p. 203). In these areas control over the pace of work rested more securely with the work-group and the productivity problem bore witness to the collapse in worker motivation. In 1973, after a three-year 'pace-setter' development programme, the Board was forced to admit that despite a concentration of investment and management effort on development work 'the general level of performance is virtually where it was'.

The Failure of NPLA

Why did the measured day-work strategy produce this poor productivity record? One reason is that the strategy widened the gap in interests between the miners and NCB management in certain important respects. The most obvious way it did this was through the removal of incentive payments, previously the most important means of achieving an identity of interests. Searle-Barnes's (1969) study of the introduction of the NPLA in Nottinghamshire, for example, revealed an immediate decline in productivity. Performance on the majority of faces operating the new agreement was found to be below that achieved on similar faces where payment by results had been in operation.

This adverse effect of the removal of incentives was compounded by the fact that it occurred in a period of unfavourable trends in earnings for many mineworkers. One objective of the NPLA was to compress internal difficulties. This required restraining the wages of higher-paid groups involved in direct production underground, while the level of surface workers' pay was increased (Handy 1981, p. 192). This narrowing of the internal differential of erstwhile piece-workers occurred in conjunction with a decline in their position relative to other industrial workers. The rundown of the industry in the 1960s led to wage increases below the going rate for miners. Incomes policy had a similar effect both in the 1960s and in the 1970s. Movements in face and development workers' earnings relative to other groups of miners and to workers in other industries, therefore, could be said to have themselves encouraged the restriction of effort levels. The significance of the removal of incentives in this situation was that it denied production workers in mining any means of countering the adverse trend in their earnings. The day-wage system coupled with relative decline in earnings pushed miners towards a disengagement from production and the restriction of output.

A further factor serving to widen the interests of management and work-force was the control system introduced as part of the package. In particular, the expanded ranks of supervisors were resented by miners used to controlling much of the work process themselves (Griffin, 1972; Heery, 1984, pp. 334–5). Attempts at 'direct control' initiated a 'dynamic of low trust' (Fox, 1974), as workers at the face resisted what they considered an attempt to 'drive' them. Relations between deputies, overmen, and rank-and-file mineworkers in some coalfields had tradition-ally been antagonistic.[3] As the former assumed greater responsibility for directing work at the point of production they deteriorated still further. During the day-wage era, for example, although the number of local wage disputes fell, the number of stoppages caused by refusals to accept alternative work increased (Handy, 1981, pp. 208–9). This indicated added conflict over the organization of work, the very area where it was intended the supervisor would assume more directive responsibility.

This situation was further exacerbated by the fact that many of the industry's supervisors had neither the authority, the training, nor the experience to enable them to assume a more directive role. Until 1972 supervisors' earnings lagged behind those of production workers and there was little incentive for the most able mineworkers to join their ranks. The industry's wage structure under the early phase of powerloading, therefore, existed in tension with the industry's structure of control over work in that it served to diminish supervisory status and quality. The 1975 attitude survey, conducted near the end of the day-wage era, provided evidence of the ineffectiveness of much of the industry's supervision. Although three-quarters of face-workers complained that there were too many supervisors at their pit, very few (14 per cent) complained of being under pressure to get work done. About two-thirds of face-workers reported that they were usually left alone to get on with work by themselves, suggesting that the conflict over the control of work, initiated by the day-wage system, had been resolved in most pits very much in the work-force's favour.

A second reason for the poor productivity performance under NPLA was that the mining work-force remained in possession of sufficient power to pursue and frequently realize its objectives. Expressed in the terms used above, management remained critically dependent on work-force co-operation despite its efforts to minimize that dependence. As the division of interests between the two sides emerged and widened in the day-wage era so the work-force exploited management dependence through restricting output. The relative failure of the strategy arose from the combination of its adverse effects on the interests of the work-force and the continuing collective power of the miners.

---

[3] In David Storey's novel, *Saville*, for example, which is set in a Yorkshire mining village in the 1950s, the hero's father is ostracized by his neighbours when he accepts promotion to the rank of deputy.

One significant source of work-force power has already been mentioned. Despite the mechanization of operations, several key activities at the coal-face remained dependent on worker skill and effort. In addition, the unavoidable uncertainties of the mining process created a further requirement for worker commitment. The rapidity with which the incessant crises at the coal-face were overcome and the extent to which powerloading equipment was fully utilized were matters which were largely controlled by the direct work-group. Under NPLA the miner, most emphatically, had not become a mere appendage of the mining machine.

A second factor was the weakness of the National Powerloading Agreement itself. The rules it contained which were intended to specify management's rights to direct labour were imprecise in certain important respects. This was most obvious in the clauses relating to the use of work study. At first sight the stipulation in the agreement that manning and maximum machine utilization would be determined by work study seemed like a major success for management in view of the strict limitations the NUM had previously imposed on the use of work study. However, it has been noted by Handy (1981, p. 204) that the agreement contained no mention of 'task norms'. Work study, he has written, 'was applied to the machine to determine manning with a view to maximum machine utilization. That was very different from deciding what the machine and men were capable of doing and fixing task norms accordingly.' Will Paynter, in his speech to the NUM conference recommending acceptance of the NPLA, pointed out to the delegates the inoffensiveness of the work study clauses.

Not only did the NPLA fail to provide close regulation of the use of labour, it also failed to specify sanctions to be used if work groups failed to co-operate with management. It did not contain specific disciplinary procedures, leading, for example, to a withholding of payment, if face-teams did not comply with management instructions to ensure maximum machine utilization (Gidwell, 1977, p. 11). Without such procedures, the expanded ranks of supervisors were left without an adequate tool to ensure work-force compliance with their instructions.

A third, and perhaps critical, source of work-force power was the strong local organization of the NUM. The tradition of collective organization and action in the industry permitted a further weakening of management's rights to direct labour as codified in the NPLA. The extent of union power was quite considerable, as is demonstrated in Chapter 7. To return to the case of work study, for example, the provision in the agreement that manning levels would be set by work-study engineers was not applied in several areas. On many coal-faces the size of the work-team continued to be decided by local custom and practice. According to Searle-Barnes (1969, p. 113), in Nottinghamshire, where there had previously been few union restrictions on the use of work study, the day-wage era witnessed the growth of NUM controls over its use. Workplace union organization was also effective in contesting and nullifying the rights of supervisors to direct the labour-force (Krieger, 1984, p. 95). Despite the terms of the agreement which specified flexibility in the use of labour at the coal-face, difficulties were encountered by management in many pits in securing redeployment between tasks. Union strength, therefore, acted to shield the work-force from the new formal controls acquired by management.

Within the pits, therefore, the work-force was possessed of sufficient power to contest management's strategy of 'direct control'. In the 1970s, when management's problem of low productivity was most clearly exposed, these internal sources of strength were supplemented by external shifts in the industry's product and labour markets. The rise in the price of oil increased demand for coal, and in 1974 the industry launched its expansionary 'Plan for Coal'. The change in the industry's commercial situation led to a halting of the pit-closure programme, to renewed investment, and to attempts to increase output. This switch in course arguably served to increase management dependence on worker co-operation. Pryke (1981, p. 57), for instance, has argued that the virtual cessation of pit closures on financial grounds in the 1970s removed a vital incentive for greater efficiency from the industry's work-force. Dependence arising from the need to meet new market opportunities, moreover, was supplemented by that arising from labour shortages, particularly in the Midlands, where the Board experienced difficulties in the 1970s in recruiting and retaining labour.

Management Responses to the Failure of Measured Day-work

The introduction of measured day-work was intended to reduce management reliance on labour co-operation by increasing management's power to direct the production process. The failure of this strategy, as indicated by the disappointing productivity record under NPLA, pointed to continuing work-force control over mining operations and the limitations to management's power. We want now to consider how NCB managers at both the national and the workplace level responded to this failing of 'direct control'. These responses followed two courses. On the one hand there were attempts to intensify the strategy of reducing organizational dependence on labour co-operation. While on the other hand there were attempts to elicit greater co-operation from the work-force by increasing the dependence of workers and the NUM on the actions of Coal Board management.

The principal way in which the Board sought to reduce its dependence on labour co-operation was through the continuation of the mechanization programme. Throughout the 1970s new machinery was introduced into the pits in attempts to increase production and to improve underground transport and communications. It was stated above, for example, that delays in advancing the face-ends were a major problem encountered in the move to measured day-work. The management response to this was to initiate a programme of stable-hole elimination and of introducing heading machinery. These innovations reduced the amount of labour absorbed in cutting stable holes, driving side tunnels, and supporting their sides with stone packs. By March 1976 traditional stables had been eliminated in over 70 per cent of all advancing faces and by 1978 the ripping of side tunnels had been mechanized at one or more of the ends of a third of all faces. Heading machinery was also introduced for development work, to drive the tunnels for retreat faces and the roadways to new advancing faces (Pryke, 1981, p. 52).

Despite these innovations performance remained poor. A study by the NCB in 1977, for instance, showed that advance per shift on coal-faces with fully mechanized face-ends was marginally *inferior* to that on coal-faces with no face-end mechanization. The greater use of heading machinery on development work also failed to produce an improvement in the rate at which tunnels were advanced.[4] In 1976 Derek Ezra, the chairman of the NCB, announced:

'We are not yet achieving the improvement in productivity which our massive investment programme would lead us to expect. Of course, a large part of the investment will take some time to materialize. But a good part is also spent on meeting current needs with the supply of adequate quantities of up-to-date machinery and equipment. Many pits have performed remarkably but our overall performance is poor (quoted in Pryke, 1981, p. 54).

Although 'up-to-date machinery and equipment' increased the capacity of the industry, the basic problem of its inadequate use by a labour-force lacking in motivation remained. For the Board's mechanization programme to be fully successful, the work-force had to be galvanized to exploit more fully the opportunities of new equipment.

The decision to continue the mechanization programme was obviously taken at the highest echelons of NCB management. Another high-level response to the disappointments of NPLA was to try and use the authority of the NUM over its members to raise productivity. Part of the 'political exchange' between the union and the state in the wake of the 1972 and 1974 strikes was a commitment on the part of the former to co-operate in the modernization and expansion of the industry. The 1970s were marked by attempts by the NCB to transform this commitment into a significant

---

[4] This in turn gave rise to a second attempt to reduce dependence, at least on the NCB's own employees. In the 1970s several areas of the NCB began to use contractors on development projects, in order to reduce the time required to complete work. Significantly, the contractors tended to use piecework as a motivating device. The use of contractors was a major bone of contention between the Board and the NUM in the latter phase of the daywage era.

shift in work-force motivation. The Board's support for mining unionism, its accommodation of many of its interests, originated partly in a belief that this would elicit reciprocal support for management's interests from the NUM. Fostering union dependence on management through strong bargaining relationships, through joint consultation and ultimately, in Bullock's shadow, through industrial democracy, would pull the NUM with its membership in tow, towards greater co-operation in the process of production.

The NCB sought to use the NUM to raise productivity in a number of ways. In 1974, for example, the Coal Industry Consultative Committee launched a 'joint drive for 120 million tons'. This involved each Area Consultative Committee meeting every two months to discuss necessary action to reach output targets and monthly meetings of colliery Consultative Committees to review progress. Two years later a further scheme was launched to deal with the particularly intractable productivity problems of the South Wales coalfields. This initiative involved a combined team of NUM officials and area NCB management conducting something of a royal progress. They visited pits to iron out production problems, and in their wake coal-face production teams were established to set output targets and provide suggestions for improving performance. The high-water mark of these attempts to involve the union and its membership in dealing with management's problem of low productivity occurred with the discussions between the two sides over the Bullock proposals on industrial democracy. These failed to bear fruit, but the key proposals put forward by management was the establishment of Colliery Policy Committees which would discuss and authorize the pit production plans and review their progress.

Despite some successes (the Welsh coal-face teams, for example, set their output targets significantly higher than management estimates), these experiments in consultation and involvement failed to arrest the decline in productivity. The techniques were simply not powerful enough to solve the industry's overriding operational problem. At their heart was a conviction that the union's authority over its membership could be used to encourage more intensive and more flexible working. This, apparently, was not the case. Joint discussions with union representatives at national, area, and colliery levels, though they may have produced union commitment to greater co-operation, could not eliminate the division of interests between labour and management which had produced the productivity problem in the first place. Neither was the authority of the NUM strong enough nor could it be readily directed towards solving operational difficulties. In addition, there was a profound wariness within the union of attempts to incorporate it within management. Several lodges included in the South Wales exercise, for example, refused to set output targets, arguing this was management's task. At the time of the report, many

activists, Arthur Scargill prime among them, were resolute in their opposition to any measure which could weaken the independence of the union
vis-à-vis the employer (Scargill and Kahn, 1980). Even advocates of
industrial democracy, such as Peter Heathfield, urged much fuller rights of
decision-making than the NCB was prepared to submit to and were openly
critical of the toothlessness of the proposal to establish Colliery Policy
Committees (*The Miner*, December 1978). The unwillingness of many
representatives to accept the role of urging greater work discipline, therefore, must be added to their questionable capacity to perform that role, as
a factor leading to the failure of the NCB's experiments in participation. A
further problem was that many of the Board's own managers viewed such
experiments with scepticism. A lack of management enthusiasm, as well
as union suspicion, therefore, was an important factor in choking off
experiments with briefing groups or face-team meetings.

By the mid 1970s appreciation of the failure of participation was
growing among senior NCB management. At the NUM's 1976 conference
Derek Ezra pointed out that, full union support notwithstanding, the
industry continued to suffer from indifferent performance. His
prescription was a return to incentives. A similar view was expressed in the
same year by George Tyler, general secretary of BACM, and spokesman
for the industry's powerful corps of mining engineers. He wrote,

My personal view is that whilst we want to encourage the workforce to take an
interest in the Board's organisation, particularly at pit level, the major problems of
the mining industry are not a product of poor consultation. The existing
consultative organisation is adequate, although no doubt it can be improved. The
major weakness in this industry stems from the fact that there is no incentive for
men to work harder. If the Board and the NUM can reach agreement on a realistic
incentive scheme it will open the floodgates to waves of initiative throughout the
industry. If we fail to do that, worker participation will just lead to more
committees, more 'talking shops' and probably more time lost away from
production' (BACM *National Newsletter*, Sept. 1976).

Tyler's scepticism regarding the value of worker participation and his
preference for increasing work-force dependence through the payment
system was largely shared by his line management membership. Indeed,
the third response to the failure of NPLA, and that favoured lower down
the hierarchy closer to the point of production, was to use unofficial
incentives to try and maintain output. Wet payments, overtime, early
finishing, and, on occasion, barrels of beer, were offered to coal-face and
development workers as an inducement to work harder. In the Midlands
in particular, it seemed, the strong tradition of piece-work bargaining
carried over into the day-wage era. According to Krieger (1984, p. 258),
'In Nottingham colliers . . . characteristically responded to the

introduction of the NPLA by pressing management (and the NUM) to increase overtime and revise upward the gradings of specific classes of miners.' Our 1976 survey echoed these findings and revealed that in some pits overtime payments constituted as much as 25 per cent of total earnings.

The problems with these local incentives, as far as management was concerned, were, firstly, that they necessarily remained rather marginal to the effort bargain, and, secondly, that they were agreed informally. They were not subject to higher-level scrutiny and frequently represented rather dangerous departures from national agreements on hours of work, grading, deployment, and overtime. They were a fertile source of custom and practice. Their existence did, however, illustrate management's need for some form of productivity bargain with the direct work-force. The Board's version of 'direct control' had clearly proved inadequate to meet the requirements of production. In 1977 this was effectively acknowledged when the first Area Incentive Schemes were negotiated with the NUM. Since then incentives have remained the Board's main technique for controlling work. It is to the consequences of this shift in labour management strategy that we propose to turn in the following chapter.

2
Reliance on Incentives

Introduction

Since 1977 reliance on incentive payments has formed the core of the Coal Board's strategy for labour management. In our view, this choice on the part of management is founded on an effective recognition of management's weakness and dependence on labour co-operation to achieve its production objectives. There has been a realization that the engagement of the work-force with the process of production is problematical and that the use of payment by results to motivate face and development teams is the most effective way in which management can overcome this problem of uncertainty.

This realization did, in fact, come quite early in the day-wage era. In its evidence to the Wilberforce Inquiry, established to resolve the 1972 national strike, for instance, the Board stated its belief that a return to incentives was necessary. Three years later, a national productivity scheme was established, which provided for a bonus determined by the industry's overall rate of performance. This proved ineffective and was discontinued. Eventually, though, pressure on the NUM leadership to concede a more meaningful incentive scheme, in which pay would be linked to performance at pit level, bore fruit. The union's executive agreed in 1977 to permit the negotiation of area incentive schemes, despite the result of a national ballot which had reaffirmed the NUM's policy of opposition to payment by results. By the end of 1978 all NUM areas had negotiated an incentive scheme.

A full description of these schemes (which, in fact, all conformed to a common pattern) must wait until the following chapter when we discuss management's control of the new payment system in the face of NUM bargaining pressure. For the moment, it can simply be noted that their key feature was the linking of a substantial proportion of the earnings of production workers to the performance achieved on particular 'installations', coal-faces, or development drivages. Between 1978 and 1983 average incentive earnings remained at about 30 per cent of the coal-face and development worker grade rate. In money terms this amounted to average weekly incentive earnings of £45.00 across the entire industry in 1982/3. The scheme, therefore, represented a significant shift in the employment relationship of direct production workers and a significant attempt by management to realign their own interests in production with those of the mining labour-force.

However, the incentive scheme did not simply serve to reduce the division of interests between management and labour which had appeared under NPLA, by offering workers the opportunity to earn sizeable, performance-related bonuses. It served also, for example, to improve the pay of miners relative to that of other groups of manual workers. The big strikes in the early 1970s had pushed the miners to the top of the wages league but the uneven impact of incomes policy on the public and private sectors had rapidly reduced their differential. According to Coal Board estimates, miners' average weekly earnings in 1977 stood about 5 per cent above those of adult males in manufacturing, whereas in 1975 they had enjoyed a 20 per cent advantage (Handy, 1981, p. 277). The incentive scheme was successful in arresting this contraction. In 1978 the miners' advantage over manual workers in manufacturing jumped a full 9 per cent and continued to expand in subsequent years, reaching 17 per cent in 1982.

A further and related consequence was to widen internal differentials. The narrowness of the gap between coal-face and ancillary workers' earnings under NPLA was felt by the Board to compound the problems of the declining external relativity and make it doubly difficult to motivate the production work-force. Accordingly, therefore, the scheme was designed to widen differentials. Ancillary workers do not themselves have the opportunity to earn incentive payments but receive a bonus equivalent to 40, 50, or 65 per cent of face-workers' incentive earnings depending on where they work within the colliery. Between October 1977 and April 1979 the U1 production worker differential over surface workers increased from 133.4 to 145.5 per cent; their differential over underground ancillary grades U4–U7 increased from 121.8 to 128.8; and their differential over grades U2–U3 increased from 115.5 to 123.9 per cent (Handy, 1981, p. 283).

In addition to widening the earnings gap between U1 production grade workers and those on ancillary operations, the scheme also produced a differential between the two groups who comprise the U1 grade, face-workers and development men. Although both of these groups have the opportunity to earn incentive payments at the same standard rate for standard performance, the payments accruing to development men under the scheme have generally been considerably higher than those of face-workers. The Monopolies and Mergers Commission (MMC), for instance, in its investigation of the industry in 1982, found that average incentive earnings on coal-faces were about 20 per cent lower than those on development drivages (MMC, 1983, p. 280). The incentive scheme, therefore, has restored development men to their pre-eminent position in

TABLE 2.1 Coal industry productivity in tonnes per manshift, 1976–1983

	1976	1977	1978	1979	1980	1981	1982	1983
Output per manshift	2.28	2.21	2.19	2.24	2.31	2.32	2.40	2.44
Output per manshift (all underground)	2.91	2.83	2.79	2.86	2.95	2.94	3.02	3.06
Output per manshift (coal-face)	7.89	7.75	7.91	8.53	8.88	9.09	9.56	10.10

Source: NCB (1984).

the industry's wage hierarchy. Once again they are coalmining's 'big-hitting', high earners as they were in the era of piece-work.

The Effect of Incentives on Productivity

The strategy of incentives is designed to realize management's production objectives through increasing the dependence of the mining labour-force. It links a substantial proportion of miners' pay to performance against predetermined production targets and permits face and development workers to raise their earnings and satisfy their conceptions of relative justice through co-operating with management at the point of production. However, it is conceivable that such a strategy could fail through strong bargaining pressures leading to the issuing of slack targets which do not require the work-force to raise their productivity significantly. The opportunity the NCB's incentive scheme gives to local bargaining could effectively block the attempt to increase the dependence of the work-force on co-operation with management. Research on the introduction of payment by results systems has shown that they frequently do not have a significant positive impact on performance (Bowey and Thorpe, 1986, p. 215). Consequently, in this section we want to review the impact of the NCB's turn in strategy on the productivity of the mining labour force.

Table 2.1 shows the industry's productivity for the years between the introduction of the incentive scheme and the miners' industrial action against pit closures. Clearly, this was a period when performance substantially improved. It witnessed the halting of the downward drift in the industy's productivity figures and the pushing of some indicators to record levels. In the financial year 1982/3 for example, a 5 per cent increase pushed coal-face productivity to a new peak of over 10 tonnes per manshift.

TABLE 2.2   % changes in productivity between 1977 and 1978

| | Tonnes per manshift | |
	Overall output per manshift	Face output per manshift
June quarter 1977	− 1.1	+ 1.8
September quarter 1977	− 1.5	+ 0.7
December quarter 1977	− 3.2	− 1.2
January 1978	− 0.2	+ 2.9
February 1978	+ 1.9	+ 7.4
March 1978	+ 2.3	+ 10.1
March quarter 1978	+ 1.5	+ 7.4

Source: National Coal Board.

Although the figures in Table 2.1 do indicate an association between the return to incentives and a rise in productivity, they are problematic in certain respects. Other changes were occurring in these years which could also be expected to have a positive influence on productivity. Technical innovation continued to take place with more heavy-duty faces, more retreat mining and more face-end mechanization. There were also colliery closures. Between 1977 and 1983 the number of pits shrank from 238 to 191, most of those closed being at the low productivity end of the spectrum. Fortunately, for our purposes, some statistics are available which show the effect of the incentive scheme on productivity without the clouding influence of extraneous factors. Table 2.2, for example, shows the results of an NCB study of the impact of the scheme in the first months of its existence. Most Coal Board Areas introduced incentives in the first quarter of 1978. The figures show an immediate effect on performance. A similar test applied to development productivity reveals equivalent results. Development productivity increased by 6.6 per cent between the period June–November 1977 and the period June–November 1978. As with face productivity it continued to rise thereafter, climbing to 1.62 m. per drivage shift in 1983 from a base point of 1.47 in 1978.

Statistical evidence indicates, therefore, that the use of incentives to increase the dependence and co-operation of production workers was successful. Although management did encounter severe bargaining pressures which undoubtedly limited the impact of the scheme, these were not such as to nullify its effects completely. It seems incontrovertible that the scheme was effective in reversing the trend in mining productivity and was probably important in ensuring a fuller utilization of new equipment after its introduction. In the words of one economist and expert on the industry, by any standards this was quite a 'significant achievement' (Handy, 1981, p. 286).

TABLE 2.3   The effect of incentives on motivation (%)

	Face team motivation	Development team motivation	Proportion of cutting time per shift
Increased greatly	14	25	6
Increased	80	69	68
Same	6	6	26
Decreased	—	—	—
Decreased greatly	—	—	—
TOTAL	100	100	100

Source: Colliery Manager Questionnaire, 1981.

The Effect of the Incentive Scheme on the Work-force

The national figures suggest that the incentive scheme has stimulated an increase in the pace of work. In our research we attempted to identify the various factors underlying this trend: the changes in attitude, behaviour, and work organization which brought about the increase in productivity. Our main source of information was the questionnaire completed by the colliery manager at each of the pits in our sample.

Table 2.3 shows the managers' estimates of the impact of incentives on the motivation of coal-face and development workers. All but 6 per cent said that motivation had increased and a significant minority said that it had increased greatly. The impact of the scheme appeared to be more pronounced on the motivation of development workers, probably because of their higher incentive earnings and the fact that the smaller size of development work-groups means there is a closer connection between the individual worker's effort and the amount of incentive pay earned. One result of greater motivation, according to our colliery managers, was that coal-cutting machinery was better utilized and operated for a greater proportion of the shift than under daywage. In addition, in about two-thirds of the collieries, the managers said their workers were more willing under incentives to keep machinery running in poor work conditions. Our results suggest, therefore, that the return to incentives has helped counter one of the enduring management problems of the coal industry, the inadequate exploitation by the work-force of existing capital investment.

As well as a quantitative jump in production worker motivation, our research findings indicated that the incentive scheme also produced a qualitative change in work organization. The results in Table 2.4 suggest greater flexibility and more internal discipline within production work-groups. Over 80 per cent of colliery managers, for example, agreed that the incentive scheme had led to more flexible working on the part of face

TABLE 2.4   The effect of incentives on work organization (%)

	Teams work more flexibly	Teams more willing to go light-manned	Teams more critical of poor workers
Strongly agree	3	12	3
Agree	83	77	60
No opinion	3	11	8
Disagree	11	—	26
Strongly disagree	—	—	3
TOTAL	100	100	100

Source: Colliery Manager Questionnaire, 1981.

and development teams. At only four pits did the manager not hold this opinion. Furthermore, 89 per cent of managers affirmed that production teams are prepared to work with lighter manning, while none disagreed with this opinion. A further example of more flexible working practices can be seen in the colliery managers' replies to the question on whether teams have become more critical of poor workers and more prepared to see them moved. Once again a majority of managers felt there had been a change, with concern over work-group earnings capacity overriding feelings of solidarity.

The achievement of greater flexibility under the incentive scheme has been associated with a shift in relations between work-groups and their supervisors (Heery, 1984). Under NPLA, redeployment at the coal-face was meant to be the responsibility of increased numbers of deputies and overmen. As we have seen this arrangement generated friction with work-groups. Under the incentive scheme greater flexibility has been associated with a stepping back of supervisors from the task of direct supervision. Over half the sample of colliery managers, for instance, felt there was now less need for direct supervision of workers working under an incentive agreement. This impression was supported in interviews with supervisors. 'The official has more time to do his job now', explained one overman. 'During NPLA he was like Monty leading a charge, he had to drive the men, drive, drive, drive!' Another supervisor similarly remarked that under the day-wage system he was 'continually egging, pushing men to work', but that now, under incentives, 'they push themselves'.

The gap left by the supervisor stepping back somewhat from the point of production appears to have been filled at many pits by the chargeman or team captain. The chargeman is a face-team leader, normally elected by the work-group, who has the dual function of organizing work on the coal-face, in conjunction with the supervisor, and representing the views of his face-team both to management and to the union. In the course of the study the opinion was repeatedly expressed that NPLA had emptied the role of chargeman of any significant content but that the incentive scheme had reversed this tendency and elevated its importance. The chargeman, it was widely reported, was playing an active and crucial part in directing work at the coal-face, allocating tasks and maintaining team discipline. Over 80 per cent of colliery managers said that the incentive scheme had increased the importance of the chargeman in organizing work. 'Before the captain was just a figurehead,' one supervisor told us, 'now the team listens to him more'. The chargeman therefore has organized the work-group to enable it to exploit the earning opportunities the new payment system has presented to it. The 'qualitative' changes in working practices referred to above have been administered primarily by the chargeman.

The principal significance of this expansion of the chargeman's role is that chargemen, under incentives, have assumed certain of the functions previously allocated to supervisors under the strategy of 'direct control'. Though the extent of change has undoubtedly varied across the industry, there has clearly emerged a form of work organization in which elected team leaders have assumed much responsibility for guiding the ongoing work at the coal-face. The strategy of incentives has stimulated not only greater co-operation with management and greater motivation, but also a considerable degree of work-group self-discipline. Incentives have effectively created semi-autonomous work-groups, responsible in large part for regulating their own productive activity.

Incentives in the Wake of the Miners' Strike

Although the inventive scheme introduced in 1978 was effective in fostering greater work-force engagement with the task of production there were limits to its impact. While there was universal belief among the managers we interviewed that the industry needed payment by results, complaints about the specific characteristics of the existing incentive scheme were widespread. Many of those complaints hinged on a belief that the existing payment-scheme rules did not go far enough in rendering the work-force financially dependent on co-operation with management. There was a belief that even better results could be obtained if the scheme was redesigned.

The sources of much management frustration with the incentive scheme were the checks and defences built into it by the NUM. In both national and local negotiations the union had sought to regulate the return to payment by results, to ensure that the incentive scheme complied with trade-union canons of fairness and that it did not produce excessive uncertainty in members' earnings. Fairness, for instance, was meant to be achieved by basing incentive earnings on performance against supposedly objective measurements of effort. Pay was not linked directly to productivity or output, the primary concerns of management, as this would favour miners in those pits with the best geological conditions. In addition, the scheme contained a provision enabling all the faceworkers in one pit, or even in one area, to pool and then redistribute their incentive earnings equally. The payment to non-production workers of a bonus derived from the earnings of the face-teams was also intended to satisfy the demands of fairness through restricting the growth of the U1 differential.

Guarding against the uncertainties of payment by results was attempted, in the first instance, by introducing a number of fallback payments into the incentive scheme, so that miners would not bear the costs of geological deterioration, mechanical breakdown, or redeployment away from installation work. In the second instance, the NUM leadership, particularly after Arthur Scargill assumed the presidency, attempted to restrict the proportion of pay made up through incentive earnings. And in the third instance, and perhaps more importantly, the union insisted that installation standards be negotiated at local level, thus giving the membership in each pit the opportunity to ensure that performance targets were acceptable and readily achievable.

Since the 1984/5 strike, management has moved to strip away some of the protections incorporated into the payment system by the NUM. There is diminished preparedness to accommodate trade-union notions of fairness and a desire to foster even greater work-force dependence on co-operating in management's objective of low-cost production. The opportunity for management to redraw payment scheme rules in this way has been given by the collapse of NUM strength at the close of the pit strike and the emergence of the UDM. The latter is strongest in those coalfields where miners have a tradition of support for payment by results and the new union has proved a willing partner in British Coal's attempt to increase the salience of incentives.[1] This, in turn, has put pressure on the NUM to make comparable agreements. In 1985, for instance, the Board refused to extend the annual pay settlement agreed with the UDM until the NUM renounced its opposition to payment by results and agreed to enter into negotiations on the introduction of new incentive schemes.

In the period since the end of the 1984/5 strike, then, Coal Board management has proposed and implemented a number of changes in the operation of the incentive scheme, all of which loosen union control over the payment system and accentuate work-force dependence. There has been an attempt to produce sharper incentives, with greater rewards

---

[1] In reporting the successful conclusion of its first wage negotiations with the UDM, for instance, the NCB stated that, 'in those negotiations the Nottinghamshire and South Derbyshire representatives supported the Board's intention to place greater emphasis on incentives in the industry's wage structure' (NCB *Report and Accounts*, 1985/6).

for co-operation with management and more significant financial punishments for failing to deliver that co-operation. One way in which this has been attempted is through changing the way in which incentive earnings are calculated. Since the end of the strike area and colliery managers in the Board's Yorkshire, North Derbyshire, South Midlands, and Western Areas have replaced the original 1978 incentive scheme with new local schemes at a number of pits. Without exception these are 'bulk task' incentive schemes. They dispense with the requirement of the original scheme to link payment to performance against formal effort standards and, instead, link payments to the achievements of an output target; either a tonnage figure or the number of strips cut from a coal-face per shift. This represents an explicit rejection of the idea that incentive schemes should recognize the demands of fairness by giving all production workers a roughly equivalent chance to earn bonus and constitutes an attempt to tie earnings much more directly to the achievement of management's objectives. It is also felt by many managers that 'bulk task' incentives are more clearly understood by the work-force and so are more effective. In national negotiations with both the UDM and NUM, the Board has raised the prospect of a more general movement towards such direct output incentives, though nationally a move in this direction may only supplement and not replace the 1978 incentive scheme.

Further withdrawal from accommodation with trade-union notions of fairness has been revealed in management's growing unwillingness to countenance the pooling of face-workers' incentive earnings. The most graphic example of this has been the unilateral termination of the North Derbyshire Area Incentive Scheme in 1986. The North Derbyshire scheme provided for the pooling of earnings across the entire area. In British Coal's view, 'this variation on the national scheme discriminates against the most productive pits and operates a safety net for miners in the collieries with lower output which cannot be economically justified' (IDS Report, Mar. 1986). This statement indicates a belief, firstly, that earnings should be tied to colliery output, and secondly, that workers should not be shielded from the costs of poor economic performance through collective agreements. Management's decision indicates a concern effectively to reduce the size of the incentive-earning group and enforce a tighter link between earnings and performance at pit level. Within pits, too, however, there have been attempts to reduce the size of the incentive-earning group. Several of the new local incentive schemes in Yorkshire and the Midlands remove the option to pool the earnings of workers on different coal-faces so that incentive payments directly reflect performance on a particular installation. This is also the case with a new Area Incentive Scheme negotiated with the UDM in June 1987 for the Nottinghamshire coalfield.

A third way in which British Coal has challenged union attempts to ensure relations of equity between mineworkers has been its announcement that in future incentives would primarily benefit production workers. The Board wants to break with the system, introduced in 1978, whereby ancillary workers are paid a bonus derived from face-workers' earnings. The purpose of this, as we have said, was to limit the widening of internal differentials which the return to payment by results implied. In a series of statements since the miners' strike, however, British Coal has made it clear that it wants to detach the payment structures of production and non-production workers and further widen differentials. The way this will be done is through introducing additional incentive elements into the pay of the former group which will not be 'carried over' to affect the earnings of the latter. Again, local movement towards this objective has been a feature of the new incentive schemes in Yorkshire, the Midlands, and Nottinghamshire. Several of these decouple the earnings of installation and other workers and provide the latter with an alternative bonus, normally based on the overall tonnage produced at the colliery. The new scheme in Nottinghamshire more than doubles the standard incentive payment for face and development workers, but provides only a slight increase in bonus earnings for other miners.

Reducing the influence of trade-union conceptions of fairness on the payment system has formed one element in British Coal's use of incentives since the miners' strike. This can be said to increase the dependence of the work-force by linking earnings more closely to performance and management's ability to pay while downgrading the effect of comparisons. The second way in which management has tried to foster greater dependence is by weakening union controls designed to stabilize incentive earnings. In the aftermath of the strike, for example, it seems that many colliery managers have withdrawn local agreements governing such things as the operation of the payment system (Adeney and Lloyd, 1986, p. 187; NUM, 1986, p. 69). Our research revealed that before the strike there was considerable local union control over the various fall-back payments written into the incentive scheme. It is probable that this control is now diminished and that fall-back arrangements are operated less favourably for the union, so increasing the proportion of incentive pay which genuinely derives from performance against the incentive target. In addition, where new incentive schemes have been introduced provision for fall-back payments has been reduced.

A second way in which management has attempted to push back union controls designed to limit worker dependence on raising output has been through increasing the proportion of pay which is made up of incentive earnings. The refusal of the Board to concede an increase in the basic-grade rate to the NUM in 1985 until it conceded that strikers must incur reduced pension entitlements, had the effect of forcing many miners to rely on incentive earnings to raise their incomes. As a result there was a large increase in incentive payments in 1985 and 1986, which reached £51.55 per week in April 1986, about 25 per cent of take-home pay (IDS Report, Aug. 1986). Actions by the Board suggest that it wants this trend to continue. The large increases in standard incentive payments introduced in Nottinghamshire have just been mentioned, and in 1986 the Board's pay settlements with both the UDM and the NUM included the introduction of an attendance bonus and a 'conciliation' bonus for avoiding unofficial strike action. The inclusion of such payments, alongside the existing productivity incentives, represents a broadening of the range of functions incorporated within the industry's system of payment by results. Once again, this serves to increase the financial dependence of miners on co-operation in securing management's objectives.

The final change which management has sought to introduce into the operation of incentives in the wake of the miners' strike is the reduction of local opportunities for bargaining over the payment system. Alterations to the existing incentive scheme, such as the ending of the North Derbyshire pooling arrangement and the tightening up of local agreements have been introduced unilaterally and usually in the face of union opposition. In North Derbyshire, for example, the area union responded to management's action by imposing an overtime ban. There is, therefore, a greater preparedness to refashion the payment system without union agreement, though the new local incentive schemes in Yorkshire, the Midlands, and Nottinghamshire were negotiated. A feature of several of these schemes, however, is that they limit the opportunities for the work-force to renegotiate the productivity target. The scope for adjusting the target through special allowances for delays to work caused by poor geology or mechanical breakdown has been reduced. Under the original 1978 scheme the application of such allowances has frequently been a matter of vigorous local negotiation (see Chapter 4). In removing the allowances, therefore, there is an intention to reduce bargaining pressure as well as a desire to further sharpen incentive scheme rules.

In this section we have described how the management of the coal industry has developed its use of incentives in the context of reduced union power after the miners' strike. The existing incentive scheme has been altered in certain ways. There are proposals to supplement it with new forms of payment by results and in some collieries it has been effectively abandoned. Common to all these changes, both achieved and proposed, is a concern to reduce trade-union influence over the payment system, and to sharpen the incentive effect so as to increase the dependence of the work-force on the achievement of management's objectives. The effects of this policy on the industry's productivity have so far been positive. At the end of the financial year 1987/8 the Board's chairman was able to report a 60 per cent increase in productivity since the end of the 1984/5 dispute, which compared with an improvement of 1 per cent per annum in the decade before the strike (British Coal, 1988). A substantial proportion of this increase, of course, was due to the closure of the industry's low-productivity collieries and continued technical and organizational development. The scale and extent of improved performance achieved by many pits, however, suggest very strongly that there has been a real and not merely a statistical increase in labour productivity. In the financial year 1985/6, for example, 61 of the industry's 133 collieries achieved productivity records. Improved performance was not solely due, therefore, to the elimination of low-productivity capacity (NCB, 1986).

Just as the overall contribution of the payment system to improved productivity cannot be readily quantified using published figures, neither can the contribution of the changes the Board has introduced in its operation of the incentive scheme. However, the fact that such changes have been introduced at a time of dramatic advance in productivity is likely to reinforce their adoption and encourage future development of the payment system on the same lines. There are reasons, however, for thinking that the unusual 'productiveness' of payment by results in the years since the strike may be due to the context in which it has been operating. Two factors have complemented management's attempt to make the work-force more dependent on the use of payment by results. The first of these is the indebtedness of many miners as a result of the length of the 1984/5 strike (Adeney and Lloyd, 1986, p. 4). The second is the increased rate of colliery closure and the adoption by management of explicit cost targets to guide closure decisions. Between the start of the strike and March 1988 the number of pits shrank from 170 to 94, and management adopted cost targets of £1.65 per gigajoule for short-life pits and £1.50 per gigajoule for long-life pits. The effect of the first of these factors was to increase the interest of miners in raising earnings through the incentive scheme, while the effect of the second was to encourage them to raise productivity and achieve a more cost-effective use of capital equipment in order to reduce the risk of colliery closure. It can be argued that both increased the responsiveness of miners to payment by results.

The Miners and New Technology

In this chapter we have argued that management strategy for the control of work in coal-mining has shifted in the past twenty years away from experiments with 'direct control' towards attempts to stimulate greater work-force motivation through incentives. We now want to compare this interpretation with, and defend it against, an alternative analysis of the evolution of work organization in coal-mining which has been put forward by scholars from the University of Bradford (Burns *et al.*, 1983, 1985). The interpretation offered by these writers is more or less the complete opposite to that propounded by ourselves. In their view, the mining industry in the past twenty years has witnessed 'a dramatic change in the kinds of objectives adopted by the NCB'. They argue that 'most of the human relations aspects' of work design have been abandoned in favour of patterns of work organization which 'reduce human intervention' (Burns *et al.*, 1985, p. 96).[2] The instrument of this transformation, they contend, has been new technology.

The Bradford Group's case is that coal-mining in the 1980s has entered a new 'automation phase of development' (Burns *et al.*, 1985, p. 96). This originated, they argue, in a series of decisions taken by the NCB's Central Planning Unit (CPU) in the early 1970s. These set the investment strategy for the Board for the next two decades and with it the future course of work organization in the industry. According to the Bradford Group, the principal problem the CPU identified for resolution was the inadequate use of machinery. It was concerned to cut the amount of production lost through delays caused either by inadequate or insufficient machinery or by the work-force restricting output. The means developed to achieve this was the MINOS (Mine Operating System) system of mine automation which has begun to be introduced in collieries over the past few years. MINOS, according to the authors, is 'a highly centralized, hierarchically organized system of remote control and monitoring in mines' (Burns *et al.*, 1985, p. 97). It permits the 'closed-loop control' of a number of mining processes such as coal clearance, environmental monitoring, and coal preparation. A further system, FACE (Face Advanced Control Equipment), is being developed to control the advance of the conveyor and roof supports (Winterton, 1985, p. 234). A second aim is to permit the monitoring of the work-force at the point of production in order to increase management control. FIDO, dubbed the watchdog by Yorkshire face-workers, has been developed to monitor 'man-made' delays. Information is captured by the system at the coal-face and is relayed to a control room computer located on the surface. This indicates to management the position of the shearer along the face, as well as the cause and duration of any delays in production (Winterton, 1985, p. 234).

The main thrust of these innovations, the Bradford group argue, is to reduce management's dependence on labour commitment. New technology, in their view, has been developed in coal-mining in terms of three selections from the list set out in Figure 1.1 in the previous chapter. The first of these is a desire to replace labour with machinery in order to save on labour costs and to permit greater management control of

---

[2] 'Powerloading', according to Winterton (1985, p. 231), 'increased the miners' control over the labour process by requiring new skills and by returning responsible autonomy' to face teams.

production. In their work the Bradford Group emphasize throughout the serious consequences of automation for mining employment. MINOS, and its associated computer systems, will permit reductions in the numbers of workers required in virtually all areas of mining work. At the coal-face, for example, the authors quote Department of Energy estimates which claim that teams will be reduced from an average of twenty-two to fifteen men as a result of automation (Burns *et al.*, 1983, p. 17). As well as the direct effects on employment the Bradford group also point out that automation is having indirect effects. Through facilitating an increase in productivity it enables the Board to concentrate production in the central coalfields, where the return on investment is greater, and to close pits in the peripheral coalfields. This process, they say, formed 'the background to the 1984 miners' strike' (Burns *et al.*, 1985, p. 93).

The second use to which new technology is being put, according to the Bradford group, is the deskilling of the work-force. The majority of maintenance jobs will be deskilled through the development of new diagnostic equipment and standard inspection machinery, while the FACE system will incorporate elements of the skills of face-workers (Burns *et al.*, 1985, pp. 101, 106). Reinforcing the narrowing of worker discretion through job design is the third selection by the industry's management. In the view of the Bradford group new technology will solve the previously insuperable problem of developing effective supervision of underground workers (Burns *et al.*, 1985, pp. 96, 100). FIDO provides management with detailed information of worker activity at the face and this can be used to ensure labour maintains a level of productivity congruent with management's objective.

The case put forward by the Bradford group is undoubtedly a strong one, though the structure of the argument is familiar; readers will have no doubt detected symptoms of Bravermania. Their argument that it has been the intention of senior management in the NCB to use new technology to reduce the size of the labour-force and narrow the span of worker discretion seems incontrovertible.[3] However, we would question their statement that these are novel objectives, adopted in the early 1970s. As far as we are aware they have been constant goals of the NCB since Vesting Day. They certainly formed part of the NPLA strategy and featured also in the response to its comparative failure. In addition, these objectives have been pursued in recent years not just through the adoption of microelectronic technology but also through the 'upgrading' of existing techniques as seen, for instance, in the heavy duty mechanization programme and the installation of shield supports (NCB *Report and Accounts*, 1982/3).

---

[3] Their evidence, culled from numerous management policy statements, provides support for John Child's contention that enterprises, like British Coal, which are dominated by professional engineers will tend to use new technology to eliminate the direct labour force (Child, 1985).

Apart from this, we have two main difficulties in accepting the work of the Bradford Group. The first concerns their description of the NCB's business strategy. The concentration of production in the central coalfields, the closure of pits, and the NUM's strike against those closures are all depicted as consequences of the decisions taken by the NCB's Central Planning Unit in the early 1970s (Burns *et al.*, 1985, pp. 93–4; Winterton, 1985, p. 241). This neglects the fundamental shift in the industry's business strategy instituted by the Thatcher Government. The emphasis on achieving production targets through large-scale investment, which was to be found in the 1974 Plan for Coal, has been displaced by an emphasis on financial rigour. The industry has been required to compete on world energy markets and match its output to a (medium-term) goal of profitability. This in turn has led to colliery closures and redundancies and to a concentration of production in high-productivity pits. It is incorrect to portray these developments simply as the follow-through of the decisions made by the CPU.

Further, the shift in business strategy initiated by the Conservatives has led to much closer scrutiny of capital investment decisions within the NCB (Berry *et al.*, 1986, pp. 140–1). Prior to 1986 the accounting measures used by the NCB (output per manshift, cost per tonne) were systematically biased in favour of capital-intensive as opposed to labour-intensive operations. This bias has now been offset by the introduction of a cost target of £1.00 per gigajoule for new capital investment. It is possible that this, coupled with the general financial pressure on the industry, may restrain the drive towards automation described by the Bradford Group. It is possible to point to instances where the government's enthusiasm for limiting expenditure has successfully overcome the enthusiasm of the Board's mining engineers for high technology development. Perhaps the most obvious example is the limiting of the scale of the Board's Vale of Belvoir project. While there are undoubtedly elements in the investment strategy initiated by the CPU which can be used to foster the Conservatives' aim of a self-supporting coal industry, there may also be contradictions between the two.

Our second difficulty with the work of the Bradford Group arises from their tendency to exaggerate the potential of the new technology for monitoring and directing the work of miners. Their argument is largely based on reports of the impact and potential of micro-electronic equipment made by mining engineers. They have not studied new technology *in situ*. This has perhaps led to a tendency to discount the problems management may encounter in applying new techniques.

A major theme in sociological studies of the introduction of new technology is the uncertainty of its effects. Wilkinson (1983), for example, has argued that the introduction of a new piece of capital equipment in an organization occurs through a frequently difficult and prolonged process of adaptation. New techniques have to be bedded down within the workplace. During this adaptation process, he argues, workers have the opportunity to influence the manner in which new equipment will be operated. He reports case-studies from manufacturing where workers have used this opportunity to 'claw back' control over work even where management have deliberately tried to use new technology to minimize their discretion.

In mining, we feel, the nature of the underground environment is likely to require just such an adaptation process. Geological problems pose a continual threat to production and machinery must be operated in difficult physical conditions. In this situation the exclusion of 'human intervention' from much of the mining process may prove difficult. Avoiding and reacting to disruptions to automated operations, we would argue, is likely to remain dependent on the exercise of tacit skills by the work-force. Important elements of discretion will remain within mining jobs and the exercise of that discretion by the direct work-force will determine the extent to which new equipment is fully exploited. Indeed, this has been acknowledged by the Bradford Group in one of their papers. They write that, 'an industry with a reduced and unskilled workforce and automated machinery is likely to run into serious problems in maintaining productivity' (Burns et al., 1985, p. 106).

In their work the Bradford Group make much of the monitoring capacity of new technology. Mine automation, it is argued, permits not just a reduction in the number and a deskilling of mining jobs, but also the closer supervision of those deskilled jobs that remain. However, while FIDO may increase the amount of information available to management on worker performance, the Bradford Group have little to say on how that information will in fact be used to intensify work. In terms of the framework we developed above, they neglect the fourth component of management control over work, the use of disciplinary sanctions to enforce a level of effort compatible with management objectives. Existing evidence, however, suggests that miners have had some success in resisting attempts to use information obtained through FIDO to tighten management control. The Bradford Group themselves report an agreement in Yorkshire that rules out the use of FIDO to resolve disputes over the incentive scheme, and we came across similar controls on its use in Nottinghamshire. In the wake of the 1984/5 strike, management may well have escaped from such restrictions. The point remains, however, that greater information on worker performance does not of itself produce greater management control of work. This is dependent on the relative strengths of management and labour. At one point, the Bradford Group state that a consequence of new technology could be to increase the strategic power of miners in those large, high-productivity pits which have survived the closure programme. Our analysis of workplace trade-union power presented in Chapter 8 would support this view and it seems likely that the workers in such pits will have the capacity to prevent FIDO being used to intensify work.

The effect of FIDO, according to the Bradford Group, has been to enable the NCB, 'to achieve a level of supervision that it has never previously had over underground work; the supervision and control have increased the intensity of work, removed the autonomy of the face team, and threatened jobs through increasing productivity' (Burns et al., 1985, p. 101). Their work contains several statements of this kind which, in effect, claim that new technology is being used in coal-mining to achieve the 'real subordination of labour'. Our final difference with the Bradford Group arises from the fact that if this is the case, if the significance of human intervention in the mining process is being minimized, then why does management remain wedded to an attempt to raise the productivity of labour through payment by results? In their work the incentive scheme has been described as a means to avert national pay strikes by fragmenting the bargaining structure (Winterton, 1985, p. 232) and as a means 'to incorporate the miners into the process of automation' (Burns et al., 1985, p. 101). It is argued that FIDO's success in cutting production time lost through delays has been welcomed by miners because this increases incentive payments. At no point is there recognition that incentives have proved effective as a management tool for directly raising productivity. At no point do the authors confront the argument of the industry's managers that greater use of capital equipment in the future must rest on greater reliance on payment by results.[4]

In our view, the enthusiasm of British Coal for incentives betokens much less confidence in the capacity of new technology to control workers than is shown by the Bradford Group. It suggests a conviction that management will continue to be dependent on the active engagement of labour with production even in the high-technology mining industry which is emerging. Further evidence that this is the case is to be found in the fact that management have renewed their enthusiasm for techniques of worker involvement. This baldly contradicts the Bradford Group's assertion that a concern with the human relations aspects of work have been abandoned. Since the 1984/5 strike British Coal has initiated a programme of training in 'direct communication' for its managers (NCB Report and Accounts, 1986). In the North Derbyshire and Western areas monthly team briefings have been initiated for face-workers to discuss safety and production problems (Guardian, 14 Feb. 1986). In other

---

[4] According to a statement of the Board's technical director to the House of Commons Select Committee on Energy, raising productivity 'depends on our ability to motivate the workforce, and we are increasingly suggesting that increases in real earnings can only come from productivity'.

areas, such as South Yorkshire, management has used a variety of methods of direct communication to stress the connection between productivity, continued investment, and colliery closures.[5] Unlike the experiments with worker involvement in the 1970s, this current campaign does not rest on the authority of the NUM. Indeed, one of the intentions behind it appears to be to bypass the union, reduce its 'institutional centrality' within the workplace, and build new relationships of loyalty between the work-force and the colliery management team. It therefore complements the attempts to reduce union influence over the payment system. The most important point, however, is that it is based on a recognition that full utilization of equipment depends on worker commitment; that discretion and autonomy remain at the coal-face and can be tapped to achieve management's objectives.[6]

Conclusion

In this and the previous chapter we have reviewed the various techniques managers in coal-mining have used to raise and maintain the work performance of British miners. We have identified, described, and evaluated the effectiveness of two management strategies for the control of work, the strategy of 'direct control' which was enshrined within the National Powerloading Agreement of 1966 and the strategy of incentives, introduced in 1978 but further developed in the wake of the 1984/5 miners strike. The emphasis of the first of these strategies lay on the use of techniques intended to reduce management dependence on labour commitment. The emphasis of the second strategy, on the other hand, has lain on the use of payment by results to stimulate work-force co-operation at the point of production.

In the final section of Chapter 2 we have attempted to defend our description and periodization of management control in mining from an alternative offered by writers from the University of Bradford. Whereas our analysis has stressed the importance of payment systems and the extent of joint regulation, typical objects of study of 'traditional' industrial relations writing, the Bradford Group have stressed the importance of technology and the design of tasks. This emphasis on the design of jobs in

[5] We owe this information to Stephen Wood and Ray Richardson of the London School of Economics.

[6] In terms of our framework for analysing management control of work, the industry's experiment with direct communication attempts to increase worker dependence on co-operation in two ways. Firstly, it offers 'involvement', an opportunity to participate in decisions which affect the immediate working environment. This is particularly important with briefing groups. Secondly, it seeks to communicate and emphasize to workers the extent of their dependence on co-operation with managers. This is the purpose of techniques which use direct communication to stress the financial pressures on the enterprise and the risk of colliery closure.

order to minimize discretion has been a feature of many contributions to what has become known as the 'labour process debate'. In this body of work there is a tendency to argue that the most significant resource management has in controlling work is its ability to design tasks so as to deskill the direct work-force and concentrate decision-making in its own hands. While this may be the case, an emphasis on job design must not exclude consideration of other influences on the control of work. A repeated criticism of Braverman's *Labour and Monopoly Capital*, which can also be applied to the work of the Bradford Group, is that it ignores the importance of 'tacit skills' even in the performance of jobs which have been deliberately deskilled by management (Mainwaring and Wood, 1985). Where work is performed then some irreducible discretion must remain in the hands of the work-force. This can be used to restrict output or to raise it. The use of techniques to encourage the latter result must, therefore, always form part of the managerial repertoire. In mining, we have argued, such 'tacit skills' are particularly important because of the uncertainties of the production process. In managing British miners, British Coal has discovered that payment by results is the most effective means of ensuring that these tacit skills are deployed to serve managerial objectives.

PART II   The Control of Local Pay-bargaining

3
The 'Reform' of Industrial Relations

Introduction

As the previous chapter has made clear, the reintroduction of incentives by the National Coal Board in 1977/8 proved a reasonably successful managerial innovation. An incentive held aloft in the sphere of exchange secured greater commitment from the industry's work-force in the sphere of production. The scheme, therefore, helped solve one of the most serious difficulties posed for the industry's management by the National Powerloading Agreement. Simultaneously, however, it presented a new set of problems. The scheme was intended to be self-financing. Improvements in productivity were not to be outstripped by increases in incentive payments and bonus secured through its operation. The opportunity for local, pit-head pay-bargaining which the scheme presented to the industry's work-force raised the prospect of its 'decay', a gradual shift in the terms of the effort/reward relationship in the work-force's favour. The incentive scheme, then, set the industry's management the task of preventing its 'decay', of controlling local pay-bargaining so as to avoid an upward spiral in wage costs.

The difficulties faced by the NCB, however, were not unique, and the problem of controlling payment systems has been a major preoccupation of practitioners and students of industrial relations in post-war Britain. Therefore, before describing the system erected by the NCB to control local pay-bargaining, we place it in a wider context by examining the debates surrounding current trends in payment systems and the 'tools' which, it is claimed, can assist management in their task. Interest in this area was stimulated by the publication of the Donovan Report in 1968. Since then, the analysis presented of the 'anarchic' nature of workplace industrial relations, and the prescriptions offered have been the subject of continuous debate. Our discussion of the control of pay-bargaining, therefore, starts with an examination of the Report and the responses to it.

The Donovan Analysis

According to the Donovan Report itself, and much academic writing in the 1960s (Donovan, 1968; Fox and Flanders, 1969), the British system of industrial relations was suffering from a lack of normative regulation. Its peculiar characteristics were the fragmentation of collective bargaining and heavy reliance on informal procedures and agreements. For Donovan, and his academic advisers from the University of Oxford, the consequences of this dispersed pattern of organization were grave. They included an increasing resort to unofficial strikes and other forms of work-group pressure; 'excessive' power on the part of shop stewards to determine both earnings and the nature of work organization; consequent inflation and low productivity in British manufacturing; and an attendant and inbuilt resistance in the economy to the strategies of national policy-makers revealed most clearly in the frustration of attempts to control incomes (Donovan, 1968, pp. 261–2).

The origins of this pattern of industrial relations have frequently been traced to the structure of British management. Brown (1973, p. 105), in his study of piece-work bargaining, for instance, relates the growth of custom and practice and wage-drift to 'poor information and control systems within management'. Clegg, in his comparative study of trade-union organization, makes a similar point. Management in British industry, he argues, has been marked by a failure to develop, 'effective and unified control systems', and this has led to the 'greater power and independence of workplace organizations in Britain' (1976, p. 108). An important feature of this 'failure' on the part of British management has been an excessive reliance on poorly administered systems of payment by results. Fragmented bargaining and shop-floor power have been said to reach their fullest development in the context of decayed systems of incentive (Donovan, 1968, pp. 23–4). British managers have used piece-work as an alternative to developing more effective controls over production while the operation of payment by results has led to a further attenuation of their hold over work organization.

Donavan's prescription for the 'pathological' condition of British industrial relations was that management should simultaneously reform itself and workplace collective bargaining. The Report recommended that management should adopt a more proactive approach to relations with shop stewards and work-groups. The main terms of its recommendations are well known. Donovan called first of all for the formalization and standardization of collective bargaining within the individual enterprise. Written and agreed rules should govern the relationship between employer and employee, importing greater predictability and stability into shop-floor industrial relations. The Report also recommended that British industrial relations should undergo processes of centralization and specialization. Although it advised a switch from multi-employer to single-employer bargaining, within the firm the Report's programme of reform implied a limitation of the discretion of line management, and particularly foremen, to agree matters and yield concessions to the union.

Greater responsibility for the conduct of industrial relations should instead be devolved to personnel management whose numbers should be expanded and status enhanced. Such changes were necessitated by Donovan's call for firms to devise 'effective personnel policies to control methods of negotiation and pay structures' (1968, p. 25). It was personnel specialists who were to design, implement, administer, and monitor such policies.

The Donovan Report, therefore, advocated a managerially initiated reform of industrial relations procedures within the individual enterprise. *Ad hoc* decision-making and casual bargaining, it advised, should be replaced by formal rules and the practice of 'muddling through' should be replaced by explicit industrial relations policies establishing company objectives in this sphere. Integral to these recommendations for a bureaucratic ordering of industrial life, were calls for the reconstruction of payment and grading systems. Donovan envisaged a rationalization of systems of pay and grading through a process of productivity bargaining which would increase management control over work organization and permit a tighter link to be established between earnings and company performance (1968, pp. 83–5). The Report implied that the 'buying out' of incentive bonus schemes should be part of this process.

Since Donovan, a major concern of industrial relations writing has been the extent to which British industrial relations have evolved in accordance with the Report's recommendations. A number of positions have been adopted. The first argues that developments have broadly followed the lines mapped out by Donovan, though there is disagreement over the extent to which this is a direct result of the Royal Commission.[1] This argument has been put forward most forcefully by writers from the University of Warwick. In a series of publications they have contended that the ten years after Donovan witnessed the growth of more formalized single employer bargaining; the greater propensity of firms to adopt written disputes and other procedures, an increase in the number of personnel specialists, and the reform of payment systems (Brown, 1980; 1981, pp. 32–3, 44, 111; Brown and Sisson, 1983).

The interpretations offered of the consequences of these changes have tended to be cautious. There are statements from Warwick, however, which suggest that reform along Donovan's lines had the result suggested by the Commissioners, namely a restoration of management control over pay and productivity. Perhaps the boldest of these has been made by Brown who argued in 1980 that 'Employers increasingly have pay more

[1] Purcell's (1981, p. 19) insistence that the Report was influential, for example, can be contrasted with Batstone's (1984, p. 42) argument that much of the 'reform' of industrial relations since Donovan arose from broad organizational changes in British management, which themselves largely derived from the late 1960s' merger boom.

under control both by having explicit negotiations with representatives of their own employees and by doing so within the framework of job evaluation and work study' (p. 146).

Some writers, however, have taken an opposite view minimizing the extent of reform and asserting that much of British industrial relations remains fragmented and informal. Marsh (1982, p. 162), for instance, has claimed there is 'no evidence of more than a moderate movement in the "Donovan" direction', and other writers have drawn attention to continuing limitations in the use of personnel specialists and of techniques such as job evaluation (Daniel and Millward, 1983, pp. 207, 285–7).

Closely associated with a tendency to question the extent of reform is a tendency to question the significance of those changes which have occurred. Even where personnel specialists have been appointed, where more formal procedures have been adopted, and where pay and grading have been rationalized, it is argued, 'disorder' may persist in the British workplace. A representative of this position is Batstone. He claims that reform frequently had the opposite effect to that predicted by its advocates, leading to an increase in the range and intensity of bargaining and, moreover, that 'the movements towards reform do not appear to have removed informal practices, including what might loosely be termed custom and practice and unilateral worker/union regulation. Indeed, if anything, the restrictions upon managerial freedom have tightened' (1984, p. 136). Turner and his colleagues (1977, p. 68), moreover, have concluded on the basis of survey evidence that the formalization of industrial relations has led to increased rather than reduced labour conflict.

There is dispute, therefore, over the direction, the scale, and the consequences of change in British industrial relations since Donovan.

The Reform of Payment Systems

The reconstruction of payment systems, as we have seen, has been an important theme in post-Donovan industrial relations. According to Brown (1981, p. 110), the 'techniques used in payment are a central feature of workplace industrial relations. They influence the frequency with which there are opportunities for bargaining over pay and other matters. They also have powerful implications for management controls.' The effects of payment-system reform on workplace bargaining and management control has normally been approached through discussion of five issues. These are the development of new forms of payment by results; increased reliance on work study; the use of job evaluation to establish 'rational' grading structures; the diminishing ability of supervisors to negotiate with workers; and the growth of more elaborate management control systems which is associated with an increase in the numbers of specialist personnel managers. Before turning to our investigation of the NCB's incentive scheme, it is necessary to review the state of debate in each of these areas.

New Forms of Payment by Results

In the 1960s fragmented piece-rate systems of payment were seen as major causes of 'disorder' in British industrial relations. They stimulated workplace bargaining and provided opportunities for the extension of shop-floor controls over pay and work (National Board for Prices and Incomes, 1968). Since then, however, a number of innovations have been said to reduce the adverse consequences of payment by results and to improve its effectiveness as a tool of management control. The first of these is a trend towards group schemes. The advantages such schemes are presumed to hold over individual piece-work are that they simultaneously reduce and centralize workplace bargaining. The ratio of reward to effort for an entire work-group, department, or even plant is set in one single bargain, while haggling between individual workers or section stewards and rate-fixers is replaced by negotiation between senior stewards and plant managers. However, while developments such as this may make group payment by results preferable to many managers, these schemes can also have weaknesses as control devices. Frequently they are complex and difficult to understand and contain only a limited incentive effect. According to a manager in the coal industry their great disadvantage is that 'they take a man's earnings away from the end of his shovel'. Group schemes may also help collectivize workers. They may replace the 'militant individualism' of workers under traditional piece-work (Cunnison, 1966) with collective pressure on management for concessions. A survey by White, for example, found that group schemes, particularly plant-wide bonus schemes, were associated with a higher than average level of disputes (White, 1981, p. 102).

A second, widely reported trend in payment by results is the reduction in the proportion of total earnings which derive from incentives. Between 1973 and 1979 for those male manual workers receiving incentive payments, the payments fell as a proportion of total earnings from 28.6 to 20.6 per cent (Brown and Sisson, 1983). Incentives today tend to form a rather modest supplement to a flat-rate payment negotiated at workplace, company, or industry levels. One possible effect of this may be to reduce bargaining pressure on payment by results systems. As the contribution of incentives to total earnings dwindles, the need for workers to control the payment system may also diminish (White, 1981, p. 139). The commonly reported finding that workers manipulate incentive schemes to stabilize earnings would suggest this is likely to occur. Against this view, however, it can be argued that a fifth of total earnings remains a figure well worth struggling for. In addition, where incentives shrink to too small a proportion of the wage, they are likely to lose their significance for worker motivation. There is likely to be a point beyond which diminished bargaining pressure must be exchanged for diminished effectiveness.

Work Study

A further change in the operation of payment by results is that schemes are now based much more frequently, 'upon fairly rigorous work study techniques' (Brown, 1980, p. 138). The benefits considered to accrue to management from this change are twofold. Firstly, and most importantly, it is felt to increase management control over the fixing of productivity levels. The formal measurement of labour input by management specialists replaces the determination of effort levels by custom or informal bargaining. According to Brown and Sisson (1983, p. 142), the effect of basing payment by results on work study 'has been to reduce considerably the scope for the informal and fragmented pay bargaining which featured so prominently in the Donovan analysis'. A second claimed effect is that pay differences are viewed as a reflection of differences in labour input and are consequently held to be 'fair'. Work study endows management with 'the capacity to demonstrate that differences in levels of bonus paid are justified by real differences in performance' (Farningham, 1972). It can, therefore, help in combating competitive bargaining and pressures to loosen standards.

Other writers, however, have put forward arguments which suggest that the consequences of the wider deployment of work study may not be so unambiguous. Baldamus (1961, pp. 45–6), for instance, sees work study as 'a matter of intuitive judgement', the purpose of which is the discovery of 'the preconceived, habitually maintained standards of normal exertion in any type of operation'. In his view, work study does not establish a standard of effort purely of management's choosing. Rather, its use by management is invariably limited by what the workers studied consider to be a fair level of effort, given a certain wage.

If Baldamus is correct in thinking that work study does not replace but merely formalizes customary effort standards, then the second advantage said to accrue to managers may also not be realized. If workers are aware that work-study standards do not comprise 'objective' measurements but reflect such things as the relative bargaining power of work-groups, then they are unlikely to accept as legitimate differences in earnings arising from the application of such standards.

Job Evaluation

Another feature of the formalization of workplace industrial relations in the 1970s was the spread of job evaluation. As with work study, the effect of this is frequently held to be the reduction of fragmented workplace bargaining (Daniel and Millward, 1983, p. 203). Job evaluation, in this view, reduces workplace bargaining by replacing sectional haggling over differentials with a single, centrally negotiated wages structure. It can also reduce bargaining pressures by simplifying the grading structure. The advantages to management of drawing senior shop stewards into the evaluation process are also mentioned frequently. The new grade hierarchy is thereby given legitimacy and work-force representatives assume responsibility for preserving its integrity.

Once again, however, the link between payment-system reform and 'orderly' industrial relations can be questioned. Like work study, job-evaluated wage structures may themselves become the target of sectional bargaining. Workers dissatisfied with their position on the scale may pursue regrading, despite the fact that this may lead them into conflict with those stewards committed to the system's defence. Where relatively strong groups of workers do achieve grading concessions this is likely to reduce the legitimacy of the scheme in the eyes of other workers, leading to further demands for exceptional treatment. Where such demands are not met worker co-operation with management may well diminish. According to Batstone (1984, pp. 167–8), 'the very attraction of job evaluation—its integrity and coherence—may become serious problems, particularly given multi-unionism and a tradition of fractional organization and bargaining'.

Pressures on job-evaluated wage structures are likely to be more intense in workplaces where job evaluation coincides with payment by results. Although the underlying logic of the two techniques is at variance—one is concerned with linking rewards to effort, the other with establishing equitable differentials—they do coexist in a substantial number of plants (Daniel and Millward, 1983, p. 206). Payment by results is likely to disrupt job evaluation because it tends to produce differential incentive earnings which upset neat, rational pay structures. Workers who find themselves doing badly out of payment by results may seek compensation through regrading, while workers who feel undergraded may exert pressure for slack incentive targets.

The Changing Position of the Supervisor

The rationalization of payment systems and wage structures since the 1960s has been linked to broader changes in the structure of management organization. The management of industrial relations, within the workplace and within the individual firm, has undergone processes of centralization and specialization. There have been movements towards plant-wide or company-wide collective bargaining, in part associated with the adoption of group incentive schemes and job evaluation. There has also been a growth in the number of specialist industrial relations managers at the workplace and on company boards. Both of these developments have major implications for the generalist at the base of the management hierarchy, the supervisor.

A number of studies in the 1960s and 1970s traced the origin of shop-floor power to the relationship between work-groups and their foremen and other junior line managers. Such managers, it was argued, were possessed of considerable discretion and were overwhelmingly concerned with maintaining production in their particular section or department. The maintenance of wage structures or payment systems tended to be considered secondary. Junior managers would collude with work-groups in the subversion of formal industrial relations rules and procedures in order to avoid disruption to production. Faced with assertive workers, and lacking in effective sanctions, they were compelled to yield concessions. The result was the 'inevitable growth of informality' (Terry, 1977).

The reform of workplace industrial relations is believed to have altered this situation in a number of ways. The adoption of more comprehensive written agreements, for instance, can provide rules to guide supervisors in their management of staff. Formalization can bureaucratize the foreman's role and minimize the need to take *ad hoc* decisions under conditions of pressure. Even more important has been the elevation of the power of decision in workplace industrial relations. Supervisors have been replaced, as the work-force's principal bargaining partner, by more senior management representatives. Such figures are believed to be less exposed to work-group pressure and are also felt to be more aware of the long-term costs of short-term concessions. Centralizing the power to bargain, therefore, is seen as an effective way of eliminating managerial weakness and shutting off a major source of custom and practice.

There are grounds for believing, however, that the supervisor's 'creative' input into workplace industrial relations may have survived the reforming process. Even if standardized procedures have been drawn up to guide supervisory behaviour, substantial areas of discretion may remain. Supervisors may be in a position to decide whether or not to apply formal rules or to choose either a lax or a strict interpretation of their meaning. The interpretation of rules, indeed, may be used as a means to bargain with workers, failure to activate procedures being exchanged for work-force co-operation (Marchington, 1982, pp. 89–90).

Supervisors, therefore, despite change, may yet retain sufficient power to exert perhaps a modest but still significant amount of influence over workplace industrial relations. Even where their discretion has been successfully minimized, however, and the power of decision transferred up the management hierarchy, the effects may not be as is frequently supposed. More senior managers may be equally alive to the need to avoid disruption to the production process, they may be equally vulnerable to bargaining pressure and equally likely to take a short-term view. It remains a matter for empirical verification whether centralizing control of workplace industrial relations eliminates 'disorder'.

The Growth of Personnel Specialists

A final and crucial aspect of the reform of workplace industrial relations is frequently considered to be the growth in the number of specialist industrial relations managers. For those who claim to discern an effective reform of industrial relations since Donovan, the significance of this development is likely to reside in the commitment of specialists to the specific requirements of industrial relations management. Unlike supervisors and other line managers, they will be less prepared to sacrifice coherent wage structures or agreed procedures for short-term gains to production. They are more likely to value 'order' in industrial relations.

At the heart of this interpretation of developments is a belief that the power to innovate in industrial relations should be transferred from line management to specialists better equipped to shoulder the responsibility. Personnel managers will develop more sophisticated industrial relations policies and practices, and supervisors and other line managers will be constrained to follow their guidelines. It is considered that a degree of control must be exercised by the personnel or industrial relations department over line management. Conflict between production managers and the personnel function, however, is a well-attested feature of industrial relations (Hill, 1981, p. 82). It remains a matter for verification whether the expanded ranks of personnel specialists have been able to secure commitment to 'reformed' industrial relations among their colleagues in the line. As Brown (1981, p. 26) has noted, '[it] is one thing to have specialist managers but quite another to have their advice and policies heeded'.

One factor that has possibly militated against them in this is the traditionally rather peripheral position the personnel function has occupied in the management hierarchy. Management functions tend to be evaluated in accordance with the directness of their contribution to the process of accumulation. Accounting systems in the modern enterprise are designed to measure the cost-effectiveness of different departments. Much personnel work, however, cannot be evaluated with such quantitative techniques. As a result, personnel departments tend to suffer from low status and are frequently seen as separate from the vital, profit-producing core of the management organization. According to Legge (1978, pp. 57–8), 'management in general tend not to perceive the human resource variable as presenting uncertainties whose resolution is vital to organisation success, and in this they are supported by the value systems that dominate all cost-conscious organisations'. As the resolution of pressing uncertainties is a vital component of departmental power within organizations, personnel departments may not be in a strong position to force line management to comply with more deliberate industrial relations policies.

The reforming impact of personnel managers may be frustrated in another way; they may come to accept line management's definition of the realities of industrial relations. Conflict between staff and line may, thereby, be avoided but at the cost of the former accepting their subordination to the latter. Where this occurs, personnel managers may readily collude in the bending of agreements and the subversion of procedures by production management. They may refuse or fail to act as committed and expert innovators, as the theory of reform requires them to do. That many personel specialists may make this choice is suggested by some of the findings of the Workplace Industrial Relations survey. These established that one half of personnel specialists have no formal qualifications for personnel work and that the most common type of preparation for personnel management is on-the-job experience in the organization where people are employed (Millward and Stevens, 1986, p. 25). Several consequences may well flow from this. Personnel managers are likely to imbibe fully the existing organizational culture, to be sympathetic to established methods of practising industrial relations, and hold a heavily 'practical' rather than a professional understanding of their own job. Their induction into personnel work, that is, is likely to encourage conformity rather than challenge to the status quo.

Where personnel managers refuse to accept a subordinate position and successfully gain the compliance of line managers in the reform of industrial relations, however, the result may not be more 'orderly' industrial relations. A frequent complaint of line managers is that formalized industrial relations procedures are excessively rigid. From the viewpoint of the line manager the ability to negotiate with work-groups may be seen as an important means of developing worker co-operation. Restrictions on this ability to negotiate through the expansion of the personnel specialist's role may well lead to a build up of bargaining pressure and increased shop-floor conflict. There may well be 'dysfunctional' consequences for management, therefore, arising from the development of more formalized industrial relations. Research findings indicate that this is the case. The 1978 survey carried out by Warwick University (Brown, 1981), for instance, found that enterprises operating corporate pay-bargaining were more prone to industrial disputes. The authors concluded that this association 'appears to arise from the restrictions that these and their associated controls place upon local management: they are less able to make ad hoc concessions to their workforces than if bargaining was centred on their establishment' (Brown, 1981, p. 91). A transfer of influence from line managers to specialists, therefore, particularly when specialists are located above the establishment level, may well lead to inflexibility and more conflictual industrial relations. Where personnel specialists have proved effective innovators, formalizing industrial relations practice, the effect may have been to stimulate conflict rather than restore 'order' in the workplace.

The Reform Strategy: A Summary

Donovan's prescription for the reform of industrial relations was founded on the conviction that there was too much bargaining in British industry, too far down the organizational hierarchy. Inadequate management control systems presented workers with 'excessive' opportunities to achieve either bilateral or unilateral control of pay systems and work organization. The various components of the post-Donovan reform of industrial relations were intended to reverse this state of affairs. Taken together they can be viewed as measures to enhance management control by providing checks and restrictions on the scope and scale of workplace bargaining. They attempted to achieve this in three ways. The first was the replacement of fragmented shop-floor bargaining with a system of formal rules and standardized industrial relations procedures. Closely related to this was the second feature of the reform strategy, the centralization of collective bargaining within the plant or company which, in turn, would facilitate the third element of reform, the introduction of monitoring of the results of workplace bargaining. The task of personnel specialists would be not only to introduce new procedures but also to establish information systems to gauge their effectiveness. Corporate headquarters would develop arm's-length supervision of workplace negotiations. Each of these component elements of industrial relations reform can be discerned in the design of the National Coal Board's incentive scheme. It is to a more detailed description of this collective agreement that we now turn.

The National Coal Board's Incentive Scheme

Once the National Coal Board had decided that some form of incentive for production workers was necessary, the optimum position would have been for the scheme to have been run solely by management without

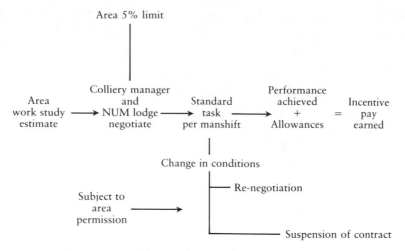

Figure 3.1. The mechanics of the incentive scheme

recourse to local bargaining. In coal-mining this optimum position for management could not be attained. The strength of the union ensured that if incentives were to be reintroduced then local branches must be given the opportunity to negotiate over standards. Given this starting-point, the NCB strove to limit the scope of local bargaining and to introduce checks on its operation. It sought to ensure that devolving collective bargaining to the pit-head would not lead to a lack of regulation in the means whereby earnings were calculated and the proliferation of *ad hoc* agreements within the pits.

This was to be done, in the first instance, by specifying tightly in a written agreement the agenda of local bargaining. The formal incentive scheme agreement produced within each Area conformed closely to a 'national blueprint' and it is this which detailed the content of local negotiations. The main features of the agreement are shown in Figure 3.1.

At the centre of this 'blueprint' was a formula under which colliery management and NUM branch officials could negotiate 'installation agreements' for each coal-face and development drivage. The key components of each installation agreement and the main subjects of negotiation were the *standard task*, expressed in the case of a coal-face as the number of lineal yards of a face to be cut at an expected depth of strip and in the case of a drivage as the distance to be advanced in lineal yards; and the *standard manning*, the number of mineworkers required to fulfil the standard task. From these figures it was possible to calculate the *standard task per manshift*, the point at which 100 per cent performance was attained. Negotiation then was purely about performance. When 100 per cent performance was achieved the men received a standard incentive payment, the size of which was fixed in national negotiations. Theoretically, however, there was no limit on the amount of incentive pay which could be earned, so if the NUM branch negotiated an installation agreement which permitted the face or development team to achieve 200 per cent performance then the men would receive twice the standard payment.

To avoid this situation and ensure that slack standards were not negotiated, the 'blueprint' imposed a further limiting condition on local bargaining. Negotiations over the standard task and standard manning were required to start from a work study assessment of what was reasonable. Colliery managers, moreover, due to a 'national edict' from Hobart House, were given instructions not to let the final negotiated standard task per manshift deviate by more than 5 per cent from that recommended by the work-study engineers.

A frequent cause of the decay of payment by results systems is the proliferation of special allowances. The NCB attempted to minimize this problem by specifying in advance when and how workers were to be compensated if geological conditions, mechanical breakdown, or redeployment inhibited their capacity to achieve standard performance. If there was a halt to production on a coal-face, for example, which had not been allowed for in the work study assessment of the standard task, which was not due to the team's negligence, and which lasted for at least twenty minutes, then the yardage which would have been cut during the period of the delay was added to the weekly total of yards actually cut, thus topping up the men's incentive pay. Similarly, it was permitted to revise an installation agreement to make the standard easier to achieve, but only if there was a substantial alteration in geological conditions which produced at least a 5 per cent drop in output and which was going to persist for at least four weeks. It was also possible to suspend an agreement and pay the men an average of what was earned on the remaining installations at the pit if conditions deteriorated so badly that the face or development became 'unmeasurable'. Before a colliery manager could do this, however, he had to seek the permission of his superiors at area level.

The intention behind these 'compensation' clauses was to make the scheme flexible in its operation so that the incentive effect was maintained when teams ran into difficulties, but also to render its operation as routine as possible. Through laying down procedures for management to follow when changes in geology or breakdowns were encountered it was hoped to limit the opportunity and need to resort to *ad hoc* arrangements and informal bargains. Negotiations were to be limited to fixing the standard task and standard manning and there was to be no return to the haggling over compensatory payments which was a pronounced feature of colliery industrial relations in the days of piece-work.

An additional feature of the incentive scheme's design, which was intended to ensure that negotiations adhered to the prescribed issues, was the centralization of bargaining within the workplace and the restriction of the negotiating role of supervisors. This, again, was in marked contrast to the era of piece-working in the mining industry when the deputy and overman had the power to determine to a great extent a man's income.[2] Under the incentive scheme installation agreements were negotiated by the colliery manager and the principal officials of the NUM branch. Supervisors and most other members of the management team were excluded. Deputies were required to record the duration of stoppages at the coal-face and the deployment of men away from installation work, but in order to combat any collusion between supervisor and work-group on such things as the overbooking of the time during which the shearer was stopped, these records were checked regularly by a member of the colliery management team. It was he, not the deputy, who decided whether a delay was already accounted for in the standard or whether it was due to the negligence of the work team.

Orderliness in the operation of the incentive scheme, however, was to be ensured principally through the fact that it was computer-based. That is, once an incentive agreement was reached so that so many men had to cut so much coal to earn the standard bonus, then the operation of that agreement and of the payment of men was intended to function routinely. Each week performance data were fed into the computer and a fortnight later the men were paid what they had earned. This 'automatic' functioning of the payment system was intended to restrict the amount of pay-bargaining and make the scheme easier to control.

In addition to being used to calculate incentive earnings, the computer was used by industrial relations staff to monitor the success of the scheme. The rapid upward flow of information relating to trends in worker performance and payment was intended to increase the visibility of colliery industrial relations. NCB area staff would be speedily alerted to any malpractice in the operation of the incentive scheme and would be in a position to intervene at workplace level to correct matters.

Incentive pay under the 1977/8 agreements was earned only by production workers, coal-face and development teams. All other sections of the work-force, including management, received a bonus calculated on the basis of what production workers earned. Surface workers and clerical staff received a payment equivalent to 40 per cent of average incentive earnings for all face and development workers at their pit. Workers

[2] Malcolm Pitt (1979, p. 52) in his history of the Kent miners has the following to say about the supervisors' role under piecework: 'A team's weekly docket was calculated on the yardage of coal and muck extracted by the men, and the official, with his notebook and measuring stick, became a petty tyrant whose favour had to be won by an ounce of chewing tobacco and a pound note left on a girder, or a night's free beer in the local pub.'

'elsewhere-below-ground' received 50 per cent or 65 per cent of this figure depending on the proximity of their work to the point of production. Craftsmen received a 100 per cent bonus if they supported a team of face or development workers, but received 50 per cent of the full rate for other work below ground and 40 per cent for work on the surface. The bonus for supervisors and managers was similarly determined by place of work and the category of labour they supervised.

The principal drawback of this arrangement, so far as management was concerned, was that there was a substantial 'knock-on effect' from any bargain struck with a team of production workers. The implications of a slack standard being issued for a coal-face were magnified considerably. According to one manager interviewed, the capacity of the scheme to generate upward drift in earnings was 'frightening'. The benefits to management were twofold. The system of derived bonuses was an effective way of widening internal differentials, which was considered necessary to raise performance on coal-face and development work. Secondly, however, it minimized disruption to the industry's 'rationalized' grade structure. Linking the bonus of non-direct workers to the incentive pay earned on coal-faces and developments was intended to limit fractional bargaining and competition over pay between different categories of worker.

The National Coal Board's incentive scheme, therefore, embodied many of the features said to be associated with industrial relations reform. It was composed of an intentionally strict framework of centrally negotiated rules; it was work-study based; it was a group incentive scheme; and it was monitored by industrial relations specialists located above the colliery level. The scheme appears to have been deliberately designed to take into account many of the widely reported difficulties managers have experienced in the past in operating payment by results. It is an excellent example of a 'reformed' incentive payment system. How effective this 'model' system was in providing a solution to these problems is the subject of our next chapter.

4
'Reformed' Industrial Relations in Practice

Our discussion of the various features of the post-Donovan 'reform' in industrial relations has revealed conflicting views on how effective they are in limiting workplace bargaining and enhancing management control over pay and work. One reason for this lack of agreement is a paucity of detailed empirical studies of the operation of reformed systems. Most evaluations are based on large-scale, but necessarily superficial surveys whose findings are open to conflicting interpretations. Our aim was to complement the broader survey research by providing detailed information on how a wage payment system designed according to 'reformist' principles operates in practice.

In this chapter, therefore, we are concerned, firstly, with establishing the extent to which the objectives discernible within the NCB's incentive scheme's design were in fact realized. We investigate, therefore, whether or not pit-head bargaining seeped beyond its allotted sphere; whether or not significant influence over the scheme slipped downwards to the supervisor and the work-group; and whether or not the relationship between colliery management and area industrial relations specialists was fraught with tension, leading to an attenuation of the latter's monitoring role. Our second concern is with the consequences which flowed from the manner of the scheme's operation. We aim to relate discussion of the *processes* through which effort bargains were established to their substantive content. The chapter concludes, therefore, with a discussion of the effectiveness of the incentive scheme as a means for the control of labour.

The Operation of the Incentive Scheme at Workplace Level

Fixing Installation Standards: The Use of Work Study

Work study, the designers of the incentive scheme intended, should limit the extent of collective bargaining in the pits and ensure a high degree of management control over the fixing of wage/effort ratios. An area

TABLE 4.1   The primary means used to devise the initial standard for coal-face and development installations

Method used	Coal-faces Numbers %		Developments Numbers %	
Synthetic work-study data based on other pits	1	3	3	9
Synthetic work-study data based on records of past performance at this pit	21	60	17	48
Actual work-study observation	9	26	10	29
What colliery management believe to be an appropriate standard without reference to work study	4	11	5	14
TOTAL	35	100	35	100

Source: Colliery Manager Questionnaire, 1981.

industrial relations   official who was interviewed, for instance, explained that 'Political pressure is greatest at the point of negotiation and, therefore, it is essential for colliery management to be given an objective basis from which negotiations begin and from which the final result will only deviate to a limited degree.' Table 4.1, however, reveals that this procedure was not always followed. In a substantial minority of pits, more than 10 per cent, it was normal for the initial standard offered to the union to be devised by colliery management. Area industrial relations officials in three areas interviewed in the course of the study intimated that some colliery managers were unhappy with the prominent position allocated to work study in the operation of the incentive scheme. One official commented that, 'Colliery managers think they can pluck a better standard from the air, than that systematically devised by the work study department'. A minority of colliery managers, therefore, had successfully resisted reliance on work study, in part because they believed they were capable of devising more accurate standards themselves, and also because they considered work study to restrict their ability to bargain with the NUM branch. At none of the pits visited was it reported that the union had prevented the use of work study.

Work study was used as stipulated, however, in the majority of pits. The job of the Area Method Study Department was to produce a task assessment and an assessment of standard manning whenever a new installation was ready to be worked. These assessments could be arrived at by two means. Firstly, a synthetic standard could be devised based on past measurements at the pit in question or from other pits in the same area or even from pits from different areas. Secondly, work-study engineers could observe work on the installation for a number of shifts, measuring both man and machine performance to arrive at a totally new standard.

Under the first system work-study engineers selected from a bank of performance measurements those they believed to be best suited to a particular installation. The advantage of this system for management was felt to be that it isolated the formulation of the initial standard from work group and union influence. An area industrial relations official, for example, explained that the 'men cannot pull the wool over your eyes' with a synthetic: they could not 'spin out the cycle time' as they did with an actual study.

Of the collieries visited just under 30 per cent used actual studies as the primary means of fixing initial standards for both coal-faces and development drivages. Most installation standards, therefore, were based on 'synthetics'. However, in all but a tiny minority of cases these 'synthetics' were drawn up from past measurements taken at the colliery for which the new standard was required.

That this was the case was indicative of mineworkers' unwillingness to accept non-customary effort standards, based on performance at other pits, even as a basis for negotiation. Anecdotal evidence was gathered to support this view. In certain areas visited in the course of the study the use of work study had been restricted, prior to the scheme's introduction, by the NUM. As a consequence, when the scheme was accepted these areas had to rely on standards derived from measurements in other coalfields. The use of these synthetic standards was objected to and resisted by NUM branches. They were viewed as an attack on customary rates of working, as an attempt to jack up output to levels achieved in coalfields with different geological conditions.

Conflict over the rigour of work study estimated had, significantly, become less frequent at the time of the research. Each area by then had built up its own bank of performance data, and initial standards were based primarily on measurements of previous performance at the pits concerned. Local union resistance, it seemed, had been successful in ensuring that the standards from which negotiations began should be devised in a manner acceptable to the work-force and should not be formulated purely by management.

Further evidence that work study was engaged in producing 'acceptable' standards, as Baldamus claims is normal, was provided by the figures for average incentive earnings at the thirty-five collieries in the survey sample. These revealed that mean performance was at or below the standard level in about 40 per cent of collieries, lay between 100 and 150 per cent of standard in about a third, and rose above 150 per cent in the remainder. That a substantial number of collieries regularly attained very high levels of performance was revealing. Performance at 120 per cent of standard, according to a recent textbook on work study, 'needs practice and skill' and is 'usually only seen on highly repetitive work', while performance at

160 per cent is 'seen perhaps once in a lifetime'. (Jay, 1981, p. 76). The recording of regular high performances at certain collieries was, therefore, probably due to the slackness of the standards issued by the work study engineers.

Slack standards, however, were more likely to be offered to workers in some pits than in others. Evidence will be presented later which shows that high earnings and, therefore, high levels of performance are very much more likely at highly productive collieries. In these pits, it can be argued, workers placed a higher value on their effort and so work-study engineers were under pressure to set fairly slack standards which would permit these aspirations for a favourable effort bargain to be satisfied.[1] Variation in mean levels of performance against installation standards, therefore, reflected variation in workers' tolerance of relatively strict work-study assessments. This in turn was related to the power of workers in different collieries; to their varying degrees of indispensability to the Coal Board's operations.

Work study is a standardized procedure administered by management specialists, the purposes of which, within the NCB's incentive scheme, were to retain a substantial degree of management control over the fixing of effort standards and to limit the scope of colliery level collective bargaining. Our survey of the actual use of work study in the pits revealed, firstly, that in a minority of collieries the technique was not used as stipulated. In addition, however, where it was used there was considerable evidence that the standards submitted by work study were not purely formal, managerially authored estimates unsullied by custom. Union insistence that estimates should be derived from measurements taken at the pits concerned helped ensure that standards approximated to past performance. Moreover, there were indications that the use of work study did not necessarily confine bargaining to the final 5 per cent of the standard. The analysis of incentive earnings suggested that work study took into account the expectations of the work-force in compiling initial standards. Where workers' aspirations were higher, generally because their strategic position was stronger, then work study took this into account. Work-study engineers, therefore, exhibited 'bargaining behaviour' in that they had a seemingly fine anticipation of the aspirations of the work-force and a fine appreciation of their power, and tailored their 'proposals', their standards, accordingly.

[1] Evidence in support of this view was gathered at one of the pits included in the initial phase of the study. During an interview the branch secretary at a highly productive Midlands pit remarked that when the scheme was introduced his lodge had decided that £10 a shift payment, equivalent to about 190% performance, was the minimum they would accept. This appreciation of the high value of their members' effort was matched by an appreciation of their power and its origins. The branch secretary in explaining they had succeeded in reaching their target remarked, 'our power comes from productivity'.

TABLE 4.2   % deviation of agreed installation standard from the work-
study estimate

Percentage deviation	Coalfaces		Developments	
	Numbers	%	Numbers	%
None	—	—	2	6
5 or under	24	70	22	69
6–10	7	21	5	16
11–15	3	9	3	9
TOTAL	34	100	32	100

Source: Colliery Manager Questionnaire, 1981.

Fixing Installation Standards: The Five Per Cent Limit

An additional restriction on local pay-bargaining was the 5 per cent
negotiating limit within which the colliery manager was supposed to
remain. Table 4.2 reveals, again, that a substantial number of pits had
escaped from this constraint. At one in every four collieries the final
standard normally deviated from the work study estimate by more than 5
per cent, and in many of the remainder it was likely that the limit had been
breached at least occasionally.

This deviation from the negotiating limit did not seem to have been
accompanied by conflict between colliery managers and their superiors at
area level. All industrial relations officials who were interviewed reported
that the '5 per cent rule' was applied flexibly. The need for flexibility
arose, it was explained, because work study was 'not an exact science' and
the union were frequently justified in demanding a more substantial
relaxation than the prescribed limit allowed. Behind such justifications,
however, can be discerned an appreciation of the problems which could
arise from an over-zealous attachment to formal rules. If work-study
standards, which affronted workers' conceptions of effort value, were
imposed then the result could be a restriction of output as workers decided
the incentive target was not worth pursuing, or an industrial dispute, as
they sought to bring the target within reach. Flexibility in the operation of
the '5 per cent rule' was then accepted as necessary by managers at Area
and in the pits. A rigid adherence to the rule, it was recognized, could sour
industrial relations or provoke a costly dispute.

*The Operation of Installation Agreements: Random Delays and
Redeployment*

Coal-mining by its nature is an uncertain business and changes in
geological conditions underground may disrupt an effort bargain agreed

by the union and the colliery manager. The standard, in such cases, may become harder or even easier for the work-team to achieve. Because the incentive scheme was supposedly based on effort rather than on output or productivity, the text of the formal agreement specified procedures which could be enacted whenever changes in conditions rendered invalid a previously concluded effort bargain. These procedures, essentially through altering the amount of work required to earn the standard payment, permitted a revision of the effort bargain in the light of changed conditions and so protected the earnings of the work-force.

The influence of minor changes in task difficulty on the effort bargain were controlled by a number of compensation clauses. The two most important of these were the random delay or interruption clause and the booking-off clause. The first stated that work-teams should be compensated for unforeseen delays in production of twenty minutes or more which were not due to their own negligence. The second stated that if a worker was redeployed away from an installation then he would not lose earnings provided his own work was available, and the number of manshifts entering the incentive divisor would be reduced to protect the earnings of remaining team members.

What was essential about these clauses was that they were to be applied routinely and by management. The agreement specified in detail exactly when the rules applied and how workers were to be compensated and stated that it was the task of colliery management to ensure their correct implementation. The day to day compensation of workers for variations in task difficulty, it was intended, would be governed by the enactment of standard procedures and would not be the subject of informal bargaining between management and union, worker and supervisor.

Table 4.3 provides evidence that this intention was not realized in the majority of cases and that the union exercised considerable influence over the operation of these rules. Although colliery managers did not rate union influence as highly as did NUM officials themselves, it is clear that in the majority of pits the union was able to exercise at least some influence over what should count as a random interruption and whether team size should be adjusted through the redeployment of men away from installation work.

That formal rules of this kind will inevitably become the subject of plant-level bargaining has been suggested by Terry. He further states that it is supervisors and lower managers, those most susceptible to work group pressure, who will indulge in such bargaining and bend or ignore formal procedures as a concession to the work-force (1977, pp. 85–6). In the course of the survey many complaints were received from colliery and area managers that supervisors did behave in this manner and constituted a weak link in the control of the payment system.

Under the incentive scheme it was the responsibility of mining supervisors to record the number, duration, and cause of interruptions to

TABLE 4.3. Estimates of NUM influence over random interruption and booking-off clauses

| Level of influence | Random interruptions | | | | Booking off | | | |
| | NUM branch representatives | | Colliery manager | | NUM branch representatives | | Colliery manager | |
	Numbers	%	Numbers	%	Numbers	%	Numbers	%
None	—	—	2	6	1	3	7	20
Very little	2	6	3	9	2	6	5	14
Some	2	6	15	43	6	17	10	29
Moderate amount	8	22	10	28	5	14	7	20
Great deal	23	66	5	14	19	54	6	17
Complete	—	—	—	—	2	6	—	—
TOTAL	35	100	35	100	35	100	35	100

Source: Colliery Manager and NUM Branch Representative Interviews, 1981.

work and the extent of any redeployment of workers away from the coal-face or development drivage. According to many senior managers supervisors' fulfilment of these duties was characterized by 'a vast amount of collusion' with work-teams to boost compensation payments. Deputies, it was claimed, over-recorded the length of delays, so phrased their descriptions of the cause of interruptions that they fell within the 'random' category, and under-recorded the number of manshifts worked on installations. The reason given for this collusive behaviour was that the supervisor's bonus was derived from the earnings of the men he supervised and so the scheme basically invited him, 'to write his own pay cheque'.[2]

Undoubtedly supervisors had used their position as the recorders of performance data to improve their own and their work-team's earnings. They have bargained with workers over the application of rules which were designed to strictly guide their behaviour. There were limits, however, to the creative role of the supervisor in colliery industrial relations. Their involvement in the procedures of the incentive scheme was monitored, and at many pits colliery managers had deliberately attempted to restrict supervisory discretion and their ability to manipulate the payment system. In more than half the collieries visited the manager estimated that between 11 and 50 per cent of random interruptions recorded by supervisors were disallowed by a member of management proper. This was a matter for resentment among deputies

[2] Various apocryphal tales concerning the extent of supervisory collusion were related. In one instance a case was reported of a deputy recording more time lost in stoppages than was available for coal-cutting in the course of the shift.

and overmen who perceived in these checks a clear lack of trust on the part of higher management. One supervisor who was interviewed, for example, contrasted the present incentive scheme with the situation under piece-work and remarked that, 'time was never taken out in the old days. Managements shouldn't be able to scrub it off. Every shift it happens; it destroys you, the atmosphere changes, the attitude changes.' Despite this policy of limiting supervisory involvement in the incentive scheme, colliery managers themselves were not averse to bargaining over compensation payments. The pressure from workers to interpret formal rules flexibly, which Terry argues is experienced most strongly in the lower reaches of the management hierarchy, could be brought to bear on the occupants of more senior positions. The operation of these supposedly routinely applied procedures could, it seemed, become the subject of regular and rather 'formalized' negotiations between the colliery manager and the NUM. In most pits, for instance, it appeared the union received a weekly list of the duration and cause of random delays and a statement of which ones had been cancelled by management. The union would then query some of these cancellations, and, through bargaining with management, exert influence over what should or should not be classified as a random interruption. This process of negotiation was not specified in the incentive scheme national blueprint which assumed that the classification of delays would be routinely performed by management with the aid of the installation work study report.

It was apparent that the number of manshifts entering the incentive-scheme divisor, a further determinant of incentive earnings, was also the subject of widespread bargaining between colliery managers and NUM representatives. At one pit, for example, both the manager and the union reported that if incentive earnings fell below a certain figure then the NUM would approach the manager and ask him to take shifts out of the incentive payment calculation so as to keep earnings at a relatively stable level. Both acknowledged that the number of manshifts going into the incentive divisor was a matter for 'horse-trading' beyond the bounds specified by the agreement.

Excessive redeployment and concealed assistance on installations was viewed by area industrial relations staff as the major managerial problem associated with the incentive scheme. The high cost of such practices, the fact that they could produce a higher rate of payment for the production of less coal had been emphasized many times to colliery managers. Many managers, it was clear, however, still permitted undermanning or adjusted the number of shifts in the divisor to maintain the co-operation and motivation of their work team.

The Operation of Installation Agreements:
Renegotiation and Suspension

The formal rules of the incentive scheme provided for major disruptions to the effort bargain through two other procedures, the renegotiation and the suspension of the installation agreement. An installation standard could be renegotiated if a 'persistent and continuing' change in conditions was encountered and could be suspended if conditions become 'non-measurable'. Neither of these procedures appeared to be activated frequently at our sample of pits. In about one-fifth of the pits there was a revision every three months and at only twelve pits was there a record of a suspension for the financial year 1980/1. The fairly restrained use of these procedures was in line with the recommendations of the scheme's designers. It was intended that neither revision nor suspension should be undertaken lightly because of the possible costs involved.

Adjusting or suspending standards shielded the work-force's earnings from the vagaries of geology and so could ensure a stable and possibly increasing level of incentive earnings. One possible reason for the relatively infrequent application of these rules, therefore, could be the ability of management to resist union pressure. There was considerable evidence, however, that this was not the case. At many pits, it seemed that colliery managers had responded to work-force pressure for the adjustment of standards by developing informal alternatives to renegotiation and suspension.

The managers were keenly aware that a failure to compensate work-teams for altered conditions could have serious consequences. The men might respond to a shrinkage of their earnings caused by adverse conditions, by allowing their effort to shrink to a commensurate degree: if a revision was not granted, an area industrial relations official explained, 'the men lie down and spend the shift'. A worsening of the effort bargain might also provoke industrial action. Over 60 per cent of the colliery managers agreed with the statement: 'The threat of a stoppage of work or restriction of output is greater if the men do not earn a roughly stable amount of bonus.' In addition to being sensitive to the possible responses of their workers, however, many colliery managers were acutely aware of the disadvantages of using the formal procedures. It was explained, for instance, that renegotiation tended to have a ratchet effect: standards were slackened when conditions became more difficult but were never fully restored if they later reverted to their initial state. Suspending an agreement had even more inherent dangers for management. Suspension amounted to a temporary abandoning of the link between effort and reward. In practice, this could mean that on a suspended installation the men simultaneously received higher wages, derived from the earnings of workers in easier conditions, and experienced a loss of incentive precisely when management required motivation to work through difficult ground.

The formal rules of the incentive scheme, therefore, could trap as well as strengthen the hand of management and this had led it to develop alternative, informal responses to union demands for the adjustment of effort bargains. It was common for colliery managers to reach an informal agreement with the NUM branch to bring the standard back within reach if conditions changed. This could be done by adding random inter-ruptions to the team's weekly output total, by increasing the manning on the installation, or by lifting manshifts out of the incentive divisor. Action of this kind was felt to be a less costly way of protecting earnings which preserved an element of incentive even in the most difficult conditions.

Reliance on these arrangements served to enlarge colliery managers' discretion in operating the incentive scheme. Instead of applying rules formulated elsewhere to the situation existing within their own sphere of authority, they were tending, either unilaterally or as a result of local negotiation with the NUM, to devise new and particular solutions to fit their own circumstances. Such an enlargement of the colliery manager's decision-making capacity, beyond the confines of what the scheme's designers intended, raised the possibility of conflict as area industrial relations officials responsible for overseeing the scheme took counter-action.

Conflict of this kind, however, did not seem to be a significant feature of intra-management relations. Those area industrial relations officials who were interviewed readily acknowledged that informal modifications to the signed effort bargain were fairly widespread and recognized that such practices had their uses. In one area, for example, an official explained that it was 'inevitable' that the colliery manager 'cooks the books a bit' and that for staff at area the appropriate response to this was 'to have the Nelson touch'; that is to let it go on provided wages costs at the pit did not run ahead of productivity. Area management, therefore, tacitly condoned the practice of flexibly applying the incentive scheme and adjusting installation standards in the face of changed conditions.

The System of Derived Bonuses

The return to payment by results had an inevitably disruptive effect on the coal industry's system of differentials. It widened differentials between grades, increasing the relative rewards for face and development workers at the expense of surface day-wage men and those working elsewhere below ground (Handy, 1981). It also produced differentials within grades. Under the terms of the incentive scheme the bonus accruing to craftsmen and supervisors varied according to place of work.

Two related problems arose for colliery management as a result of these changes. The first was dissatisfaction amongst those groups who lost out in the reshaping of the industry's pattern of differentials. In the early days of the scheme's life, for example, there were sizeable disputes involving groups such as winding enginemen and rescue teams who felt their incentive bonus was too low. The second was resistance to deployment to work which carried only a low level of bonus. This was particularly a problem with fitters and electricians who might be required to work in different parts of the pit: 67 per cent of the sample of colliery managers stated that they had encountered difficulties in deploying craftsmen to non-installation work.

The response of colliery managers to these problems frequently was to bow to pressure and develop informal modifications to the agreement. The differential of the vast majority of the industry's supervisors over industrial staff was preserved by paying them 100 per cent bonus, and a similar practice was used at many pits to avoid problems with the deployment of craftsmen. The system of derived bonus, therefore, which was intended to restrict local bargaining to the setting of installation standards, had not had this effect. Groups of workers at pit level were able to negotiate departures from the formal agreement which protected their relative earnings from the impact of the incentive scheme. The effects of payment by results on a previously 'rationalized' grading structure was limited by work-force bargaining pressure. Those groups who secured concessions, though, tended to be relatively powerful. Surface workers and underground day-wage men were less able to escape from the consequences of the incentive scheme. It appeared that colliery management were only willing to collude in the subversion of the system of derived bonuses where this facilitated the deployment of workers who made a crucial contribution to production.

The Area Monitoring Process

It was the task of area industrial relations officials located at each area headquarters to collect and analyse data relating to the incentive scheme's operation, to advise colliery management on the correct interpretation of the agreement, and to alert senior management to any incipient decay in the payment system.[3] Monitoring the scheme in this manner, it was intended, would provide a means of policing the boundaries of colliery-level decision-making, ensuring that local bargaining remained within its set limits and that formal rules were adhered to. 'Experience has shown', remarked one industrial relations official, 'that earnings would get out of hand without central control. Inevitably there is pressure on the colliery manager to give way. Pressure is greatest at the pit. We who are free from

[3] A further stage of monitoring is conducted at national headquarters.

that kind of pressure can intervene from the centre to ensure the situation does not get out of control.' The intended functions of the monitoring system, therefore, were to maintain the agreement and prevent slippage in the effort bargain to the advantage of the work-force. It has been amply demonstrated, however, that at least the first of these functions was not fulfilled with any rigour. Informality, the avoidance or manipulation of rules was found to be widespread.

The monitoring of the scheme at colliery level involved a number of different procedures. In the first place there was a weekly process of 'exception monitoring', whereby area industrial relations staff examined the earnings and performance figures for each installation at each pit and contacted the colliery manager if exceptionally high earnings or a mismatch between earnings and performance were uncovered. The second stage in the process was a more long-term monitoring of trends in performance and payments. The principal intention here was to ensure that earnings varied with productivity. The third and final component of the monitoring procedure was a detailed audit of the operation of the scheme, supposedly performed twice yearly at each colliery. The aim of this 'supervisory visit' was to monitor the monitoring process by checking on the data routinely despatched to the computer from the pits. Once this visit had been concluded a detailed report on how the scheme was being operated at a particular colliery was sent to the colliery manager and to his superiors in area line management. This was then discussed at an 'accountability meeting'.

Introducing a computer-based incentive scheme in which wages were calculated automatically from input performance data was intended to render the payment system's operation routine and minimize the ability of those at pit level to influence the effort bargain. However, it was a perfectly simple, though somewhat time-consuming, operation for those responsible for collating the performance data at the pits ready to send into area to work out with a pocket calculator what the work-force's incentive earnings would be. Once this had been done the performance figures could be changed to raise or depress the earnings figure as the colliery manager saw fit. Resort to this practice was openly admitted by managers at several pits visited in the survey, and its existence was also acknowledged by a number of area industrial relations staff. One official, for instance, claimed many managers had a notion of how much bonus they should be paying and worked all the performance figures out backwards from that point. 'It's all political', he explained, 'keep the men happy'!

In addition to managers unilaterally adjusting performance figures in order to maintain worker effort, or to link earnings more tightly to output or productivity, it appeared that at many pits these same figures were given to the union, with the result that the record of performance from

TABLE 4.4   Colliery managers' perceptions of their independence from area and the consequences for industrial relations

How much freedom of action do you have from higher management in agreeing things with the NUM?	Numbers	%	What has been the impact of the Incentive Scheme on your freedom of action from higher management in agreeing things with the NUM?	Numbers	%	How often do problems arise in your job when dealing with the men of this pit because you have to refer matters up to higher management?	Numbers	%
Total	2	6	Greatly reduced	—	—	Always	—	—
A great deal	24	68	Reduced	8	22	Most times	—	—
Some	9	26	Same	23	66	Sometimes	6	17
A little	—	—	Increased	3	9	Rarely	28	80
None	—	—	Greatly increased	1	3	Never	1	3
TOTAL	35	100	TOTAL	35	100	TOTAL	35	100

Source: Colliery Manager Questionnaire, 1981.

which earnings were calculated became the subject of bargaining. Over 70 per cent of branch officials interviewed said they always inspected the weekly figures for the performance on each installation before they were sent to area headquarters, and 40 per cent said they queried these figures every week.

Adjusting the figures in this manner gave colliery management greater flexibility in applying the incentive scheme and increased the 'unregulated' decision-making power of union and management. It also, however, through falsifying the information sent to area, reduced the validity of the monitoring process. The data from which trends were extrapolated may not have been a totally accurate record of what was occurring within the pits. Doctoring the performance data, therefore, helped shield colliery management from the gaze of the monitors. The 'supervisory visit', the check on the validity of the information entering the system, however, should have provided the basis to reverse this situation. That this procedure had frequently not had this effect was due, in the first place, to a failure to operate it. In no area visited were the 'statutory' two visits carried out, and in those making use of the procedure collieries were inspected once a year at the most.

That 'supervisory visits' were not carried out as frequently as instructed was primarily due to the fact that colliery managers had resisted the implementation of this procedure. Colliery managers are highly paid, experienced personnel with a great deal of legal and financial responsibility. They occupy, in Alan Fox's (1974) terminology, 'high-trust' positions within the employing organization. Monitoring such high status personnel, it seems, initiated, again in Fox's words, a 'dynamic of low trust'. Managers resented their autonomy being threatened; they resented the very fact of being monitored as it implied they were not competent to run the scheme unsupervised, that they were not to be 'trusted'.

A second, and possibly more fundamental, reason why colliery managers should resist the monitoring process has already been advanced: in doing so they could enlarge their capacity to bargain freely with the NUM. Mining is an unpredictable process and maintaining output is crucially dependent on the co-operation of the work-force. Boosting payments by manipulating performance data, it seemed, was the surest way of guaranteeing this co-operation. Considerations of output, therefore, encouraged managers to resist the control system and expand their ability to decide what level of incentive pay was 'earned'.

It was revealed by the survey that a less conflictual relationship with the NUM was found at collieries where the manager believed himself to enjoy more independence from his area. Table 4.4 gives the pattern of responses to three questions from the Colliery Manager Questionnaire. Most managers, the table reveals, considered that they had a great deal of autonomy in agreeing things with the union, that the incentive scheme had not altered this, and that difficulties rarely arose through the need to seek area clearance before reaching an agreement with the work-force. Some variation was encountered, however, and perceptions that the incentive scheme had reduced autonomy or that problems arose rather more frequently through the involvement of higher management, were associated with a belief on the manager's part that the incentive scheme had increased the propensity of the work-force to take industrial action.[4] It was also the case that very strong associations were discovered between the colliery manager's estimate of the frequency of problems due to area involvement and the degree of conflict reported by both manager and union over the six incentive scheme 'decisions' about which they were interviewed.[5] At pits where difficulties arose rather more frequently through the need to clear matters with area, the procedures which compose the incentive scheme were more contested.

These findings support the view that reduced bargaining autonomy for local management tends to promote inflexibility and conflict in relationships with trade unions. Colliery manager strategems to increase their independence, their scope for flexible response, did therefore have a 'rational' basis: greater autonomy was associated with better industrial relations.

Although a proportion of the data upon which the monitoring process was based was subject to manipulation, it was the general opinion of industrial relations staff that sufficient was gathered to let them know roughly what was happening in the pits. None the less, the extent to which monitoring information was used was dependent on the attitude of senior line managers at the apex of each area organization. Industrial relations officials reported to management at this level and it was they who decided whether action should be taken on the basis of these reports. Senior line management was essentially the arbiter in a conflict between colliery management, which was concerned primarily with maintaining output, and the industrial relations officials, who were concerned to contain wage costs and ensure a consistent application of the formal agreement. It was intimated in at least some areas that senior managers chose almost invariably to support their fellow line managers at pit level; to favour the claims of output over procedural rigour.

An example of this was supplied by an industrial relations official from one of the areas where the 'supervisory visit' had been restricted. He

[4] Pearson's R for the two correlations were 0.48 and 0.34, both statistically significant within the 5% level.
[5] The correlations of the colliery manager's perception of problems due to area involvement with his own and the NUM's perceptions of conflict over the 6 decisions were 0.68 and 0.41, both significant at the 0.001 level.

reported that at one pit in the area it had become apparent that performance data were being manipulated to produce a very high earnings figure. Industrial relations had raised the matter with the colliery manager who replied, 'you can either have coal or control, you can't have both'. Shortly afterwards the annual profit for the pit was announced to be £8m. and the colliery manager was 'patted on the back' by the deputy director, and promoted to the position of production manager. The official concluded the example by stating, 'The Area Director doesn't want control. When he wants control, we'll get control.'

The reason senior management was prepared to grant colliery managers a fair degree of autonomy was that this was supportive of good industrial relations and seemed the surest way of maintaining output. As one production manager expressed it, 'We are not going to come down hard on a colliery manager who is getting results even if it means bending the Agreement a bit. After all its good business for the men, its good business for the pit, and its good business for the Board.' Senior managers, though they may have possessed a wider vision, were as aware as their subordinates of the possible costs of a strict application of agreements. Very similar pressures to those which impelled lower managers to depart from formal rules were experienced by those higher up the ladder of authority. These pressures, indeed, were transferred upwards with the flow of information from the pits arising from the computer monitoring process.

The rigour of management control, therefore, is not simply dependent upon the level and quality of management information. It depends also on the preparedness of higher management to act on such information. One area manager, for example, when asked under what circumstances the information gathered through monitoring was acted on, replied that whether or not 'unsatisfactory procedures' were eliminated, 'would depend on a managerial assessment of the consequences and benefits'.

Although some industrial relations staff who were interviewed clearly resented the autonomy of colliery managers and their degree of support from area line management, most accepted the situation. The priorities of many of those involved in monitoring the incentive scheme had shifted, it seemed, since its introduction. From an early concern with ensuring a correct and consistent application of the agreement there had developed a more limited concentration on the primary indicator of the scheme's success, the relationship between incentive earnings and productivity. Provided these two figures moved in tandem it was widely acknowledged that a degree of latitude for the colliery manager in applying the agreement was permissable.

Thus, the monitoring process had effectively been adapted over time to complement the dominant system of management control used in the industry, management by objectives. This emphasized the autonomy of the colliery manager and established the reaching of output targets as the principal organizational goal. Industrial relations managers, in the main, accepted the priority of production and this had minimized the extent of conflict between them and their colleagues in the line.

The Operation of the Incentive Scheme:
Summary

The preceding survey has revealed a considerable growth of unprescribed and informal practices flourishing beneath the formal rules and standard procedures which composed the incentive scheme. The purposes of these rules and procedures were to confine local negotiations to a nationally set agenda and to ensure an orderly operation of the payment system in the constituent coalfields and collieries of the NCB. These aims, in large part, were not met. Local bargaining came to embrace a wider set of issues than those specified in the formal agreement; there was some fragmentation of bargaining activity, with supervisors and work-groups reaching informal understandings over the operation of compensation clauses; and industrial relations at the workplace escaped from close supervision by personnel specialists located at area headquarters. Although the incentive scheme made use of many of the features of the post-Donovan reform of workplace industrial relations the result was not more 'orderly' and rule-bound collective bargaining. Many of the elements of piece-work bargaining reappeared in the administration of this sophisticated group incentive scheme.

It has been demonstrated, for instance, that work-study estimates, which were intended to restrict local bargaining, were tailored to meet the expectations of the workers studied. The application of intentionally unambiguous rules governing the compensation and redeployment of workers was the subject of negotiations involving colliery managers as well as supervisors. The disruption caused to the established wage hierarchy by the reintroduction of payment by results also generated an increase in informal bargaining. And industrial relations staff, those charged with monitoring the scheme, proved unable to prevent colliery managers widening their area of discretion and manipulating the agreement. Indeed, over time, they came to accept the legitimacy of line management's actions.

The reason for informality in the operation of the incentive scheme was that it served colliery managers' interests. In the first instance it provided the opportunity to build good relations with work-teams, based on flexibility and an ongoing and mutual exchange of favours. Local bargaining could foster strong relations with the union and ensure the co-operation of the work-force in the fulfilment of output targets. It would be wrong, however, to trace the origins of informality solely to the power of the NUM and the manager's need to treat with them. A second reason why management at pit level saw fit to bend or dispense with formal rules was that it could inflate the cost of incentives. Some managers, therefore, restricted the role of work study because they felt it erred on the side of generosity, while others had developed alternatives to suspending agreements which compensated the men for declining conditions but which did so at less cost. Supplementing the pressure from the union to extend bargaining, therefore, was an element of 'managerial custom and practice' (Armstrong & Goodman, 1979; Edwards, 1987): a failure on the part of managers to apply the agreement because it could operate to the benefit of the work-force.

Informality in the administration of the incentive scheme could, therefore, be substantively rational for colliery managers. It could facilitate the achievement of their primary objectives. However, local agreements, *ad hoc* arrangements, and informal bargaining may not be substantively rational when viewed from the position of the management organization as a whole. In the next section, therefore, we look at the consequences of the scheme in more general terms.

The Consequences of Informality

The Level of Industrial Conflict

Systems of payment by results are widely held to be associated with industrial conflict, as it is assumed that the frequent opportunities they present for renegotiation of the effort bargain increase the likelihood of disputes (Brown, 1981; Clegg, 1979). Certainly, the coal industry's own experience of payment by results in the piece-work era would support this view. The industry was then infamous for its disproportionate contribution to the national record of 'stoppages of work due to industrial disputes'. Between 1958 and 1968, for example, it accounted for 44 per cent of all industrial stoppages while constituting only about 2 per cent of the labour force (McCormick, 1979, p. 155). With the removal of the contentious issue of pay-bargaining from the local level under NPLA, however, the number of local disputes dropped. The reintroduction of an element of pay-bargaining, therefore, might have been expected to increase substantially the incidence of disputes. Examination of the quarterly statistics for the number of disputes in the industry over the period 1976 to 1981, however, reveal that this was not the case (see Fig. 4.1). The scheme was introduced in the period between early October 1977 and the summer of 1978. It can be seen that after an initial increase, the number of disputes settled down at a level only

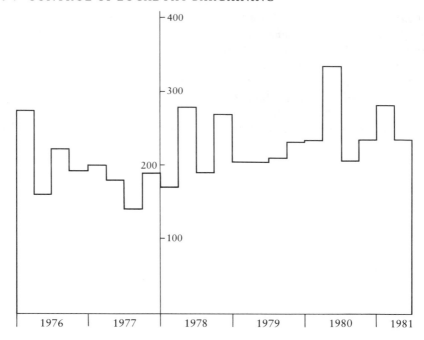

Figure 4.1. Number of disputes per quarter

slightly higher than that which was normal in 1976 and 1977. (Figures for the numbers of tonnes and manshifts lost through disputes reveal a similar pattern.) The early peak in the number of disputes is explained by the efforts of the management and union at the inception of the scheme, seeking to establish precedents which would govern the relationship between payment and productivity for a considerable time to come. Later peaks are explained by senior management's efforts to tighten up on the application of the scheme in a number of pits mainly in the Yorkshire area. However, overall, the reintroduction of incentives produced a surprisingly small increase in disputes.

These national statistics are supported by information from our two surveys which show little or no deterioration in interpersonal relations between union officials and management and supervisors during this period. In fact, 27 per cent of the branch officials in the 1981 survey said that the scheme had actually improved relations with management, and only 9 per cent that relations had worsened. Our data then would support the contention of writers such as Paul Edwards (1987), that systems of payment by results are not necessarily associated with industrial conflict. We have demonstrated that this is the case, moreover, even in the presence of a relatively powerful union.

The reason for the relatively low incidence of conflict is clear from our previous discussion—management applied the rules of the scheme flexibly, introducing informal practices in order to retain the co-operation of the work-force. However, informality may have promoted harmonious industrial relations and ensured the fulfilment of output budgets but it may also have inflated the overall cost of the incentive scheme and advanced its decay. Whether this was the case, whether departure from the formal rules and standard procedures acted to reduce the value of the payment system for management as a whole, is the subject to which we now turn.

The Effect on Earnings

In general terms the 1978 incentive scheme proved a successful innovation so far as the NCB was concerned. It succeeded in halting the downward drift in productivity which occurred in the 1970s and helped push many performance indicators to new levels. However, it was certainly the case that the scheme proved costlier than the NCB initially anticipated. In mid-1978 a review carried out by the Board found that the incentive pay being earned was twice the level expected for the level of productivity achieved. In 1980, however, a further report concluded that the scheme had attained its self-financing objective. This used a different calculation from that of the earlier assessment and argued that break-even point was a 10 per cent increase in annual saleable output above the 1977–8 base level. By 1979/80 this had been achieved.

Since then the Monopolies and Mergers Commission has criticized the industry for its high level of labour costs and commented that the 'statistics provided to us on earnings under the incentive scheme led us to question whether the controls maintained are adequate' (1983, pp. 281–2). In general, the Commission gave the scheme a rather guarded approval. It was critical, however, of some elements of its design, most notably the facts that work study formed only a basis for negotiation and that non-production workers received a bonus which was not conditional on their own performance. It expressed most concern over the minority of coal-faces achieving very high levels of performance and attributed this to the slackness of work-study standards and the tendency for conditions to change substantially in the course of an installation's life.

It can be surmised, then, that informality in the operation of the incentive scheme pushed earnings upwards and diminished the cost-effectiveness of the payment system. It would be wrong to conclude, though, that management lost control of the scheme. The Board may have paid out more in incentive and bonus payments than it intended but overall costs did remain at or near the self-financing limit. Possibly the clearest indicator that the scheme was not subject to wholesale decay is the very close association which obtained between average incentive earnings

TABLE 4.5. Colliery performance and average incentive earnings

Performance indicator	Correlation coefficient[a]
Face productivity (output per manshift)	0.73
Overall productivity	0.68
Profit per tonne	0.67
Annual output (tonnes)	0.50
Increase in profit since 1976	0.49
Increase in output since 1976	0.37
Manager says face motivation increased	0.38

[a] Pearson's correlation coefficient significant at 5% or less. $n = 35$.

levels and the various indicators of colliery performance shown in Table 4.5. It can be seen that across the thirty-five pits in the survey sample there are very high correlations between average incentive earnings per manshift and face productivity, overall productivity, profits per tonne, and annual output.

However, increases in output and profitability since the inception of the scheme which could be indicators of increased effort were only moderately correlated with incentive pay. The best indicator we have of increased effort, moreover, the managers' estimate of the scheme's effect on face motivation, yielded only a modest correlation with average incentive earnings. Clearly workers were being rewarded largely according to the *value* of their effort to the Board. The principal factor determining the distribution of incentive earnings was management's ability to pay.

This close association between the economic performance of collieries and the economic return to workers indicates, firstly, that the scheme had not functioned to reward 'effort'. When it was introduced the miners were promised by the NCB and by Joe Gormley that the opportunity to earn incentive pay would be equivalent in all pits regardless of conditions. The October 1977 edition of *The Miner*, for instance, reported that, 'the Agreement for each installation will be negotiated separately. The machinery in use, the method of work, the working time, the statutory regulations and the prevailing geological conditions will all be fully taken into consideration when agreeing standards. Thus, each installation will have an equal chance of earning incentive pay.' This patently was not the case. That earnings reflected pit performance, which in turn was largely determined by such factors as seam thickness and quality and level of investment, indicated that the scheme had not operated as the formal description said it should. Equality of opportunity in practice did not exist: miners in high performance pits had a much greater chance of receiving high payments than those in less valuable pits.

The association also indicated that management was largely successful in containing pressures for equivalent payment in less productive pits. Competitive bargaining between groups of workers has in the past been isolated as a major factor encouraging the decay of payment by results. In the NCB areas included in the study, however, competitive bargaining between pits had not proved a major managerial problem and had not generated an inexorable upward creep in earnings levels. One industrial relations official, for instance, remarked that there had been 'a lot less competitive bargaining than you might think', and that what little had occurred had been successfully resisted. Our survey data support this view, revealing that as many as 43 per cent of local union officials had no information on the standards set at other pits, and that about one-third had no information on the bonus paid. Of those who did have this information, all but 6 per cent said that they rarely used it in their negotiations with management. The union officials, therefore, largely bargained on the basis of what they thought their pit could afford rather than what they thought others were getting.

The lack of competitive bargaining in the areas we studied is partly explained by the deeply ingrained culture of payment by results in the industry. With the exception of the interlude of NPLA, mineworkers have been paid for the value of the coal they produce rather than the effort expended. The questions being raised about the future of the industry and the long-term 'economic' viability of the less profitable pits no doubt also served to dampen the demands of those in the less productive collieries, strengthening the correlation between productivity and bonus pay. Management and unions, therefore, in many pits, were under pressure to reward the work-force in line with its perceived 'productivity'. Miners it appears, largely expected, or at least accepted, that their bonus should reflect the fortunes of the pit rather than the sweat of their brow.

This was not the case, however, in parts of the Yorkshire coalfield which were not included in the survey. In two of the Board's Yorkshire areas the scheme had been subject to fairly rapid decay at some collieries, leading to a managerial crack-down to restore control of the effort bargain. This was due to colliery managers yielding to pressures to follow a 'high earner'. The Yorkshire area of the NUM is unique in possessing a system of 'panels' intermediate between the branches and the area leadership. These panels are akin to combine committees, being composed of representatives from pits in each NCB administrative area. In the past, under piece-work, they played an important role in formulating a common policy on price list revision (Taylor, 1984, p. 176). In the first years, at least, of the incentive scheme's life it seems they played a similar role, co-ordinating bargaining tactics in an attempt to raise earnings throughout Yorkshire. The absence of supra-branch organization of this type in the areas included in the study helped minimize the pressures on management to equalize earnings.

Managing Incentives Since the Miners' Strike

Since 1979 a concern with the extent and effects of the reform of workplace industrial relations has been partially displaced within British industrial relations studies by concern with the impact of recession. Scholars have been presented with a new research agenda, examining the effects of mass unemployment on the power disparity between management and labour and the success of the Thatcher Government's attempts to liberate economic activity from trade union influence. In mining the impact of recession has been experienced most sharply since the defeat of the NUM in the 1984/5 strike. This has given management the opportunity to refashion the industry's employment relations. In this section we want to examine the consequences of this shift in the balance of power for the conduct of local pay-bargaining.

Perhaps the most important point that should be made with regard to this issue is that local bargaining over incentive payments continues to take place throughout the industry. There have been some significant changes, however, in how this process is managed. In particular, central co-ordination and supervision of incentive scheme bargaining has declined. The striving of colliery managers to acquire greater control over local bargaining which has been described in this chapter has been permitted greater expression.

A major feature of the 1978 incentive scheme was the inclusion of a variety of checks designed to contain local bargaining pressure from the union. One way in which this was to be achieved was through confining bargaining within a nationally fixed framework of rules. Since the strike this framework has been openly abandoned at a considerable number of collieries. The 1978 incentive scheme continues to be applied in some areas such as South Wales, Scotland, and the North-East, but in Yorkshire, the Midlands, and Nottinghamshire there have been significant departures from it. At some pits in these areas the national scheme has been replaced by completely new schemes which have been devised by colliery and area managers and negotiated with NUM branch officials, while in Nottinghamshire a new area incentive scheme was negotiated with the national leadership of the UDM in 1987. The Nottinghamshire agreement covers all pits in the Nottinghamshire coalfield. In the NUM-controlled areas there is less standardization. In some cases the new schemes have been applied at a number of pits within one area. A scheme, known as the Doncaster Option, for example, has been introduced at seven collieries in South Yorkshire. In other cases, schemes have been tailored to the requirements of particular pits. Wistow in North Yorkshire and High Moor in North Derbyshire, for instance, employ their own, made-to-measure agreements. In all cases, though, there has been an emphasis on local management developing incentive arrangements which can best stimulate increases in productivity within their pit or area, and a switch away from a concern with limiting the discretion of such managers for fear that they will yield excessive concessions to the work-force.

Associated with this change of emphasis has been a reduction in the influence of specialist managers in the management of incentives. Some of the new schemes, for example, reward workers for achieving output targets and dispense with work-study estimates. Much more significant, however, has been the cessation of the monitoring of incentives by industrial relations staff. Computer monitoring of incentive payments and performance no longer takes place. At the time of our research it was clear that line managers were able to escape, at least in part, from the supervision of area and national industrial relations staff. In the aftermath of the miners' strike they have achieved even greater independence. The influence of industrial relations specialists has been deliberately reduced. This has occurred as part of a general attempt to strengthen and streamline the industry's system of management by objectives. There has been a simplification of colliery managers' objectives so that they are now evaluated primarily in terms of the financial performance of their pits. They have been given wider discretion over how they achieve this overriding objective, and this has involved the abandoning of any attempt to ensure that incentive agreements are being correctly applied. In our research we recorded the adaptation of the industrial relations monitoring process to the effective power of the line. The further concentration of decision-making in the hands of the colliery manager has required its complete abandonment.

In addition to the ending of central supervision there have been two other significant developments in the management of incentives since the miners' strike. The first has been an attempt to reduce the scope for local bargaining through simplifying the terms of the incentive contract. A feature of the new incentive agreements which have been introduced in Yorkshire, the Midlands, and Nottinghamshire is the avoidance of allowance payments. As we have shown, under the national scheme these were frequently the object of vigorous local bargaining. Under the new schemes compensation payments have been 'bought out', by increasing the size of the standard payment. In 1986, for example, the standard payment for 100 per cent performance under the original incentive scheme was £6.80 per shift. Under the Doncaster Option, however, it was £10.80 per shift, though without compensation for random interruptions or redeployment. South Yorkshire miners working in pits where the Doncaster Option operates are only compensated if difficulties at the face lead to the loss of an entire machine-shift. This is the case with most of the new incentive schemes which have been introduced.

In minimizing the opportunities for haggling over allowances, the new incentive schemes have also acted to reduce the involvement of supervisors in the management of incentives. Where the new schemes have supplanted the 1978 original, the recording function of mining supervisors has been diminished. The restriction of supervisory discretion which was a feature of the original incentive scheme has, therefore, been extended. In addition, in 1986 NACODS negotiated the consolidation of bonus payments for deputies and overmen. It was felt at the time of our research by many senior managers that paying supervisors incentive bonus encouraged them to collude with work-teams in misrecording levels of performance. The value for management of consolidating supervisors' bonus is that it reduces the incentive for such collusion.

The second significant development in the management of incentives since the miners' strike has been a move to 'decouple' the incentive earnings of production workers from the incentive bonus paid to non-production workers. Under some, though not all, of the new incentive schemes operating in Yorkshire, the Midlands, and Nottinghamshire bonuses have ceased to be tied to the earnings of face-workers. Under the Doncaster Option, for example, non-production workers receive a completely separate bonus based on the tonnage produced at the pit. The purpose of the system of derived bonuses which operated under the 1978 scheme was to minimize the disruptive effect of the reintroduction of incentives on the industry's wage structure. Management has now withdrawn from this objective. There is less concern with accommodating trade union notions of fairness and with maintaining a coherent and limited structure of internal differentials.

What then do changes in the management of incentives tell us about how managers in British Coal have made use of the recession and the defeat of the NUM in the 1984/5 strike? In the first place it is clear that commitment to collective bargaining remains. There has been no break with the practice of negotiating both incentive schemes and specific incentive contracts with the unions. Where new incentive schemes have replaced the 1978 agreement they have been negotiated, albeit with local officials, and they all provide for the joint regulation of the effort bargain. However, management has used its position of strength to amend or replace existing agreements where they have obstructed management's purposes.

In Chapter 2 we described how management has attempted to produce a much sharper incentive for the direct work-force. Complementing the moves in this direction have been the 'decoupling' of incentive earnings and bonus at some collieries, the consolidation of supervisory bonuses, and the 'buying-out' of compensation payments. Management has used the post-strike situation to excise some of the disadvantageous clauses of the 1978 agreement which were catalogued in the main body of this chapter. It is noteworthy that the 'buying-out' of allowances, for example, represents a formalization of the 'managerial custom and practice' we encountered in the course of our research.

The final critical feature of the post-strike management of incentives has been a decline in the concern with containing union bargaining pressure. This loomed large in the design of the 1978 incentive scheme and led, in particular, to the introduction of the computer-monitoring process. The same concern has survived into the post-strike period as seen, for instance, in the reduction of supervisory involvement and in attempts to remove the opportunity to 're-negotiate' incentive contracts by ending compensation payments. However, the ending of computer monitoring and the delegation of greater responsibility to the colliery manager for the management of incentives betoken reduced management anxiety over the decay of payment by results. There is a confidence that forceful management and the new financial discipline which operates in the industry will prove sufficient to hold local bargaining pressures in check. With the NUM weakened, the restriction of local bargaining to a nationally set agenda and its supervision by industrial relations specialists can be safely dispensed with.

Whether this proves to be an accurate and prudent assessment on the part of the industry's managers remains to be seen. However, there are some grounds for believing that the vigorous local pay-bargaining which we have described and which characterized the pre-strike era could re-emerge, particularly in pits with a secure future. There is clear evidence that the management of incentives continues to be contested at pit level. Between the end of the miners' strike and January 1987, British Coal recorded a total of 748 disputes at collieries, with a combined loss of 197,000 manshifts. One hundred and eight of the disputes (14 per cent) arose over incentives. These produced a total loss of 40,400 manshifts (21 per cent of the total). Pressure, therefore, continues to be exerted on local managers and can prove effective in extracting concessions. In several of the large, profitable collieries which have introduced new incentive schemes the standard incentive payment per shift lies between £15 and £20. It is also the case that adjustments to standards to take account of variations in task difficulty are frequently made at these pits, despite the claim that this practice has been bought-out. Informality and the accommodation of union bargaining pressure, therefore, continue to characterize the leaner, more commercial mining industry which has emerged in the wake of the pit strike.

Conclusion

In this and the previous chapter it has been argued that the return to payment by results in the mining industry presented the Board with a major management problem: how to contain bargaining pressure at pit level in order to prevent a decay of the payment system and without a return to the high level of local disputes prevalent before NPLA. Management responded to this problem, it was further argued, by introducing a range of checks and limits on the pay-bargaining process at colliery level, which were designed to ensure that the setting of effort standards remained very largely in management's hands. These constraints, it was said, corresponded to a Donovan-style reform of workplace industrial relations, with their reliance on the principles of formalization, centralization, and specialization.

In this chapter the operation of these constraints on bargaining was investigated in detail. It was shown that the appetite for negotiation of managers, workers, and trade-union representatives, had escaped the limits set down in the formal incentive scheme agreement and that the operation of the payment system was characterized by a great deal of informality. Our, more detailed, work supports the conclusion of Batstone (1988) that the reform of workplace industrial relations has not proved overly successful in regulating workplace bargaining.

The consequence of this in the coal industry, we believe, was to increase wages and increase the cost of the return to payment by results. We would also suggest, however, that informality had beneficial consequences for management in that it offered a means to resolve conflicts over pay and the conduct of work, and provided the basis in many pits for the emergence of 'strong bargaining relationships' with NUM branch officials. A further vital point is that earnings levels across our sample of pits remained closely tied to measures of colliery performance. Indeed, it is probable that the growth of informal bargaining helped produce such an association because it meant that each NUM branch was rendered more reliant on its own internal sources of power. The formal rules of the incentive scheme were intended to reward worker 'effort' and not productivity as such and so should not have led to a strong statistical association between earnings and measures of colliery economic performance.

In the period since our study of the incentive scheme was completed academic debate on British industrial relations has focused on the effects of recession on union bargaining power. Accordingly in the final section of Chapter 4 we examined the effects of the NUM's defeat in the 1984/5 miners' strike on the conduct of local pay bargaining. Perhaps the major finding reported in this section was that local bargaining remains a feature of the industry, but that management has seized the opportunity to alter its structure. Three major changes have been introduced. Firstly, the content of the industry's incentive scheme rules have been altered so as to suit the purposes of local managers. Incentives now operate with less allowance for trade-union conceptions of fairness. Secondly, there has been a transfer of control of incentive schemes away from higher level and specialist managers towards line management in the pits. And thirdly, and perhaps, most crucially, there has been a decline in management concern with containing local union bargaining pressure. There is a new assertiveness in the way that incentives are managed in the coal industry and a confidence that in the late 1980s management strength and economic pressures are adequate to control the bargaining process.

PART III Workplace Trade-unionism and the
Control of Labour

5
The 'Bureaucratization' of the Rank and File

Introduction

The aims of this chapter and the one which follows it are twofold. The first is to offer a description of workplace trade-unionism in coal-mining, paying particular attention to the processes associated with incentive pay-bargaining. The second is to use this material to assess a particular theoretical framework which has been adduced for the analysis of workplace trade-unionism. This is the theory of trade-union bureaucracy which has recently been extended to encompass the study of relations within workplace trade-unionism.

In its essentials the theory of trade-union bureaucracy sees the emergence of a hierarchy of specialist representatives within trade unions as problematical, leading to a divergence in goals between leaders and led. The result of this is held to be an incxorable moderation of union objectives and tactics as the goals of the 'bureaucracy' displace those of the 'rank and file'. In Britain, in the past, active workplace trade-unionism, embodied in the figure of the shop steward, has been viewed as a powerful restraint on such tendencies. More recently, however, it has been suggested that British workplace trade-unionism has itself been subject to a 'bureaucratization of the rank and file' (Hyman, 1979, p. 58). Indeed, this process has been widely identified as the major consequence for trade unions of the post-Donovan reform of industrial relations. According to the bureaucratization thesis hierarchical shop-steward organizations have become heavily implicated in the control of labour. It is this claim which we wish to explore below. We are interested in the extent to which the workplace union in the mining industry has been employed as an instrument of management control. First, however, it is necessary to review the theory of trade-union bureaucracy, and its application to workplace trade-unionism, in greater detail.

The 'Bureaucratization' of Workplace Trade-unionism

In his 1984 postscript to *Working for Ford*, Huw Beynon states that the years since Marx's analysis of British capitalism have witnessed 'a continuance of the guerilla war' against capital which Marx himself described, but that 'in all these struggles the role of the trade unions has been to de-escalate rather than extend the struggle between labour and capital' (p. 369). This theme of the limitations of trade-unionism has been reiterated many times by socialist writers. Although trade unions are vehicles for the advance of the working class they are drawn relentlessly into relations of accommodation with employers which defuse class conflict and frustrate the realization of workers' essential interest, the destruction of the capitalist mode of production. According to Hyman (1984, p. 214),

Trade unions are the collective instruments through which men and women in shop and office, factory, mine and mill, seek to increase their control over the conditions of their working lives. . . . Yet in their day-to-day activities, trade union representatives . . . are under intense pressures to behave as if capitalist relations of production are unalterable . . . The maintenance of orderly relationships with employers can then easily become an overriding priority.

The pull to accommodation with capital is commonly seen to be associated with the emergence of a hierarchy of specialist representatives, a development which is itself encouraged by 'external agencies' (Hyman, 1975, p. 90), employers, managers, and state officials. On the left, this process has typically been designated the problem of trade-union bureaucracy. Hyman, for instance, remarks that the term 'trade union bureaucrat' is more of 'a derogatory epithet' than an 'aid to scientific analysis' (1980, p. 73), but then goes on to state, 'of course there *is* a "problem of bureaucracy" within trade-unionism, in that full-time officials typically acquire interests, perspectives and resources which tend to channel union policies towards accommodation with employers or governments and containment of membership activism' (ibid. p. 74).

The limitations of trade-unionism in much left analysis, then, derive in large part from the growth of specialism and representative democracy in trade unions and from the associated divergence in goals between the 'bureaucracy' and the 'rank and file'. The former is held to be wedded to the preservation of stable relationships with capital and its agents, while the interests of the latter can be served only by the sundering of such relationships.

A variety of explanations for this divergence in interests has been put forward by socialist writers. One tendency has been to emphasize the differences in material conditions between the trade-union official and the workers he or she represents. Such an emphasis is to be found, for example, in Robert Michels's 'iron law of oligarchy', which has structured so much analysis of trade unions. Michels believed labour leaders would betray the revolutionary goals of the labour movement because, as leaders, they had effectively escaped the working class and joined the bourgeoisie. Their policies would thus serve bourgeois interests and not those of the workers they ostensibly represented (see Crouch, 1982, p. 164). Lane (1974, p. 239) has also remarked upon the 'essentially middle-class life' of the local trade union official and the insertion of national officials 'in the rather more sophisticated circles of the metropolitan middle class'.

A second tendency, which is frequently found alongside the first, emphasizes the structural determinants of the union leadership's activities. This line of argument is a notable feature of Hyman's work. Hyman has offered an interpretation of union officials' activities which stresses their role as the guardians of the 'institutional needs' of trade unions (1975, p. 90). Once trade unions become established as permanent organizations they develop 'needs' which may contradict the presumed interest of members in challenging the domination of capital. The prime 'institutional need' of trade unions as organizations is considered to be self-preservation. To ensure this the union 'must cultivate the goodwill or at least acquiescence of employers and the state' (Hyman, 1971, p. 17). The preservation of the union, then, is believed to require union officials to enter stable relations with employers and offer guarantees of orderly industrial conduct. Their role as guardians of the union 'may thus involve the suppression of irregular and disruptive activities of the rank and file which challenge managerial control' (Hyman, 1975, p. 91). Hyman's analysis of the 'organizational interests' of trade unions, therefore, leads him to conclude that *union* control and *workers'* control may face in opposite directions, and the element of power over the members inherent in union organization be turned against them' (ibid. pp. 91–2).

Within the 'rank-and-filist' tradition of the British left, it is typically argued that bureaucratic domination of trade unions and accommodation with employers are inherently unstable. The forces making for hierarchy and stable industrial relations are believed to be beset by powerful counter-tendencies. This is the substance of Hyman's criticism of Michels. Borrowing from Gouldner he asserts that the 'iron law of oligarchy' is continually opposed by the 'iron law of democracy' (1971, pp. 28–32). Michels, according to Hyman, offers 'an overdetermined model of oligarchic development'.

Such a response is understandable from writers on the left. If the antagonism between capital and labour is viewed as the fundamental organizing principle of society, and if it is held that this antagonism promises social transformation, then the institutionalization of class conflict through bureaucratized trade unions must be prone to collapse. If the role of trade unions has been to 'de-escalate' class struggle, then class struggle must have originated independently of trade unions and, presumably, would have escalated towards its denouement if trade unions, at least in their present form, had not existed and intervened. For 'rank-and-filist' writers, class struggle, logically and historically, precedes the formation of trade unions (Clarke, 1977, pp. 11–21). Indeed, within this conception, trade unions are viewed as vehicles for the distorted expression of this basic force. It is the continual reproduction of the class struggle which is believed, in the last instance, to impose limits on the bureaucratization of the labour movement.

Offe and Wiesenthal (1985, p. 199) have described such a belief as a conviction in the 'class instinct' of the proletariat. Although in much 'rank-and-filist' work this 'instinct' is left untheorized, in Hyman's sociology there are clues as to its components. In a number of places in Hyman's work can be found references to 'processes of spontaneous solidarity' (1975, p. 157) or the 'immediate collective solidarity' (ibid. p. 161) of workers on the shop-floor. One element in Hyman's conception of the 'class instinct' of the working class, therefore, is a belief that collective action comes naturally to workers. A second element refers more to the goals than the form of working-class action. According to Hyman, workers' struggle against capitalism does not simply embrace an economistic campaign to achieve a more favourable distribution of wealth, but 'also raises issues of power and control' (1971, p. 37). The concrete expression of this urge is the attempt by workers to amass 'job control'. For Hyman, 'the final source of conflict within our system of industry [is] its impact on workers as total human beings' (1984, p. 102). Labour under capitalist relations of production is deeply alienating and its inherent deprivations impel workers to resist management control and develop inchoate demands for more autonomy and forms of production more congruent with their essential needs: 'from disputes which are trivial in themselves a conscious aspiration for real industrial democracy may at times be generated'.

The value of shop stewards and shop stewards' movements in this framework is that they are held to reduce the contradiction between the necessity of organization and the 'self activity' of workers. Representation through shop stewards diminishes the distortion of workers' inherently radical aspirations. 'Both the rise of the shop stewards' organisations and the number of unofficial strikes are symptoms', wrote Cliff of the experience of the 1960s, ' . . . of the common aspirations of the working class towards workers' control' (1970, p. 201). Shop stewards are believed to be capable of this because they work on the shop-floor alongside the workers they represent. The steward is 'highly visible, subject to the same experiences as his comrades, and subject to the same group pressures' (Lane, 1974, p. 198). Stewards can thus be more easily controlled than higher-level representatives but also, and perhaps more importantly, are driven by the same deprivations as the rank and file. Shop stewards are perceived to be *embedded* in the rank and file and it is from this that their radical potential and their threat to the 'bureaucracy' are considered to derive.

This 'optimistic' appreciation of the shop steward was invariably qualified even in the most hopeful left-wing statements of the late 1960s and early 1970s. Two main points regarding the inadequacies of shop-steward organization have tended to be made. The first is that rank-and-file movements have normally been highly sectional in character. Beynon (1984, pp. 369–70), for example, writing of the militancy of British car workers in the 1960s, has stated,

The car workers in this period were at the centre of the class struggle, yet the struggle never extended beyond the 'guerilla war'. They struggled bravely and their resolve has frequently demanded admiration. Yet there was little evidence that they have been able to link their struggles positively with those of other workers. Neither did their battles produce radical political demands.

Workplace opposition to capital, therefore, produces only 'a partial and sectional consciousness' (Hyman, 1971, p. 37). Shop stewards, who articulate this opposition, are necessarily sectional in their objectives and in their demands (Cliff, 1970, pp. 202–4).

The second point partially conflicts with the first because it emphasizes the differences of interest between shop stewards and the rank-and-file members they represent. According to Hyman 'workplace trade unionism has always displayed contradictory tendencies, involving certain parallels with the role of full-time officialdom' (1980, p. 74). The workplace shop-steward organization can develop an 'institutional' stake in 'orderly' industrial relations. The reason Hyman gives for this is the shop stewards' dependence on 'management's goodwill' (1975, p. 168). It is argued that the need to preserve the workplace organization together with the quest for incremental concessions, draws shop stewards, as it does full-time officials, into stable bargaining relations with management. Integral to this process is a pressure on shop stewards to discipline their members for management, so that they become, in McCarthy and Parker's famous phrase, 'more of a lubricant than an irritant' in the industrial relations machinery (quoted in Hyman, 1975, p. 168).

This point brings us to the issue of the *bureaucratization of the rank and file*. It has been widely argued[1] by left-wing commentators on industrial relations that developments in British workplace trade-unionism, in the post-Donovan 'decade of reform', have accentuated this second tendency. Workplace trade-unionism has shifted from facilitating rank-and-file mobilization towards its restraint. The argument has been neatly summarized by Hyman (1980, p. 74):

[1] For example, see Beecham (1984), Beynon (1984, pp. 348–9), Cliff (1970, p. 204), Hyman (1979; 1980, p. 74; 1984, pp. 188, 227–8), Lane (1982), and Terry (1983b). Not all of these authors use the phrase the 'bureaucratization of the rank and file' but their interpretations of recent developments in British workplace trade-unionism, we feel, are broadly similar.

Hierarchical divisions within workplace unionism have rapidly elaborated; there are now far more full-time convenors than full-time union officials. The centralisation of plant and company negotiations has concentrated bargaining power within the shop steward leadership at the expense of ordinary section stewards. The disciplinary powers of joint shop stewards' committees have increased, often providing a new channel for curbing militants. The place of workplace organisation within the official structures of many unions has become more closely defined. Thus, there has emerged a substantial stratum of (more or less) full-time senior shop stewards, wielding considerable power within their workplace organisation, and performing a key mediating role between employers, union officials and the ordinary membership (including first-line shop stewards).

This is a clear application of the theory of bureaucracy to workplace trade-unionism, in that the moderation of union objectives and methods, the 'curbing' of militants, is linked to the growth of hierarchy in union organization.

For writers who have developed this interpretation, the bureaucratization of the rank and file has a number of components. The first is an attenuation of, at least some, shop stewards' links with their constituencies. Organizational change within workplace trade-unionism is believed to have widened the gap between the interests of representatives and members. The growth of hierarchy, of full-time convenors, of senior stewards, and shop-steward committees has generated a difference in material condition between the workplace leadership and the rank and file. A crucial feature, therefore, of what Terry (1979) has described as the 'lay élite' is believed to be its removal from the alienating conditions of labour which remain the lot of the workers it represents. The experience of labour alongside the membership under capitalist relations of production has in the past been seen as a guarantee of shop-steward militancy and representativeness. For many workplace leaders this guarantee has vanished and it is presumed that this alteration in their condition has led to a reduction in their effectiveness, and, according to some commentators, to their corruption (Beecham, 1984, pp. 103–4).[2]

Removal from the shop-floor has exposed full-time convenors and senior shop stewards to a new set of pressures and determinants of behaviour. Prime among these, and the second component of the bureaucratization thesis, are pressures from management on the 'lay élite' to discipline their membership. The new tier of workplace leaders is believed to be particularly vulnerable to such pressures because its own

---

[2] Beecham's argument is worth reproducing: 'It does not take a genius to see that the interests and ideas of workers and their representatives begin to diverge quite sharply under such circumstances. Only more recently have we learned of the detailed systems of corruption which began to emerge in this period—full time convenors on 100% earnings plus bonus, plus night premiums, plus unlimited time off site. . . . '

position and the organizations which it leads are dependent on managerial support (Terry, 1983b, pp. 53–4). The 'institutional needs' of the bureaucratic workplace organizations, which emerged in the 1970s, are felt to compel shop-floor leaders to adopt moderate policies because the growth of such organizations was permitted, and indeed encouraged, by management. Continuance of such organizations and of the privileges of those who lead them is considered to depend on the 'lay élite' operating to serve management's interests.

It is the manner in which bureaucratic workplace organizations have been created, therefore, which is felt to provide the key to their function. They are not considered to be the creation of workers themselves, but of sophisticated managerial attempts at control. This is believed to be the case particularly in those sectors of the economy where shop-steward organization largely came into being as a result of the industrial relations 'reform' of the 1970s. Even in industries with well-established trade-union traditions, however, it is argued that there was a shift towards greater dependence on the employer. Beynon (1984, pp. 348–9), for example, has detailed management sponsorship of the 'convenor system' in Fords.

Four developments in workplace trade-unionism in the 1970s are typically presented by adherents of the bureaucratization thesis as indicators of increased dependence on management. The first of these is the increase in the numbers of convenors and senior shop stewards who are paid by their employer to spend all or most of their time on union business. The second is the provision by management of office space and other facilities for the workplace union. The third is the provision of industrial relations training for shop stewards. And the fourth is the assumption by management of the responsibility for maintaining workplace organization through closed shop and check-off agreements.[3]

The final component of the bureaucratization thesis is the suggestion that the concerns and activities of senior stewards have been more fully integrated with those of the national union leadership. This is said to have occurred through constitutional change within the unions themselves, which has increased the scope of lay representation on national executive and other committees (Hyman, 1979, p. 57). It is also believed to have occurred through institutional change in the realm of collective bargaining, through the allocation of seats on national negotiating committees to senior lay figures (Beynon, 1984, p. 348). For the adherents of the bureaucratization thesis these developments do not represent an opening-up of trade-union decision-making to membership influence but

---

[3] It is worth noting that all four of these arrangements, which are believed to increase steward dependence on management, could also be said to widen the difference of condition between representatives and members which is the first component of the bureaucratization thesis.

rather the imposition of a top-down strategy of control (Strinati, 1982, p. 139). In Hyman's (1979, p. 58) view,

The internal politics of trade unionism today involves a complex system of linkages between the relatively inactive membership on the shop or office floor and the top leadership in the TUC Economic Committee. The ability of national leaders to contain, control and manipulate the ordinary membership depends to an important extent on their success in establishing loyalties, understandings or trade-offs with groups at different levels in this elaborate hierarchy who are able to deploy a variety of forms of influence and sanctions.

As far as we are aware all formulations of the bureaucratization argument are equally vague about the processes through which greater institutional integration is transformed into tighter control. It seems to us, however, that two factors might be considered of importance. In the first place, the sheer fact of sitting on committees with full-time officials exposes shop stewards much more fully to their arguments for moderation. In the second place, and more importantly, sitting on such committees exposes the 'lay élite' to the same pressures from employers and government which full-time officials experience and which lead them to favour moderate policies.

In setting out the components of the bureaucratization thesis it has, hopefully, become clear where its advocates believe the origins of workplace bureaucracy to lie. The growth of hierarchy in workplace trade-unionism is viewed as an effect of managerial, governmental, and official union policies. Although some commentators (Hyman, 1979, pp. 59–60) mention the desire of shop stewards themselves to co-ordinate their activities and combat sectionalism, the process of centralization is presented largely as an instance of the overdetermination of union organization by 'external agencies'.

It is argued that management encouraged the growth of hierarchy in workplace trade-unionism as part of a wider reform of workplace industrial relations (Terry, 1983b, pp. 52–4). This was distinguished by moves to centralize collective bargaining within the workplace and to formalize industrial relations procedures. Both initiatives encouraged more elaborate and centralized shop-steward organizations. Fragmented bargaining and piece-work were replaced by job evaluation and group incentive schemes so that the capacity to negotiate with management over pay was concentrated in fewer hands at establishment level. More formalized contacts between management and union, greater use of written disciplinary and disputes procedures, and more standardized pay and effort fixing techniques, in addition, promoted specialization within the workplace organization. The result, it is argued, was that senior stewards became more like full-time officials, professional negotiators equipped for their role through TUC and other courses in bargaining skills (Terry, 1983a, p. 70).

The intentions behind this managerially authored reform of industrial relations are taken to be the securing of peaceful or 'orderly' industrial relations and the re-establishment of management control over pay and work organization, which had been lost in the shop-floor battles of the 1960s. In pursuing these goals management is believed to be supported by state policy. In most statements of the bureaucratization thesis there is reference to the Donovan Report and its programme for the reform of workplace industrial relations (Hyman, 1979, p. 56). Beecham (1984, p. 106) indeed, in an appalling phrase, has referred to the 'Donovanisation of the workplace'. In general, though, there is no attempt by the theorists of bureaucratization to assess the actual impact of state initiatives such as the Royal Commission. It is assumed that managerial action within the workplace and governmental pronouncements are complementary elements in the strategy of an undifferentiated 'capital' to integrate and neutralize workplace trade-unionism.

Whereas the discussion of state policy, by adherents of the bureaucratization thesis, tends to stop short at the description of motives, the discussion of union policy does not even get this far. It is simply taken for granted that the interest of union leaders, the 'bureaucracy' proper, lies in recreating workplace trade-unionism in its own image. The impulse to control is left largely unexplained. We would suggest, however, that the key assumption underlying such theorists' interpretation of union policy is that the leadership's 'direct responsibility for their organisations' security and survival' (Hyman, 1979, p. 55) has led them to try and moderate workplace trade-unionism in order to preserve stable relations with employers and government. Given the impracticality of any attempt to dismantle shop-steward organization, this project has necessarily taken the path of control through integration in the established union machinery.

How effective have managerial, state, and official union policies been? The answer contained in most statements of the bureaucratization thesis is that they have been very successful. Workplace trade-unionism has been bureaucratized and this has produced a 'downturn' in the level of class conflict in Britain. However, there are qualifications to this argument. Beynon (1984, p. 371), for example, has commented on the emergence 'of a new rank and file organisation within the Ford plants' during the 1978 pay strike. This, he notes, called itself the *'workers'* combine committee' and grew out of disaffection with the 'convenor system'. Hyman (1983, p. 44) meanwhile has noted that 'there have been intimations of greater autonomy' from those workplace organizations most dependent on official union sponsorship and support. He cites the militant action of NUPE members in the winter of 1978–9 as evidence. Behind such statements, we believe, it is possible to detect the 'rank-and-filist' conviction that the contradictions of capitalism must eventually undermine any attempt to stabilize relations between capital and labour. Trade-union bureaucracy in the workplace, as at higher levels, must eventually be challenged by the 'class instinct' of workers themselves.

In the main, however, it is the effectiveness of the changes in workplace trade-unionism which is emphasized in most statements of the bureaucratization thesis. These are said to have had two chief consequences. The first of these is the relative success of the Social Contract in holding down working-class incomes under the last Labour Government (Hyman, 1979, p. 58). While the second is the muting of workplace opposition to the closure of plants, the restructuring of industries, and the intensification of work since the Callaghan Government's demise. According to Hyman and Elger (1981, p. 139), for example, the success of the Edwardes plan for British Leyland was due, in part, to the fact that senior shop stewards had become detached from their membership through involvement in BL's company-wide 'participation machinery'. A similar argument, that 'bureaucratization' has induced apathy in the rank and file and so eased the way for a reassertion of the managerial prerogative, has been made by Terry (1983b, p. 55). Commenting on 'the relative absence of worker resistance' to attempts by management to remove full-time status from senior stewards, Terry has remarked that: 'While this can partly be accounted for by the existence of other, more pressing concerns for union members and by the general lack of confidence within unions, it is also often a symptom of a degree of rank and file alienation from the established steward leadership.'

In summary, it can be said that the notion of the 'bureaucratization of the rank and file' encompasses a number of statements about recent developments in workplace trade-unionism. The first is that the growth of hierarchy in shop-steward organizations, the consolidation of a 'lay élite', has been the deliberate creation of managers, national trade-union officials, and government. Each of these three 'external agencies' is believed to have embarked on successful strategies of incorporation since the 1960s in order to further their own control over workplace trade-unionism and bend it to suit their own purposes. The alleged consequences of these strategies have been a growing divergence of interests between the 'incorporated' shop-floor élite and the workers they ostensibly represent and a moderation of shop-steward objectives and tactics.

Because such moderation is believed to be contrary to the interests of ordinary workers on the shop or office floor, bureaucratization is considered to be unstable. The new 'lay élite', the theorists of bureaucratization believe, is subject to challenge from below as workers' 'class instinct' drives them to butt against the new restraints they encounter within their own workplace organizations. In most statements of the argument, however, this challenge is regrettably seen as muted. The key to the bureaucratization argument is the presumed effectiveness of the controls achieved over dissident members and sectional shop stewards by those who cap the new workplace hierarchy. Control by this group is believed to result in apathy towards trade-unionism among the membership and in the moderation of workplace pressures on employers. The bureaucratization of the rank and file, it is argued, has produced a 'downturn' in class conflict since the heady days of the late 1960s and early 1970s and has facilitated the imposition of incomes policy, redundancy, and new working practices on the British working class. The effectiveness of the bureaucratization of workplace trade-unionism as a strategy for the control of labour, therefore, is believed to be measured in the outcomes of workplace industrial relations.

Workplace Trade Union Organization in the Mining Industry

Mining, in many ways, provides an ideal site for investigating the adequacy of the bureaucratization argument. A 'lay élite' of full-time branch or lodge officials (the industry's equivalent of senior shop stewards) is a well-established feature of union organization in the coalfields. The industry's industrial relations are highly formalized and management, at least until the 1984/5 miners' strike, has been supportive of workplace trade-unionism. Since nationalization a *de facto* closed shop has existed throughout the industry, though this has been complicated by the recognition of the UDM by the Coal Board in 1985. In addition there are close formal links between the union at workplace level and the area organizations which comprise the NUM. The representatives within the pits are the formal branch officials of the union and each branch sends a delegate to the executive committee of the appropriate area.

In Chapter 6 we aim to describe the objectives of the workplace leadership in mining and to examine whether its relationships with managers and the external union match the predictions of the bureaucratization thesis. Before then, however, it is necessary to map out in greater detail the contours of workplace trade-unionism in the coal industry, to describe the extent of 'bureaucracy' in the pits. It is also necessary to assess the degree of accountability of the workplace leadership to the mining rank and file.

Hierarchy is particularly well developed in workplace organization in the mining industry. Table 5.1, for example, shows the number of working hours spent on the conduct of union business by the branch representatives who were interviewed at the thirty-five pits in our survey. These figures show that a majority of branch representatives

TABLE 5.1 Time at work spent on union business

Hours Per Week	Number	%
Less than 20	11	31
20–39	6	17
All the time	18	52
TOTAL	35	100

Source: NUM Branch Representatives' Questionnaire 1981.

interviewed spent all of their working week on union business. A 'lay élite' is thus clearly discernible in the mining industry. The figures, however, underestimate the percentage of pits which have a full-time union representative. This is so because in six cases it was not possible to interview the senior figure on the NUM branch, usually the secretary, the equivalent of a convenor in other industries. If this is taken into account then the percentage of collieries with a full-time representative rises to between 60 and 70 per cent. In the Workplace Industrial Relations Survey (WIRS) of 1980 it was found that 70 per cent of establishments employing more than 1,000 manual workers had full-time convenors (Daniel and Millward, 1983, p. 34). Only half of the collieries in our sample employed over 1,000 workers but the number of full-time representatives was equivalent. Clearly the 'professionalization' of workplace trade-unionism is more advanced in mining than elsewhere.

Although a tier of workplace 'bureaucracy' clearly exists in mining, the picture must be qualified. Not all full-time branch secretaries are paid by management. There is a tradition of NUM branches paying the wages of their representatives themselves and this persists at a minority of collieries. Thus, at four pits in our sample the branch secretary was completely or partially paid by the membership. The position of senior representatives at a minority of pits, therefore, is not dependent on management support and this should, according to the bureaucratization argument, reduce the liability of such representatives to incorporation. However, even these 'free-standing' branch officials are subject to two other alleged determinants of bureaucratization, integration into the external union hierarchy and separation from the membership and its conditions of work.

Although some NUM branches may pay their own officials they are likely to remain dependent on management support in other ways. Another frequently cited indicator of bureaucratization is access to office facilities. Table 5.2 illustrates the extent of facilities provided by the NCB for union business. Also shown are comparative results from the 1980 WIRS (Daniel and Millward, 1983, p. 44).

The mining industry again scores highly on at least two of these

TABLE 5.2   Facilities for union business

	NCB survey numbers	NCB survey %	WIRS % among establishments with over 1,000 employees
Own office	33	94	61
Own telephone	30	86	62
Secretarial help	11	31	54

Source: NUM Branch Representatives' Questionnaire, 1981. n = 35.

indicators of management support. Comparison with the WIRS figures, furthermore, establishes that trade-unionism is assisted by management to a greater degree in coal-mining than is usual. This is especially true given the discrepancy in enterprise size between the two sets of figures presented.

In statements of the bureaucratization thesis it is invariably argued that dependence on management for time off work and office facilities necessarily distances representatives from ordinary members and reduces the effectiveness of workplace trade-unionism. This overwhelmingly negative assessment is perhaps unwarranted. Resources provided by management may have very real practical benefits for the workplace union. The existence of full-time branch officials in mining, for example, means there is a representative at hand, available at shift change-over times, to take up issues raised by any section of the work-force. The presence of full-time representatives housed on site, in a union box or office, can therefore facilitate contact with the rank and file.

The provision of facilities may also have beneficial consequences for the workplace union. In mining, for instance, not only is it the norm for office space and equipment to be made available but it is also common for management to provide rooms for workplace mass meetings. This was said to be the case by twenty of our NUM representatives. Management support, therefore, has in this case positively encouraged and not hindered workplace accountability and the form of direct democracy usually favoured by adherents of the bureaucratization thesis.

A major weakness of the argument on trade-union dependence on management, then, is that it dismisses the practical benefits which can accrue to workplace trade-unionists from management support.[4]

[4] Lane (1974, pp. 208–9), for example, notes the immediate benefits for stewards of time off work and office facilities but then declares: 'in the long run the solid advantages mostly accrued to management. The affording of facilities to senior shop stewards and convenors did not mean that they had been fully integrated into the management structure, but it did mean that the ever present conflict between labour and capital was contained and perhaps even masked.'

Advocates of the argument, however, would presumably contend that such benefits do not outweigh the disadvantages of being dependent on management. It is believed, essentially, that such dependence produces a sense of obligation within the 'lay élite' which leads, in turn, to the moderation of its activities. In our view the offer of a telephone or of an office may not inspire a very powerful sense of obligation. Nowhere have we seen any evidence produced that demonstrates a direct connection between the provision of facilities for shop stewards by management and the curbing of militancy. In our experience workplace representatives tend, in any case, to be deeply suspicious of managerial offers of assistance and wary of the danger of being compromised. The result of this is that management offers of facilities will tend to be treated opportunistically and exploited without the assumption of any sense of obligation. More importantly, however, is the fact that concessions, such as time off work, office space, and rooms for meetings, once granted, tend to be perceived as rights by workplace trade unionists. And, because they are seen as rights, rather than gifts, they do not inspire a sense of obligation.

A further point is that the extension of trade-union facilities in coal-mining in the 1970s, if not in some other industries, occurred after a wave of trade-union militancy. Given this, it seems to us slightly perverse to view the extension of branch officials' rights at work as the effect of a sophisticated managerial strategy of incorporation, rather than a simple effect of greater union pressure. In the wake of the NUM's defeat in the 1984/5 miners' strike there have been reports in the press (*Pitwatch* 1, June/July 1985; Kahn, 1985) of colliery managers reducing branch officials' facilities and amounts of time off work. According to the theory of bureaucratization such action should be beneficial for trade-unionism. We believe journalists have been right to portray it as an attempt to diminish the effectiveness of branch organization in the pits.

An important component of the notion of the bureaucratization of the rank and file is the belief that the moderation of workplace trade-union leaders has been achieved, in part, by training in 'responsible' industrial relations behaviour. Training, it is asserted, furthers professionalism among the shop-floor leadership and provides an alternative standard for the guidance of action to the needs and desires of the rank and file. Virtually the entire sample of NUM branch officials had received some form of industrial relations training. Table 5.3, reveals something of the content of that training and by whom it was provided.

Clearly most training for trade-union representatives is provided within the industry and by the NUM. Over 60 per cent of the sample had been on at least one NUM training course. A considerable amount of training, however, is provided by management, either on its own initiative or in conjunction with the union. Over half the sample had received industrial relations training which was at least partly devised by management. This

TABLE 5.3   Content, source, and % attendance at training courses

| | Course run by | | | |
Type of course	NUM	NUM/NCB	NCB	Other
Health and safety	54	29	20	17
Industrial relations practice	34	31	9	26
Incentive bonus scheme	20	23	3	—
Work study	9	17	6	—

Source: NUM Branch Representatives Questionnaire, 1981. n = 35.

TABLE 5.4   Attitudes to work study

	Positive	Qualified	Negative
Trained in work study	5	2	3
Not trained in work study	3	7	14
TOTAL	8	9	17

Note: (N = 34) x^2 5.58, significance 0.06.
Source: NUM Branch Representatives Questionnaire, 1981.

included training on such things as the proper working of the incentive scheme and the use of work study. It is education of this sort which proponents of the bureaucratization thesis claim is particularly likely to foster the incorporation of the 'lay élite'.

On one issue, attitudes to the use of work study, we were able to investigate the impact of training courses. Branch officials were asked whether they thought work study provided an 'objective and fair means' of devising installation standards. Their replies, cross-tabulated with their replies on work-study training, are set out in Table 5.4.

This does provide some evidence that attendance on work-study appreciation courses is associated with more 'positive' attitudes towards work study, although the association just failed to reach the 5 per cent level of significance. Whether such attitudes encourage attendance or derive from attendance we are not in a position to say. However, two points must be made by way of qualificaton. The first is that half of those who have attended work-study courses have negative or qualified attitudes towards it. The second is that across the entire sample attitudes to the use of work study are generally unfavourable. Despite occupying 'bureaucratic' positions within their workplace organizations, over two-thirds of our respondents were either sceptical or downright hostile in their evaluation of this supposedly objective managerial technique.

The Accountability of the Workplace Leadership in Mining

In the previous section we demonstrated that a 'lay élite' of full-time representatives is a feature of the mining industry, that this grouping is supported in its activities by NCB management, though to a lesser degree since the 1984/5 strike than at the time of our research, and that it has been equipped for its representative function through industrial relations training. We now want to turn our attention to the activities of this tier of representatives and to its relations with the ordinary membership. A central claim of proponents of the bureaucratization thesis is that the recently created layer of full-time workplace representatives is remote from the membership and lacking in accountability. The alleged effect of this is said to be rank-and-file apathy and alienation from trade-unionism. In this section, therefore, we want to use our survey material to examine the degree and nature of the contacts between branch officials and members in the mining industry and to investigate what checks, if any, the members impose on their activities.

The NUM has a reputation, partly tarnished by the failure to hold a national ballot during the 1984/5 strike, for high membership involvement in its affairs (Edelstein and Warner, 1975, ch. 8). At workplace level it is usual for branch officers to be elected to office either through a secret ballot of the membership or through a show of hands at a branch meeting. Officials normally have to stand for re-election every year and turn-outs tend to be high, as is the case with most elections in the NUM. It is also common for elections to be contested. We interviewed several branch officials who had either achieved office by unseating an incumbent or had themselves been defeated whilst holding office in the past. A particularly spectacular rejection of the sitting workplace leadership by the members was seen in the Nottinghamshire area in 1984 when pro-strike branch officials were voted out of office by working miners.

The formal, electoral controls on workplace leaders in the mining industry, therefore, do provide genuine accountability. Indeed, the electoral tests which branch officials have to undergo are rather more rigorous than those experienced by the 'lay élite' in other industries. In manufacturing, for example, senior shop stewards, particularly at larger establishments, tend to be elected by shop-steward committees rather than by the membership as a whole (Batstone, 1984, p. 93).

How accountable are NUM branch officials between elections? One way of answering this question is to look at attendance at formal branch meetings. Workplace branches are the norm in coal-mining, and so it might be anticipated that attendance at branch meetings would be high. This, most emphatically, is not the case. Across our sample an average of 35.4 members, including branch officials, regularly attended branch meetings. This meant that at the vast majority of pits less than 5 per cent of the membership were involved actively in formal branch life. However, it was pointed out at a number of collieries that branch meetings called to discuss matters of importance, such as overtime, bonus, or strikes would greatly increase the proportion of members attending. This indicates that on issues of greater salience to the rank and file, scrutiny of branch activities, as manifested through attendance at branch meetings, tends to be higher.

The pattern of formal branch activity in coal-mining, therefore, indicates the accuracy of Willman's (1982, p. 19) argument that the capacity of workplace leaders to pursue policies independently of the rank and file will be dependent on whether or not those policies impinge on issues which are 'normatively central' to the ordinary membership. Where issues are 'normatively central' branch policy will have to be tested before larger branch meetings than are normal.

The fact that the independence of the branch leadership varies from context to context is also demonstrated by contrasting the relative lack of involvement of the majority of members in routine, formal branch life with their much greater interest in the collective bargaining activities of the branch. This distinction between membership involvement in the institutional processes of the union and in collective bargaining is usually presented as a distinction between orientations toward the wider union and toward the domestic organization at the workplace (Hill, 1981, pp. 138–9). Our survey revealed, however, that in mining this distinction operates within the workplace union. The responses of branch officials indicated that they believed their involvement in workplace pay negotiations to be subject to a great deal of membership scrutiny. All but 17 per cent felt they were under more pressure since the incentive scheme had restored an element of pit-head pay-bargaining, 80 per cent of branch officials said the volume of complaints about wages from the men had increased, and 43 per cent reported the membership to be more critical of lodge officials. This impression was supported by evidence from the colliery manager questionnaire. Over half the sample of colliery managers (54 per cent) reported that NUM branch officials have more difficulty with their own members as a direct result of the incentive scheme.

Branch officials' involvement in the running of incentives is therefore a matter of considerable concern to NUM members. Branch officials, however, may still resist membership pressure and retain a relatively free hand in the negotiation and operation of incentive agreements. Table 5.5 presents rather contradictory perceptions of whether or not this is the case. Over 90 per cent of branch representatives estimated they had at least a 'great deal' of independence from the membership in pay negotiations, while only a quarter of the managers interviewed were prepared to say that representatives had this much freedom of action.

TABLE 5.5 Independence of branch from membership in pay negotiations

| | Union estimate | | Management estimate | |
	Numbers	%	Numbers	%
Complete	11	31	—	—
Great deal	22	63	8	23
Moderate amount	2	6	8	23
Some	—	—	10	29
Little	—	—	5	14
None	—	—	4	11
TOTAL	35	100	35	100

Source: Colliery Manager and NUM Branch Representatives Questionnaires, 1981.

Which of these two sets of responses is nearer the truth can perhaps be gauged from some additional information. According to the formal terms of the 1978 incentive scheme, installation agreements are to be negotiated by the colliery manager and the officials of the NUM branch. The research revealed, however, that it was normal at many collieries for more people than this to be present at the negotiating table. At twenty-four collieries (69 per cent) it was reported that the chargeman or other team representatives were included in coal-face negotiations. At twenty-two pits (63 per cent) it was reported that the chargeman or team representatives were present at negotiations for development drivages. Of course these figures do not prove that the branch secretary was not playing the major part in negotiations on the union side. The fact, however, that at such a high proportion of collieries team members had come to be included in the wage-fixing process indicates that branch official leadership on this issue was constrained within reasonably tight limits.

Further indication that this was so is provided by Table 5.6. This shows the NUM officials' views of the frequency with which the objectives of branch officials conflict with those of individual face and development teams. Although at only a minority of collieries was a conflict between branch officials and work-teams felt to be frequent, at the majority it arose at least on occasion. This again demonstrates that the independence of senior workplace representatives in wage-bargaining is by no means total and that challenges to their adopted policy from the membership can occur.

One important source of membership pressure on branch officials appeared to be a relative lack of success on the part of workplace representatives in satisfying members' pay aspirations. Batstone and his colleagues (1977, pp. 51–2) have suggested that success in prosecuting members' interests is a vital condition for the emergence and reproduction of shop steward leadership. In the mining industry, where the equivalents

TABLE 5.6 Conflict between NUM branch officials and individual work-teams over the incentive scheme

	Face Teams		Development teams	
	Numbers	%	Numbers	%
Always	1	3	—	—
Frequently	—	—	2	6
Sometimes	16	47	14	40
Rarely	12	35	8	23
Never	5	15	11	31
TOTAL	34	100	35	100

Source: NUM Branch Representatives Questionnaire, 1981.

of senior stewards were not overly successful they tended to experience challenges to their position from below. Across the sample of pits, for instance, there was a tendency for branch representatives to report more criticism from the membership and more frequent conflict with face teams where average incentive earnings were lower.[5]

If relative failure can lead to the questioning of the branch leadership then, by the same token, relative success can confirm it in its position. A number of NUM officials, at both collieries and area headquarters, claimed that the devolution of pay-bargaining had enhanced the stature of many branch representatives and enabled them to consolidate their leadership. An area official, for instance, remarked that the introduction of the incentive scheme had raised the 'status' of branch secretaries. Previously, under NPLA, he argued, they had been mere 'welfare officers'. An NCB industrial relations manager from one of the Midlands areas made an identical point. He said that the NPLA had 'neutered' the branch secretary but that with the return to local incentive-bargaining he had regained a position of importance in the pits. If these impressions are put next to the evidence on membership scrutiny of local pay-bargaining, then it would appear that greater accountability of representatives may well be associated with an increase in their independence. However, it must be emphasized that the greater ability of workplace leaders to take decisions on behalf of the membership in such situations rests on their success in realizing members' objectives. Their independence, that is, rests on their effectiveness and not on membership apathy and alienation from the trade union. Expressed rather differently, such workplace leaders exercise legitimate authority rather than bureaucratic domination.

To summarize this section, therefore, it can be said that the 'lay élite' in coal-mining operates under conditions of genuine accountability. Formal

[5] Pearson's R equalled 0.35 (sig. 0.02) in the first case, and 0.32 (sig. 0.03) in the second.

electoral controls, superior to those in many other industries, provide checks on branch officials' independence and are occasionally used to remove them from office. Perhaps even more important is the fact that their involvement in local pay-bargaining is subject to a great deal of membership scrutiny. The rank and file in coal-mining does not appear to be hopelessly alienated from workplace trade-union organization. Turn-out in branch elections tends to be high and there is a readiness to challenge branch officials' record in collective bargaining. The internal politics of workplace trade-unionism in mining, therefore, tend to be considerably more vital than is suggested by the proponents of the bureaucratization thesis. Our evidence suggests that such writers have over-emphasized both the independence of the 'lay élite' and the alienation of ordinary trade-union members from hierarchical or 'bureaucratic' workplace organizations.

6
The 'Interests' of the Workplace Leadership

In the previous chapter we outlined the theory of the 'bureaucratization of the rank and file' and began to assess its validity in the light of evidence from the mining industry. In this chapter we want to complete our examination of workplace trade-unionism in coal-mining by presenting evidence on the objectives or 'interests' of NUM branch officials. We review the practice of the workplace leadership in mining by looking at the lay élite's attempts to unify or 'collectivize' the membership, at its relationship with management and the extent to which it is prepared to control the rank and file for the employer, and, finally, at its attitude to full-time officials located at NUM area headquarters.

The Preservation of Unity

Although there are very definite limits to the ability of NUM officials to act contrary to members' wishes, they are not totally constrained, and strong leadership is a feature of workplace unionism in coal-mining as it is in other industries. NUM branch officials are certainly not mere delegates. That this is so is suggested by the evidence of conflict between the branch and sections of the membership over the operation of the incentive scheme which was presented above. The existence of such conflict suggests a divergence of interests, at least on certain matters, between the workplace leadership and the rank and file. In this and the following section we want to examine this divergence of interests in greater detail, to analyse why NUM branches are occasionally at odds with sections of their own membership. According to the bureaucratization thesis, such conflict is likely to arise from the incorporation of the 'lay élite' and its consequent attempts to restrain worker militancy. In our view, however, this interpretation of intra-union conflict is unsatisfactory, among other reasons because it neglects the specific interest of workplace leaders in building and maintaining the unity of the workplace organization. It was the pursuit of this interest, largely unrecognized by advocates of the bureaucratization argument,[1] which produced much of the conflict between leaders and members uncovered by our research.

Branch officials were asked, for example, why they believed they occasionally came into confict with individual coal-face or development drivage teams over the operation of the incentive scheme. The following were typical of the responses we received: 'This is due to the fact that branch officials take into account the overall effect on the pit and the Area'; 'The team is only concerned with themselves and their bonuses, whereas the branch officials are concerned with the pit as a whole'; 'They don't take account of the effects some things have on the whole membership.' These statements indicate an appreciation that the particular interests of individual work-groups may conflict with the general interest of the membership as a whole. They also indicate a preparedness to protect the latter by sacrificing the former. Senior branch representatives consider themselves the guardians of pit and wider solidarities. Acting within this role can lead them to try and discipline sections of the membership and this can generate conflict within the domestic organization.

One major consequence of the incentive scheme was a wider scatter of earnings throughout the mining industry. As we have shown in Chapter 3, wages could vary considerably between pits according to the rigour of the performance standards negotiated. They could also vary significantly within pits for the same reason. Differences in earnings frequently occurred between groups of production workers (face and development men who have the same grading), and the scheme widened the differential between these groups, at the top of the industry's wage structure, and other colliery workers. Table 6.1 shows the branch representatives' assessment of this pattern of change. While just under a third of respondents readily accepted the effects of the incentive scheme, the majority did not approve of the more varied pattern of remuneration.

Apart from the question of its intrinsic unfairness, representatives viewed the wider scatter of earnings with regret because of its implications for pit solidarity. The scheme at many pits was felt to be loosening the ties of solidarity by splitting the economic interests of work-groups and

---

[1] Hyman (1979, p. 60) for instance, qualifies his argument about the bureaucratization of the rank and file by stating that greater centralization within steward bodies can limit 'arbitrary acts of opposition by isolated individuals or groups [which] may dissipate the strength of factory unionism'. Three pages earlier, however, he suggests that though shop stewards' committees in the past 'tended to fulfil the functions of co-ordination rather than control', it has since become 'far more common for such committees to exercise a disciplinary role'. It must be said, though, that other writers, who share Hyman's estimate of recent development in workplace trade unionism, most notably Beynon and Lane, have produced valuable descriptions of the collectivizing work of senior shop stewards (Beynon, 1984, ch. 9; Lane, 1974, ch. 6). Presumably, they now also believe that the benign 'co-ordinating' function of such work has increasingly given way to malign 'control'.

TABLE 6.1   Branch representatives' assessment of the equity of the incentive
scheme

	Numbers	%
Just	10	31
Not very just	2	6
Rather unjust	7	21
Very unjust	14	42
TOTAL	33	100

Source: NUM Branch Representatives Questionnaire, 1981.

different grades. 'It has created an attitude of self first among faceworkers', one respondent commented, 'and a sense of injustice with the men on bonus.' One response of branch officials to this problem was to try and hold down the earnings of those groups of workers who had benefited most from the scheme. To quote another respondent, 'the nature of the scheme allows for development workers to "earn" more bonus than faceworkers. When the difference in earnings becomes too great, I intervene to bring the earnings into line with faceworkers (I make moral judgements on an immoral scheme)!' Significantly, there was a tendency for branch officials who reported the incentive scheme to be unjust also to report more frequent conflict with face and development teams over its operation.[2]

Another response of branch leaders to the fragmenting effect of payment by results was to encourage production workers to pool their incentive earnings. Under the terms of the scheme, incentive earnings could be distributed in two main ways. Workers on each individual coal-face could simply receive the money they themselves earned against their own target or else they could throw their incentive pay into a pool of earnings from all coal-faces at the pit, which was then divided equally.[3] There was an inducement for branches to elect for the first option because, under this system, fall-back payment, when no incentive is earned on a face, was paid by the NCB rather than by the workers in other teams.

Because of this inducement some area and branch officials had advised members to choose the individual option. In rather more cases, however, it seemed there was pressure from the teams themselves to go in this direction. Across our sample 54 per cent of pits averaged earnings, 34 per cent had used the individual system from the beginning, and 12 per cent had changed to the individual system. The shift, therefore, was away from the pooling of earnings. 'It started off on this beautiful socialist principle

[2] Pearson's R for the correlations between the responses to these questions were -0.38 and -0.37, both significant at 0.02.
[3] Development teams did not have a choice. They were excluded from the pooling option.

that all men are equal,' commented one manager on this issue, 'but going individual makes a difference.'

In our sample of NUM areas, eight had a policy, decided by delegate conference, of averaging earnings, while two favoured the individual system. Five of the pro-averaging areas had experienced breaches of their policy at colliery level. It was the opinion of most union officials and managers who were interviewed that this was due to pressures from face-teams who perceived averaging to be a brake on their earning potential. A branch secretary at a South Wales pit with two coal-faces, for example, reported that 'We succeeded in holding the men to a colliery bonus for a long time, but in the end we failed.' The team on one face was doing much better against its target than the team on the other. A similar tale was recounted by a branch secretary from the North-east. At his pit a policy to pool incentive earnings had survived two years before crumbling. Again, there were differences in the level of achieved performance between coal-faces. Interviews with area industrial relations managers confirmed this impression of lodges struggling to maintain the pooling system against pressure from individual work groups. In four of the seven interviews it was said that the trend towards the individual system originated amongst the rank and file, and in defiance of branch policy.

Our research on the incentive scheme, therefore, revealed that the workplace leadership in mining frequently attempts to maintain relations of equity and solidarity among the membership. It does this by striving to reduce differences in earnings which arise from payment by results and the associated fragmentation of collective bargaining. Although many branches have undoubtedly been successful in regulating the impact of payment by results in this way, it is apparent that there are limits to their abilities to impose regulation. Conflict has arisen with work-groups who have experienced the leadership's pursuit of equity and solidarity as a restraint. And on occasion such work-groups have been able to shake off the branch's restraining hand. The important point, however, is that combating sectionalism and collectivizing workers, albeit within the confines of an individual colliery, are major concerns of the workplace leadership.

The Theory of Collective Action

The question of how collective organization among workers is created and maintained has attracted a good deal of attention among sociologists in recent years. Frequently this issue has been discussed at very high levels of abstraction. Starting from tightly defined assumptions about the costs and benefits likely to accrue to individual workers from joining in collective action, game theorists have attempted to deduce the steps which are necessary for that action to occur (Lash and Urry, 1984). Whereas theorists of trade-union bureaucracy tend to assume that workers are 'endowed with a vast reservoir of latent power' (Zeitlin, forthcoming) and adopt as their principal theoretical problem the frustration of this potential, game theorists have largely been concerned with a prior issue: how collective activity among workers comes to exist at all. Their focus has been on the collectivization of workers, the difficult process through which workers come to be organized and act collectively in trade unions and political parties.

A particularly interesting contribution to this body of writing has been made by Offe and Wiesenthal (1985). Their starting-point is the differential capacity of the two parties to the employment contract, labour and capital, to become organized in order to prosecute their interests. According to Offe and Wiesenthal, labour is at an automatic disadvantage in conflict with capital because of its 'insuperable individuality' (p. 177). The capital of each firm, they argue, is 'always united . . . whereas living labour is atomized and divided by competition' (p. 178). In addition, capital can readily add to its strength through accumulation and merger. Workers, however, 'cannot "merge"; at best, they can *associate* in order to partly compensate for the power advantage that capital derives from the liquidity of "dead" labour'. A further difference is that among workers there exists a multiplicity of individual needs and desires which cannot easily be reduced to a set of common demands. 'In contrast', Offe and Wiesenthal claim, 'capitalist firms as well as business associations do not have to take into consideration a comparative multitude of incommensurable needs. All the relevant questions can be reduced to the unequivocal standards of expected costs and returns; i.e. to the measuring rod of money' (p. 179).

In tracing labour's 'logic of collective action', therefore, Offe and Wiesenthal start from an assumption that workers' interests are multifarious and competing. Given this, they suggest that two things are necessary for collective action by workers to occur. The first is that individual workers must be persuaded not to evaluate the cost–benefit trade-off of indulging in collective action in a purely instrumental way. 'Only to the extent that associations of the relatively powerless succeed in the formation of a collective identity, according to the standards of which the costs of organisation are subjectively deflated', write Offe and Wiesenthal, 'can they hope to change the original power relation' (p. 183). The second is that there must be a process of deliberation among workers to select from the multiplicity of available objectives which are considered worthy of collective pursuit.

Although Offe and Wiesenthal's reasoning is rather opague, they seem to argue that securing both of these conditions for collective action is dependent on the prior organizational work of trade unions. On the question of the preparedness of workers to risk collective action, for instance, they argue that the power of a union to launch such action 'depends upon its ability to generate a willingness to "act" on the part of its members' (p. 186). And on the question of the unification of workers' interests, Offe and Wiesenthal similarly emphasize the active, creative work of the trade union. The organizations of workers, they argue, must 'simultaneously express and define the interests of the members' (p. 184).

Much of this argument we find persuasive. Before returning to the mining industry, however, and demonstrating the analytical utility of what Offe and Wiesenthal have to say, we would like to offer a few words of criticism. Our main point of dissent with these writers is that they appear to us to exaggerate the atomization of the working class. They adopt a starting-point for their theory of collective action, which seems to us equally as unsatisfactory as the assumption of the proletarian proclivities of workers which underlies the theory of trade-union bureaucracy.

If we take their argument concerning the essential non-rationality of collective action for individual workers first. It seems to us questionable whether all collective action is dependent on workers refusing to make purely instrumental calculations. Workers in strategically placed industries, factories, or departments may, in fact, make sound calculations that the cost of collective action, loss of wages or threat of dismissal, do not outweigh the likely benefits. Where an employer's ability to pay is high and where workers are not readily replaceable then the decision of individuals to attach themselves to a collective organization need not rest on a distortion of the cost–benefit trade-off. It is perhaps for this reason that workers in such strategic locations find it much easier to organize than those who are not (Crouch, 1982, pp. 67–74). It is also the case that where collective action has once been proved effective, where its rationality has been demonstrated, then the propensity of workers to choose the same course again is likely to increase. In many real situations, not least in the mining industry, the decision on whether or not to join in collective action is much less fraught with uncertainty than Offe and Wiesenthal's abstract presentation suggests.

Their argument on the fragmentation of workers' interests, we feel, is also difficult to sustain. Although most trade-unionists belong to very large trade unions with membership running into hundreds of thousands, the locus for much union activity is the company, workplace, or department. Within such contexts the identification of common interests among workers may not be as difficult as Offe and Wiesenthal suggest. Indeed, the organization of labour by management serves to create such interests by providing workers with common work and labour market situations. It is a commonplace of industrial sociology that patterns of collective action frequently follow the division of labour created by employers (for recent research findings which demonstrate this see Thompson and Bannon, 1985). Moreover, systems of management control may deny workers the ability to pursue individual interests through individual courses of action. An example of this is the lack of internal promotion possibilities for many British manual workers arising from the failure of British employers to develop forms of labour control based on internal labour markets.

However, although we feel Offe and Wiesenthal's emphasis on the difficulty of securing collective action to be exaggerated, we nevertheless think their work is useful because it directs attention towards the collectivizing activity of trade unions and trade union leaders. Much trade-union action does depend on the preparedness of workers to disregard cost–benefit calculations, for example sympathy strikes and secondary action. And much action does depend on workers forgoing the pursuit of individual interests. Both situations were to be seen in the 1984/5 miners' strike, when thousands of mineworkers in pits which were not immediately threatened with closure struck in support of pits that were, and when mineworkers eligible for relatively generous severance payments opted to support the dispute.

Offe and Wiesenthal offer no suggestions as to how trade unions foster a 'willingness to act' among their members or persuade them to accept a collective definition of their interests. These problems have been pursued, however, in the rich empirical tradition of British industrial sociology and most notably in the work of Batstone, Boraston, and Frenkel (1977, 1978). They have provided a detailed examination of the processes through which workplace trade union leaders can foster collective organization and action.

The main focus of the research conducted by Batstone *et al.* was an engineering plant, which like the collieries in our study had a sophisticated shop-steward organization. The goals of the workplace leadership were also similar. Prime among them was 'an emphasis upon unity and the collectivity', which involved the leadership in action to prevent 'the fractionalization of the domestic organization' (1977, pp. 27–8). A second important goal was the preservation of relations of equity within the membership. This involved ensuring that there 'should be no discrimination against the less fortunate, while the unbridled pursuit of self-interest should be minimised' (1977, p. 28).

Batstone *et al.* describe two means used by the shop-floor leadership to realize these objectives and ensure membership compliance. The first of these was the shop-steward organization itself. This provided a means of integrating the various sectional interests in the plant. The Joint Shop Stewards' Committee (JSSC), for instance, provided a forum at which common policies could be debated and formulated (1977, ch. 4). The power of the organization could also be used to punish members of the union who were believed to threaten the objectives of unity and equity. This could be done formally, for example, by banning dissident stewards from JSSC meetings (1977, p. 79), or informally by denying advice, information, or access to management to groups deemed to be acting in contravention of union principles.

The second method used to secure membership compliance with union goals was the dissemination of union values. 'The condition for plant unity', the authors state at one point, 'was the reaffirmation of the values of trade unionism' (1978, p. 206). These values included commitment to 'mutual protection, looking after the less fortunate in the collectivity', ideas of 'fairness and justice', and 'an emphasis on unity', on maintaining the collectivity (1977, p. 11). The preparedness of the membership to act in accordance with these principles, Batstone *et al.* make clear, was uncertain and depended, in large part, on the continual educational role of the steward leadership. This, in turn, they say, was facilitated by the role of many stewards as 'opinion leaders' within their work groups and sections (1977, p. 128). Batstone *et al.* summarize the ideological work of the shop-steward leaders as follows: 'they consistently foster the collective identity of members in their sections, departments and the domestic organisation as a whole. The core of their ideological reaffirmation focuses upon a factory consciousness' (1977, pp. 249–50).

Within the mining industry the workplace branch fulfils a similar integrating function to that of the JSSC described by Batstone *et al.*, and the branch leadership is also involved in the continual reaffirmation of trade-union principles. To conclude this section, however, we want to draw attention to another means through which workplace leaders attempt to preserve the unity of the workplace trade union. The purpose of much workplace activity, we believe, is to secure common circumstances and common treatment by management for the entire membership. These objectives are seen as desirable in themselves but they are also pursued because they facilitate the identification of shared interest among workers and so assist in sustaining the memberships' willingness to act collectively. The pursuit of equal conditions and equal treatment for trade-union members, that is, can help realize the two requirements for collective action specified by Offe and Wiesenthal.

In our earlier discussion of branch officials' objectives *vis-à-vis* the incentive scheme we provided examples of workplace leaders striving to equalize members' earnings precisely because this was believed to facilitate solidarity. We now want to present two more examples of workplace leadership which illustrate the role of the NUM branches in securing equality of treatment by management. The first of these concerns the distribution of overtime. Almost without exception across our sample the NUM branch had achieved control over the allocation of overtime, and in most pits this was done by means of a rota. For individual workers this arrangement might well be experienced as a constraint on the pursuit of their interests. By virtue of their reputation as hard workers or the warmth of their relations with their supervisors, they might, in the absence of this arrangement, secure a larger share of overtime for themselves. The system enforced by the NUM however, places collective interests before those of the individual. It strives to ensure that all workers experience this aspect of their employment relation in an identical manner.

The second example concerns the allocation of workers to face-teams. Union control over this is not as extensive as is control over the distribution of overtime. In some NCB areas, however, it was customary for the union to regulate the allocation of face-team places by means of a seniority system. This was the case in South Wales, the North-East, Scotland, and Lancashire. The precise nature of the seniority rules governing the deployment of labour varied from pit to pit and area to area. The reasons given for the need to control deployment, however, were fairly standard. Branch officials mentioned the need to ensure fair and equitable treatment and to prevent management fostering division by allocating the best work to 'blue-eyed boys'.

In both of these examples the effect of NUM control is to remove the opportunity for individual furtherance of interests and to attach union members much more securely to the collectivity. A further effect is the imposition of restrictions on management's freedom to manage labour. Where controls of the kind described are in operation, management is obliged to treat each of its employees in an identical fashion regardless of whether this conflicts with its interest in maximizing output or profits.[4] The effect of the union's search for equity and solidarity, therefore, is to *bureaucratize* the employment relation of its members. The workplace union is involved in establishing and maintaining rules which ensure standard treatment of individual workers.

To summarize, therefore, we have argued that a central institutional interest of the workplace union in coal-mining is the preservation of unity. Theorists of 'trade-union bureaucracy' have tended to neglect or minimize the pursuit of this interest by trade-union leaders, largely we feel because they tend to assume that collective action by workers arises directly from the experience of exploitation. Writers in other traditions, however, have given priority to the examination of this issue. Offe and Wiesenthal have concluded that it is the task of the labour movement to furnish workers with a 'collective identity', while Batstone, Boraston, and Frenkel have

---

[4] This does not mean that such controls are necessarily experienced as a constraint by managers. At the pits where deployment was done through seniority the managers were generally glad to be excused 'an onerous decision', as one put it. Elsewhere, however, where control had not been secured by the union, there was considerable emphasis among managers on the need for them to be involved in choosing teams in order to ensure the best mix of men. One manager, for example, described seniority rules as 'giving up management'.

described and analysed the processes through which this can be achieved at workplace level. We feel our research supplements theirs. We have shown that, in order to preserve unity, the workplace leadership in coal-mining attempts to ensure common conditions and common treatment for its members. It attempts to collectivize workers by standardizing their experience of work. Whether or not sophisticated workplace organizations can rightfully be described as 'bureaucracies', the effect of much of their activity is to bureaucratize the employment relations of their members.

The Preservation of Good Relations with Management

Whereas advocates of the bureaucratization thesis have tended to minimize the interest of workplace leaders in the preservation of unity, they have emphasized their interest in the preservation of co-operative, bargaining relations with managers. As we have seen in Chapter 5, theorists who adopt this position argue that dependence on management for time off work, office facilities, and the like, leads them to treat managerial requests for co-operation sympathetically and to control militancy emanating from the shopfloor. The evidence we gathered from the lay élite in coal-mining concerning its attitudes towards management did provide some support for this view. Branch officials did report that they were controlling the membership for management. However, we believe that such results need not be accepted as convincing evidence of the incorporation of workplace trade-unionism.

All but one of the colliery managers interviewed agreed that a strong NUM branch official is more of a help than a hindrance to management, and that it paid to involve branch officials at an early stage when taking decisions which might be unpopular with the work-force. Just over half of the sample said they could rely, most of the time, on branch officials 'to sort things out' when the men took unofficial industrial action. There were strong indications, therefore, that management perceive the workplace leadership as a means to import stability into the relationship with employees.

The responses of branch officials generally support this impression. All but 10 per cent, for instance, said that they could usually ensure membership compliance with collective agreements. Eighty-five per cent, moreover, agreed with the statement, 'An NUM official must persuade his members on occasion to accept unpopular management decisions for the good of the pit as a whole.' Most representatives, then, considered it part of their task to lead the membership in a direction which it did not want to go. The most frequently cited example of an unpopular management decision which the branch had recommended to the membership was a change in shift starting times. Thirty-seven per cent gave this as an example. Other examples given included new safety procedures, re-deployment of labour, an end to early finishing and the use of work study to set incentive scheme standards.

Branch representatives, therefore, do, to a certain extent, perceive their relationships with management and membership in a manner predicted by the theorists of bureaucratization. They see their task as involving the disciplining of the rank and file and the securing of compliance, on occasion, with unpopular management decisions. Many of those interviewed clearly accepted as a central priority the need for efficient production and so acceded to management requests for altered shift patterns and re-deployment. They also clearly accepted the need to abide by formal agreements to which their union had been party, and so prevailed upon the membership to remain at the pit for a full working week and accept work study. In our view, however, it would be wrong to conclude from these instances that the majority of senior representatives interviewed in the study were hopelessly incorporated and accepted a managerial definition of their members' situation.

Adherents of the bureaucratization argument have tended to see leadership co-operation with management as arising from dependence on management for the privileges of office. In our view, however, a different sort of exchange is going on. We believe that representatives' ability to pursue their members' interests is, paradoxically, often dependent on their capacity to 'deliver' the co-operation of the work-force to management. Labour represents a major source of uncertainty for management in many industries, including coal-mining. Control of that uncertainty constitutes a major power resource for the trade union. Such control can be exchanged for concessions which further both the procedural interest of trade unions and the substantive interests of members in better pay and conditions. And this, we believe, is what occurs within coal-mining. In Chapter 7 we provide detailed evidence from the decision-making survey which demonstrates that, at the time of our research the workplace union in coal-mining exerted considerable influence over many issues affecting its members' experience of work.

Advocates of the bureaucratization thesis, however, can respond to this argument in two ways. The first is to declare that the exchange of labour discipline for concessions has become more unfavourable from the perspective of the rank-and-file member, as a result of the growth in hierarchy in workplace organization. Again the evidence in Chapter 7 suggest that in mining this has not been the case. At 60 per cent, of the pits included in our survey, the NUM representatives reported that the amount of time off work allowed for union business had increased in the previous five years. The decision-making survey revealed that this increase in management support for the lay élite had been accompanied by an increase, not a decrease, in union influence over decisions taken at the pit.

The second possible objection to our argument is that more would be achieved for union members if the maintenance of strong bargaining relations with managers was eschewed by workplace leaders: that is, if there was a complete rejection of any accommodation with management. This anti-accommodation argument is commonly voiced by socialist writers on industrial relations. There is a tendency to assume that more will be achieved by trade unions if they reject compromise and sustain a militant assault on employers. In our view such an assumption about the relationship between the form and fruits of trade-union action is mistaken. Of course, on occasion the rejection of existing forms of accommodation in favour of more militant action can yield spectacular benefits for trade unions and their members. The rejection by the NUM in 1972 of what had been, in effect, a moratorium on national strikes provides an obvious example.

If we take the example of the 1984/5 miners' strike, however, different lessons can be drawn. In that case the union refused to abandon its demand for a complete withdrawal of the Coal Board's pit-closure programme and rejected two possible compromise settlements with the employer in June and October of 1984. The result of this rejection of accommodation was defeat and a collapse of the NUM's ability to influence developments in the mining industry. The refusal to compromise through negotiation led to an outcome which was arguably far worse than would have resulted if initial demands had been modified.

This example indicates that determination to impose trade-union objectives on employers without negotiation can carry very high risks. Spectacular advances may be achieved but the danger of failure may be correspondingly high. The failure of the 1984/5 miners' strike arguably resulted from two key factors, the inability of the NUM to call all its members out on strike and the ruthlessness with which the state was prepared to counter the union's action. These factors are illustrative of the risks involved in following an anti-accommodation policy. Such a policy requires the union to rely solely on its own internal sources of strength in pursuing its members' interests. Because the exchange of concession for concession with employers is held to be unsatisfactory, the union must depend on its members' 'willingness to act'. There are always limitations, however, on the willingness of trade-union members to embark on and sustain industrial action. Trade unions can themselves take measures to extend these limitations, as we have seen, but they must always remain as an ultimate brake on trade-union militancy.

The first risk associated with the rejection of accommodation, therefore, is that members may not be prepared to sustain the necessary costs of this policy. The second risk is that an unwillingness compromise will call forth an equivalent response from the employer. Employers will respond ruthlessley to union attempts to impose unilateral regulations of employment conditions, as the British government responded ruthlessly to the challenge of the NUM. Because employers are generally possessed of greater power resources than trade unions and better equipped to withstand major confrontations, any rejection by unions of the regulation of industrial conflict through compromise must carry very real dangers indeed.

Our response, then, to the argument that workplace trade-unionism in coal-mining would be more effective if workplace leaders rejected strong bargaining relations with management is to point to the very real risks involved in adopting such a course of action. The limitations on the membership's willingness to act and other aspects of the power disparity between employers and trade unions, require the latter to seek forms of accommodation. As Hyman has remarked, 'No doubt *some* form of accommodation with external forces is inevitable (at least outside a revolutionary situation)' (1979, p. 55). If this is accepted then the origins of the generally co-operative relations between NUM branch officials and colliery management need not be located in the incorporation of the lay élite. They can be seen instead as tactically astute responses on the part of the workplace leaders to the difficulties inherent in their situation.

In summary, then, we have observed that workplace leaders in coal-mining do display an interest in the presentation of strong, co-operative bargaining relations with colliery management. This interest leads them, on occasion, to control their own membership *for* management. Branch officials do, therefore, act in a manner predicted by the advocates of the bureaucratization thesis. However, we believe those who maintain this position have misinterpreted the origins and the significance of this 'interest'. According to the bureaucratization argument the disciplining of members and a co-operative stance towards management form part of an exchange, the other element of which is the preservation of the workplace leadership in its relatively privileged position. It is assumed that workers' interests are sacrificed in order to maintain time off for senior representatives, free office accommodation, secretarial help, and the like.

We do not believe this sort of exchange is a significant determinant of workplace industrial relations in coal-mining. The privileges of the workplace leadership which have been yielded by management, we believe, are considered as rights which impose little or no obligation. In our view co-operation by workplace leaders in the resolution of management problems tends to be exchanged for co-operation by management in the union's fulfilment of its representative role. Managers assist branch officials in satisfying the interests of the rank and file. There is an exchange, therefore, which tends to raise the 'institutional centrality' of the union within the workplace and also produces improvements in pay and conditions for union members.

NUM Branch Officials and the Wider Union

So far we have reviewed the relationship of the lay élite in coal-mining with the rank-and-file membership and with management. In this final section we propose to review the nature of its relationship with the wider union and specifically with the full-time officials of the NUM areas.

A central contention of the bureaucratization thesis, as we have seen, is that closer links between the workplace leadership and full-time officers have fostered the 'incorporation' of the former. Involvement with those yet more remote from the shop-floor, and more readily assimilated into the world of business and government, has encouraged the lay élite to adopt perspectives inimical to their members' interests. It is argued, essentially, that senior workplace representatives have become more dependent on full-time officialdom in the years since Donovan; that their activities have been much more fully integrated into those of the union hierarchy.

This image of a growing convergence in objectives and growing integration of activities between lay and full-time officials can be usefully contrasted with the rather different theory of internal union relations offered by Crouch (1982, pp. 174–89). According to Crouch (p. 182), 'the biggest conflicts between different levels of the labour movement will be between national and local organisations'. He sees the line between lay representatives and the union leadership as a continuing site of tension and conflict. His is not a restatement, however, of the optimistic 'rank and filism' of the 1960s, which considered shop stewards as the bearers of workers' interests against a conservative union oligarchy. He criticizes this view for treating workplace activists 'as synonomous with the membership *as a whole*'. For Crouch, trade unions are composed of a largely passive membership, which has an overwhelmingly instrumental orientation towards the union, and different levels of officials, both lay and full-time, who compete for the right to represent this membership. The authority of each level of officialdom is dependent on its ability to secure concessions for the membership and this in turn is dependent on its success in securing access to collective bargaining with employers. In Crouch's view, then, relations between workplace leaders and higher-level officials are likely to be characterized by competition rather than integration. Each level will be jealous of its autonomy and anxious to extend its negotiating territory.

Which of these two arguments most accurately represents relations between branch and area officials in the NUM? We have attempted to

TABLE 6.2 Frequency with which branches consult area during pay
negotiations

	Numbers	%
Always	—	—
Very often	1	3
Sometimes	6	17
Rarely	9	26
Never	19	54
TOTAL	35	100

Source: NUM Branch Representatives Questionnaire, 1981.

answer this question by looking at the involvement of the two reasons for doing this: firstly, because theorists of bureaucratization have argued that a principal effect of the closer integration of workplace and higher-level leaders has been to moderate workers' pay demands (Beecham, 1984, p. 102); and secondly, because Crouch's theory emphasizes competition for the right to participate in collective bargaining.

We did not encounter much evidence of dependence by the branch officials in local wage-bargaining on the support of area full-time officers. There did not appear to be a close integration of the activities of the two levels as is suggested by advocates of the bureaucratization thesis. Table 6.2, for example, shows the infrequency with which NUM branch officials consulted their area organizations during the negotiation of incentive-scheme agreements.

Clearly the areas were largely excluded from the pay-bargaining process, which was very much the province of the workplace union. Area full-time officers became involved if there was a failure to agree a standard at pit level, but generally branch officials and colliery managers strove to prevent this occurring. Those area officials who were interviewed generally acknowledged that they had limited involvement in incentive-scheme pay-bargaining. Four of them did say they would intervene informally if they felt incentive earnings were not high enough at a particular pit and two of these also said they would intervene to try and reduce unusually high earnings. The typical situation, however, was that branch officials would be left to conduct their own bargaining unless they themselves requested area assistance.

These indications of the general independence of the lay élite in coal-mining confirm the findings of other researchers. Edwards and Harper (1975, p. 48) have reported from an earlier study in the coal industry that there 'was little evidence of issues being passed up and down between colliery and Area level. Perhaps rather surprisingly, each level appeared to generate and for the most part resolve its own issues'. Boraston, Clegg, and Rimmer (1975, p. 188), meanwhile, found, in a study of several industries, that independence from the external union tends to be associated with shop-steward hierarchy and the granting of facilities by management. It seems, therefore, that where a lay élite is clearly discernible the workplace union is more likely to devise and execute policies without calling on the assistance of full-time officers. 'Bureaucratization' at the workplace is associated with less, not more, integration into the union hierarchy.

The independence of the branch leadership in wage-bargaining is compatible with Crouch's theory. Our evidence could be interpreted as showing a successful defence of negotiating territory by branch officials. Certainly we came across branch secretaries who were very jealous of their autonomy, who were anxious 'to sort their own washing', as one put it. This impression was reinforced in some of the interviews with full-time officers. One area leader remarked, for instance, that 'my people like to be left to get on with the job and keep the Area out'. However, although there is a marked reluctance to involve the external union in pit business, because the resolution of problems at colliery level is considered a key attribute of the successful leader, our research did not completely support Crouch's argument. There were two principal points of divergence. The first concerned the attitude of union representatives at both area and colliery levels to the introduction of pit-head wage-bargaining. Crouch's theory would suggest that the workplace leadership would be enthusiastic about this opportunity to extend its representative function, while the full-time officers would perhaps be more trepidatious and concerned about the attenuation of their own control. Attitudes towards the devolution of pay-bargaining, however, did not assume this pattern of horizontal division. The line separating supporters from opponents of the incentive scheme ran vertically through the union. Forty per cent of the sample of branch representatives for instance, counted themselves as supporters of the scheme, while 60 per cent were opposed. This division was politically based. The opponents of the incentive scheme were overwhelmingly on the NUM left. Commitment to the left and its policy of maximizing the power of the national union led to a preparedness to sacrifice an opportunity to expand their own negotiating territory. In the unusual circumstances of the NUM, therefore, factional allegiance was a more important determinant of attitudes to bargaining structure than the competitive desire of sets of officials to maximize their own responsibilities.

The second divergence from Crouch's framework concerned the attitude of the full-time officers who were interviewed to the near monopoly of incentive-scheme bargaining held by the branches. Without exception they were enthusiasts for branch independence. None of them suggested that the areas should become more actively involved. There was no evidence that they considered their relationship with workplace leaders to be characterized by competition.

Listed below are a number of statements made by area leaders on the respective involvement of themselves and branch officials in local wage bargaining.

'I make the secretary as important as I can—they save me a lot of work. You've got to educate.'

'The incentive scheme has given back a feeling of achievement to the pit official.'

'Area let them know their rights and conditions and leave it to them.'

'I would not like to be involved. It needs to be done on the job where people have a familiarity with the situation.'

'We encourage them to handle their own matters.'

These statements indicate, first of all, a perception that the union leadership is dependent on pit-based representatives to ensure effective collective bargaining. Branch leaders have local knowledge and the area leadership simply do not have sufficient time to get deeply involved in local bargaining. We feel, however, that the statements also reveal a positive endorsement of workplace independence. The full-time officers clearly believed it to be a good thing that branches should manage their own affairs. The overwhelming impression, therefore, was of a co-operative and not a competitive relationship between workplace and higher-level leaders.[5]

Conclusion

This chapter and the preceding one have attempted to use data from the mining industry to test the validity of recent attempts to extend the theory of trade-union bureaucracy to workplace trade-unionism. The overall effect of the bureaucratization of workplace trade-unionism, it is argued, has been to produce a 'downturn' in the industrial class struggle and to stabilize existing patterns of exploitation. We believe our evidence provides grounds for rejecting this interpretation of recent developments. A lay élite of senior workplace leaders is clearly discernible in the coal industry but the extent and quality of its relations with the union membership, with colliery management, and with higher-level representatives diverge significantly from the patterns predicted by the advocates of the bureaucratization thesis.

[5] Crouch, it must be said, having developed his formal model of competitive relations between tiers of representatives, remarks that the 'tension between levels of organisation should not be exaggerated'.

Regarding relations with the membership, one major finding was that NUM branch officials experienced considerable pressure from their constituency and that, as a result, their scope for independent action remained limited. Theorists of workplace bureaucracy, we feel, therefore, have tended to exaggerate the distance between the lay élite and the membership and have been wrong to claim that the former have the capacity to act persistently against the interests of the latter. In the mining industry this does not appear to be the case. Both the formal mechanisms of branch democracy and membership interest in the collective bargaining activities of their representatives require branch officials to be acutely responsive to the demands of the rank and file.

Although there are very definite limits to the independence of the lay élite in coal-mining, within those limits branch officials do engage in 'leadership' activity. They initiate action, discipline their members, and clarify their collective interests. Our research has shown that a major concern of the branch leadership in mining is to collectivize workers. This is done by striving to ensure standardized treatment of union members by management and through fostering commitment to trade union principles of equity and solidarity. The significance of this organizational and ideological work, we believe, has been minimized by adherents of the bureaucratization thesis. They tend to take for granted that there is a deep-seated and continually reproduced challenge to capitalist relations of production within the containment of this pressure. Their framework of assumptions, we feel, encourages them to see the role of trade-union leaders in a purely negative light.

Regarding relations with management, the evidence from our survey does provide some support for the bureaucratization argument. Branch officials were, by and large, committed to preserving co-operative relations with management and were prepared, on occasion, to try and secure membership compliance with unpopular management decisions. However, in our view, theorists of workplace bureaucracy have misunderstood the nature of the exchange relationship upon which such approaches to management are based. They argue that the other element in this exchange is management support for the bureaucratic union hierarchy, through paid time off for union duties and other subsidies. In the cruder versions this degenerates into accusations of corruption. In our view, co-operation with management is exchanged in return for managerial assistance to the union leadership in the performance of its representative function. It is an exchange, therefore, which embraces and does not exclude the interests of ordinary union members.

In response to the more general argument that all such relations of exchange promote accommodation between capital and labour and that they should be eschewed in favour of 'unilateral' regulation, we have two main points to make. The first is that it cannot be assumed that union policies founded on the refusal to accommodate with employers will yield greater benefits to union members. Such policies require very powerful unions and so carry very heavy risks. One of these is that members will not endure the costs of this necessarily conflictual attitude. Another is that it will lead to counteraction by management to nullify the power of the union. This brings us to our second point. The pressures on unions to develop relations of accommodation with management, we believe, arise from the overall power disparity between capital and labour and the dependence of the latter on the former for employment. Concentration on the specific interest of trade union 'bureaucrats' in maintaining relations of accommodation obscures this fact.

However, it could be argued that the terms of accommodation, of exchange between labour and employer, are likely to be less favourable where trade unions have become bureaucratized. This hypothesis remains to be operationalized and proven. There are good prima-facie reasons, however, for thinking that the obverse is likely to be the case, that the more sophisticated and centralized union organizations will achieve better rates of exchange. One of these reasons has been mentioned above. Such organizations are likely to be possessed of the organizational and ideological resources to collectivize workers and build up a more effective counter to the power of the employer.

Our final concern in this chapter has been with the relationship between branch officials and the wider union organization. Theorists of workplace bureaucracy have argued that the lay élite has become much more fully integrated into the external union hierarchy. In our examination of workplace pay-bargaining we did not find evidence of this tight integration. Relations between branch and area officials seemed to be generally co-operative, but it was a co-operation founded on the acceptance and endorsements of a wide degree of branch autonomy by the full-time officers.

The theory of the bureaucratization of workplace trade-unionism has been advanced to explain the 'downturn' in class struggle since the heady, militant days of the late 1960s and early 1970s. Indeed, it can be seen as a response on the part of socialist intellectuals to the failure of the British shop-steward movement to live up to the revolutionary hopes the left had invested in it. Since our research was completed, the miners have mounted a truly titanic but unsuccessful struggle against pit closures. The existence of a bureaucratic lay élite in coal has clearly not neutralized the miners' capacity for collective resistance. Indeed, in our view, the ability of the union in the striking coalfields to sustain the struggle was dependent on the sophistication of workplace organization and on the collectivizing work of NUM branch officials. Without a branch leadership of the type described in this chapter it would be very unlikely that the strike would have been continued for so long.

PART IV   Trade-union Power in the Workplace

7
At the Frontier of Control: The Power of the NUM in Collieries

Introduction

Previous chapters have discussed the way in which the NUM officials and the mineworkers they represent have attempted to exercise control over work organization and the payment system. Until now, however, the term 'control' has been used in a loose way, often interchanged with the term 'power'. In this chapter, therefore, we define trade-union power more precisely and present the results of our attempts to systematically measure union power in the workplace. Our main sources of information are two surveys of union involvement in colliery decision-making, one in 1976/7 under NPLA and the other in 1980/1 after the introduction of the incentive scheme. We use these data to assess the outcomes of the processes of bargaining and union activity which have been the focus of our discussions in previous chapters, and, to gauge the extent to which the managerial prerogative in the coal industry has been invaded. However, before presenting our results, we turn to the more general debate surrounding the extent and significance of union power in the workplace and discuss the vexed question of how 'power' can be meaningfully defined and measured.

The Significance of Workplace Power

The importance of the workplace and the extent of the power of the work-group and the shop stewards within it are said to be unique to British industrial relations. Hugh Clegg, writing in 1979, for example, identifies three features of the system which are 'exceptional': the wide scope awarded to most workplace organizations in sizeable manufacturing plants to manage their own pay agreements; the considerable control that many such organizations exercise over the management and conduct of work; and the high proportion of strikes which are conducted unofficially.

This widely accepted view of workplace power, embodied, as we have seen, in the Donovan Report, was mainly based on studies carried out in the 1960s and 1970s (see, for example, McCarthy and Parker, 1968; Brown, 1973; Batstone *et al.*, 1977), a period that witnessed an expansion in shop-steward organization and activities in some industries. The encroachment of shop stewards into areas of decision-making previously assumed to be the sole responsibility of management was interpreted as evidence of their significant power and of a considerable shop-floor challenge to the managerial prerogative. The validity of these conclusions, however, have been challenged on two counts.

First is the point that the extent of the 'challenge' to managerial control at that time may have been exaggerated because research was focused on the very areas where shop-steward power was most developed, namely private manufacturing industry and engineering. Storey's (1980) inter-industry comparison of the types of issues negotiated and controlled by stewards at workplace level provides evidence that the disproportionate attention given to the engineering industry may well have had this effect. His survey showed that steward penetration into managerial prerogatives had progressed furthest in the engineering (and transport) industries. He also noted considerable variation within industries as well as between them. Certainly, where researchers strayed outside the 'traditional' area of investigation, their conclusions concerning steward power were very different. Nichols and Armstrong's (1976) study of chemical workers, for example, portrayed weak and ineffective shop stewards unable to mobilize the support of a deeply divided workforce. Similarly, Goodman *et al.*, (1977) found little evidence of a 'challenge from below' among the shoe-manufacturing workers they investigated.

Second is the fact that most studies of workplace power were based on outcomes of manifest conflict or observations of bargaining activity and paid little attention to the wider structure within which such bargaining took place. There often appeared to be an assumption that management and shop stewards start from a position of equality in the bargaining process and that wins and losses can be taken as an indication of the balance of power between the two.

However, bargaining activity alone is only part, and some have argued an extremely unrepresentative part, of the overall power process (Fox, 1973; Hyman, 1979). Workplace bargaining does not take place in a vacuum, but is bounded by a 'web of rules' formal and informal, that govern the behaviour of the parties involved. The 'rules' of collective bargaining, for example, constrain power play by defining who may take part in the bargaining process, what issues may legitimately be discussed, how they may be resolved and so on. Thus, any party which is able to manipulate these procedural rules to its own advantage has a significant power resource at its disposal. In this view, any comprehensive study of power should take into account the degree to which the established 'rules of the game' operate to the benefit of one side or the other (Bachrach and Baratz, 1962, 1970).

There is, moreover, yet another 'face' to the power process. Several writers, most notably Lukes (1974) have pointed out that the most efficient means of exercising power lies in the ability to control the 'hearts and minds' of potential opponents. Effective normative control can ensure that opposing policies are not even formed, let alone pursued, and thus relieves the dominant party of the need to draw on resources in order to defend its privileged position. Beliefs about the legitimate functions of management and employees, about what constitutes a 'reasonable demand' or a 'legitimate' tactic, the acceptance that some kind of agreement between management and unions must be reached, and so on, all are said to shape the behaviour of those involved (see Hyman and Brough, 1975). Some however, have questioned whether an acceptance of the prevailing power structure reflects the socialization of subordinate groups into a dominant ideology (notably Abercrombie et al., 1980), or the fact that 'they see the power arrayed before them as so overwhelming as to make that basic framework appear inevitable, or challengeable only at a disproportionate cost to themselves and the things they value' (Fox, 1974, p. 278). Whatever the reason, the net result is that the structure is only challenged at the margins and the outcomes of bargaining activity therefore may have little effect on the overall distribution of power.

Thus, studies of workplace power should ideally take into account the latent ideological and institutional constraints on its exercise as well as overt bargaining behaviour. Such a requirement, however, presents a supremely difficult task for empirical study. None the less, where researchers have attempted to study even part of the latent power process, they have concluded that steward power is extremely modest, if not negligible in relation to that of management. Most of these have turned their attention to 'non-decisions', the area of managerial prerogative which is rarely the subject of bargaining activity. Leijinse (1980), for example, shows that although the stewards he studied were able to exert some control over job-related issues, they were unable to transfer this control to 'industrial democracy' type issues over company policy-making (see also Wilson et al., 1982). Wilkinson (1983) demonstrated the weak and reactive position of shop stewards faced with the introduction of new technology. In only one of the four cases he studied was a formal agreement made on the new technology, and this was after the change had been implemented and concerned only pay and effort levels. Beynon (1984) concluded of his Ford car-workers, usually considered at the forefront of the challenge from below, 'essentially the controls obtained over the shop floor union activities involved little more than a different form of accommodation to the more general controls imposed by management' (p. 149). Similarly, Marchington (1979), having surveyed the area of shop-floor control insists that 'shop floor control cannot exist in any real sense in any hierarchical organisation subject to market constraints. Even if the steward controls the line, takes a whole series of strategic decisions and is skilled at his job, he can do no more than shift power or control at the margins . . . shop floor control does exist, but not much' (p. 153).

Our discussion of the study of workplace power so far has revealed considerable disagreement amongst scholars on its extent and the degree to which it constitutes a significant challenge to management's control of work. We have suggested that many of these differences stem either from the choice of research site, or, and more importantly, from the way in which power is conceptualized and measured. Where researchers have concentrated on the outcomes of bargaining over a narrow range of issues to do with work and pay, for example, they tend to conclude that shop stewards and the work-groups they represent do indeed constitute an effective constraint on management's will. Where they have cast their conceptual net wider, however, to embrace the structure within which bargaining takes place, or the role of shop stewards in strategic decision-making, they conclude that the constraints imposed on management by stewards are marginal in terms of the overall balance of power between the two.

These problems of interpretation and measurement are also reflected in scholars' attempts to assess the impact of two major developments in industrial relations which are said to have diminished the power of unions in the workplace in recent years. We have already dealt with much of the contention surrounding the first of these, the growth of 'reformed' systems of industrial relations, in previous chapters. The second, equally contested, area concerns the impact of recession, high levels of unemployment, and a government hostile to trade unions on union power and shop-steward activity. Contentions regarding the effect of these developments appear to rest largely on which indices of union power are used in support of a particular argument. For example, Eric Batstone in *Working Order* (1984) points to the continued survival of shop-steward organizations, the continued growth of real incomes, and the continued high level of strike activity (at least until 1984) as evidence that workplace trade-unionism remains an effective shield for those employed in organized plants and companies. Although he acknowledges that change has occurred and that there has been a strengthening of managements' hand, his overall conclusion is that 'what is striking is not the efficacy of market forces, but their limited effect upon the plants that survive'. Others, however, basing their conclusions on case-study evidence, have recorded widespread and largely successful attempts by management to regain control over work and performance (see Terry, 1986). Brown (1983), in addition, argues that high unemployment has markedly increased the dependence of workers on the fortunes of individual firms as alternative job opportunities have diminished. This, he says, has forced workers to acquiesce in a managerial drive to eradicate job controls built up in the 1960s and 1970s. Commenting on the findings of the 1984 Workplace Industrial Relations Survey, moreover, which show a substantial reduction in negotiation over non-pay issues in 1984, especially at the level of the workplace, he concludes that 'there has been less challenge from below' (Kelly et al., 1987, p. 294). Thus, not only is there little agreement amongst scholars on whether union power was a significant force in the workplace during its apparent peak in the 1960s and 1970s, but contention now surrounds to what extent such a force has survived into the 1980s.

Our study in the coal industry allows us to intervene in this debate in two main respects. Firstly, despite the importance attached to workplace power in industrial relations writing, it has been the subject of relatively little systematic empirical research. (For some exceptions see Storey, 1980; Poole, 1976; Marchington, 1979.) In the course of our research, however, we have obtained measures of power across relatively large samples of workplaces which are both precise and far more comprehensive than the usual indices based on the outcomes of bargaining activity. This allows us to make a more systematic analysis of the scope and nature of union power in the workplace than is usually undertaken. We apply these measures, moreover, to the study of a union which, at the time of our first survey in 1976, was considered to be among the most powerful in Britain. The mineworkers had recently emerged victorious from two titanic battles with the Coal Board, and the future for the industry looked secure. The union itself also had a number of the attributes that have been associated with high union power, namely that it was an industrial union, its membership enjoyed a superior strategic position within the production process, and it possessed a very well-developed workplace organization. The system of collective bargaining and consultation also allowed many more opportunities for union involvement in the industry's affairs than is usual in private industry. The coal-miners and their union, therefore, might be expected to be at the frontier of control at that time. Our systematic study allows us to make an assessment of this assumption and in the course of our analysis to reflect on the probable extent of union power in other industries. By the time of our later survey in 1981 the market position of coal was deteriorating rapidly and industry in general was gripped by deep recession. Although, as we will argue in later chapters, the industry was shielded from the full impact of market forces, questions of economic viability and the prospect of closures were coming to the fore. Comparison of the results of the two surveys therefore provides us with a unique opportunity to assess the impact of these changes on workplace power in the coal industry over this critical period in British industrial relations.

Finally, we conclude our discussion of the consequences of 'reform' on industrial relations in the workplace. As we have shown earlier, the coal industry exhibits a number of features of 'reformed systems' which were aimed, if not at curbing the power of shop stewards completely, at least rendering it more uniform and predictable. Our previous analysis has thrown considerable doubt on these assumptions. Here we attempt to confirm these conclusions by presenting one of the few systematic empirical evaluations of union power in the workplace in a 'reformed' system.

In this chapter, therefore, we explore several aspects of the debate about the significance of union power in the workplace. We examine the amount and range of union power in 1976, when the reputation of the NUM as a powerful union was at its peak, and again in 1981, when the general industrial climate was not so favourable to union power. We look also at how far union power is constrained or facilitated by formal rules and procedures. More specifically, we ask whether the centralization of pay-bargaining under NPLA reduced the power of the local NUM officials, and whether the reintroduction of incentives can be said to have increased it.

Measuring Union Power

Before commencing our analysis, however, we describe in more detail the measures of power which were employed in the study. We have argued earlier that studies of workplace power should take into account ideological and institutional structures as well as the outcomes of overt bargaining behaviour. There are difficulties associated with this approach in that the determinants of power in the workplace can logically be said to embrace the overall structure of power in society. An empirical analysis of power, however, must be contained within manageable limits. In this chapter, therefore, we do not attempt to estimate the overall balance of power between management and the NUM. We do, however, attempt to provide a more systematic analysis of workplace power than has generally been utilized and, moreover, to extend its scope to areas of the organization and workplace which are not usually the subject of bargaining activity. We adopt a deliberately broad definition of power as 'the ability of any individual or group to determine, by *any* process, the behaviour of another person or group'. In the course of applying this definition we examine a number of aspects of NUM officials' involvement in colliery decision-making including their involvement in the initial decision-making process, influence over the decision outcome, priorities, conflicting objectives, and the outcomes of conflict. Together these form a much more comprehensive examination of union power than is usual in studies of the workplace. The measures are used to identify variations in the range and nature of workplace power between collieries and shifts in these over time. They may merely represent marginal adjustments within the overall power structure, but they do none the less have important consequences for the individual managers' and mineworkers' control of work.

In this chapter and the next, therefore, we present an extensive examination of the power of the NUM branch officials in collieries. In subsequent chapters we attempt to place our necessarily limited study of workplace power within the wider context of national bargaining and in the political and economic context of the country as a whole.

The Power Measure

Measures of the 'power' of the colliery managers and the NUM lodge leaders in the 1976 study were constructed in the following manner: the colliery managers and NUM officials in the pilot collieries were each asked to make a list of decisions which they felt were representative of colliery decision-making as a whole. The lists were combined and used as a basis for the personal interviews in the main survey. The decisions identified, twenty-seven in all, ranged from 'traditional' industrial relations issues such as overtime, extra payments, and deployment, mainly contributed by the NUM, to strategic decisions such as planning, budgeting, and appointments, mainly contributed by the managers. Comprehensive study of management–union interaction over a period of a year at eight of the pilot collieries had shown that bargaining over or even discussion of these latter decisions was relatively rare (Edwards, 1983). Thus, their inclusion extended the scope of the research well beyond the usual areas of study which are delineated by workplace bargaining.

In the 1981 study the decision list was revised by colliery managers and NUM officials in the pilot collieries in order to reflect the changes which had taken place since 1976. A representative list of decisions developed in this manner inevitably reflects the constraints placed on local management and unions by higher levels of their respective organizations about what may be decided at the local level. They do have the advantage, however, of being instantly recognizable and meaningful to the participants. (For a list of the decisions and the interview schedule see Appendices I and II.)

Colliery managers and NUM lodge leaders in 1976 and 1981 were interviewed separately and asked a number of questions about each of the listed decisions in order to examine various aspects of their power. They were asked to respond, not as individuals, but on behalf of the groups they represented—the management team and the workforce. It is clear from our discussion of the relationship between senior and local management and between NUM officials and their members that conflict frequently occurs within these collectivities, but respondents had no difficulty in summarizing the position for their 'side' (also see Edwards and Harper, 1975, for a discussion of intergroup bargaining). There were questions about who made the decision in the first place; their own and each other's estimate of influence over the decision outcome; the importance they attached to influencing the decision; how often they disagreed on what the outcome should be; and, in the case of disagreement, who usually won. In this way standardized measures of various aspects of power in decision making were obtained for each of the thirty-five managers and NUM officials in the samples.

NUM Involvement in Decision-making

Workplace decision-making, as we have explained, is subject to a number of constraints, which limit the behaviour of the parties involved. One such constraint is the formally recognized or informally evolved custom and practice which determine the distribution of decision-making between management and unions, a 'hidden' or taken-for-granted aspect of the power process rarely taken into account by researchers.

Measures of the established mode of decision-making were obtained by asking the colliery managers and NUM lodge leaders 'who usually makes' each of the twenty-seven representative decisions. Their responses were recorded on a scale as follows:

(4) Made by management alone.
(3) Mainly the manager.
(2) Joint.
(1) Mainly the union.
(0) The union alone.

Figure 7.1 shows the distribution of the mean responses of the NUM leaders in 1976 and 1981. The results have been simplified by grouping the decisions. 'Budgeting', for example, includes setting the production target, and the manpower and overtime budgets; 'Promotions', selecting supervisors and managers; 'Redundancy' in this case concerns which older or sick workmen should be allowed to take redundancy. In 1976, the decisions labelled 'incentive standards and procedures' concerned relatively small extra payments for water money, carrying a powder canister and regrading. (The decisions included in each group are shown in Appendix I.)

The pattern of decision-making under NPLA (depicted by the dotted line) shows the initiative to be firmly in management's hands. Only in the case of redundancy is any decision even considered a joint one. By 1981,

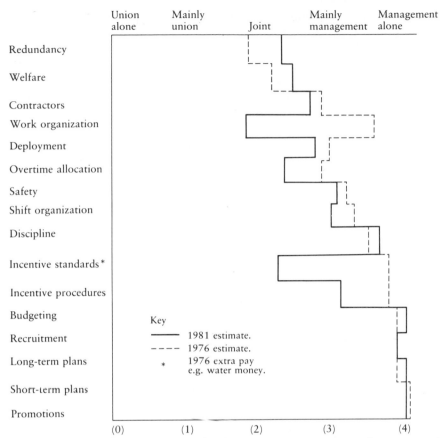

	Union alone	Mainly union	Joint	Mainly management	Management alone

Redundancy

Welfare

Contractors

Work organization

Deployment

Overtime allocation

Safety

Shift organization

Discipline

Incentive standards*

Incentive procedures

Budgeting

Recruitment

Long-term plans

Short-term plans

Promotions

Key

—— 1981 estimate.
---- 1976 estimate.
*   1976 extra pay
     e.g. water money.

(0)   (1)   (2)   (3)   (4)

Fig. 7.1   Who decides? Average of colliery manager's estimates for 1976 and 1981

however, the picture had changed with significant inroads into the managerial prerogative in the area of work organization, deployment, overtime allocation, safety, shift organization, and, as might be predicted, incentive pay. The only area where the union is less involved in 1981 is discipline. This marks the withdrawal of NUM officials from joint disciplinary committees set up to combat the high rates of absenteeism in the 1970s. NUM officials explained to us that they had increasingly found their dual role of prosecution and defence untenable, as it compromised their ability to defend their members' interests. The average response for the managers (not shown) suggests a lesser degree of involvement for the NUM over the range of decisions. Nevertheless, the pattern of their response is very similar to that of the NUM leaders, as is the direction of change between 1981 and 1976. The responses of both management and union revealed a significant increase in union involvement between the two surveys.[1]

At one level this general move towards increased participation could be interpreted as a dramatic move in the direction of industrial democracy within the industry. Indeed, comparisons with work on other industries (Storey, 1980; Millward and Stevens, 1986) would suggest that the NUM have achieved a relatively high degree of encroachment into the managerial perogative. It should be noted, however, that the significant areas of union involvement lie within the area of job control—routine decisions largely associated with the immediate work-task and pay. There was little or no involvement in the major strategic decisions to do with budgeting, planning, promotions, and recruitment under NPLA, and this largely remained the case in 1981. Thus, despite the well-established machinery for consultation on these issues, the union officials at local level considered they had little involvement in the strategic decisions which were discussed in this forum.

There was some variation within the sample, and at a small number of collieries the NUM officials claimed to have some involvement in strategic decision-making. In virtually all cases, however, the degree of involvement on closer inspection proved to be largely marginal. For example, some NUM officials were 'involved' in choosing new machinery, but this constituted being given details of the new machinery selected for the pit by higher management before it was installed or occasionally visiting the factory or another pit where it was in operation to discuss potential difficulties in its use. Participation in long-term planning generally indicated that plans agreed between area and local managers were laid before the local officials for comments. Instances of effective local opposition to these plans were very few indeed. Several union officials drew our attention to their lack of expertise in such matters, which made it difficult for them to assess the consequences of long-term planning for their members. For example, a series of poor decisions made over a number of years which could render a pit 'uneconomic' are unlikely to be picked up before a crisis occurs. Some area unions employ mining engineers to provide expert advice, but they clearly are not in a position to regularly scrutinize every colliery plan. As in other industries, therefore, participation at the local level was confined almost exclusively to the decisions most closely related to production, that is the area where the union power resources lie (see Storey, 1980; Wilson et al., 1982). The NUM at area and national level, however, was involved in strategic decision-making, but with a more general perspective. The fate of individual pits would usually only become the

---

[1] Pearson correlations coefficient between the managers' and union estimates of union involvement ranged from 0.6 to 0.9 with an average of 0.7, all significant at 1%.

subject of bargaining in the case of a major change such as the merger of two collieries or closure.

So far we have assumed that having the right to participate in making a decision in the first place confers certain advantages in terms of power play in that it sets the agenda for further discussion. However, other commentators (notably Scargill and Kahn, 1980) have argued that such involvement weakens rather than strengthens the ability of unions to protect their members' interests if it is not backed up by sufficient power resources. It does so by involving representatives in decisions where their lack of expertise, information, and influence renders them unequal partners in the process and robs them of the opportunity to oppose the eventual decision outcome. Such mock participation, it is argued, merely acts to legitimize managerial decisions and emasculate union opposition without any tangible benefits to the workforce. These arguments underline the need to look not only at participation in the initial decision-making process but also at the ability to influence the final outcome of the decision.

Influencing the Decision Outcome

Although the majority of decisions were generally recognized by both sides to lie within management's prerogative, the NUM from time to time attempted to influence the outcome. Observation in the pilot collieries identified a number of ways in which this was pursued. Managers consulted the NUM officials during the decision-making process, particularly where a national agreement gave the branch a right to be involved. The NUM officials frequently approached management, at all levels, with demands and requests. Occasionally, the NUM officials acted unilaterally, by, for example, forbidding their members to accept overtime, or withdrawing them from a place of work. Finally, there was the unmeasurable and subtle process of anticipated reactions where management or the NUM official did not pursue a course of action because both knew from past experience what the reaction of the other side would be.

An attempt to capture the impact of all these processes on the decision outcome was made by asking the colliery managers and NUM lodge leaders to say for each decision 'how much influence they had on what actually happens'. Their responses were recorded on a scale:

(5) Get your own way completely.
(4) A great deal of influence.
(3) A moderate amount.
(2) A little.
(0) None at all

The measure of influence is not zero-sum and both parties may feel that they exercise considerable 'influence' over the outcome.

As might be expected, this exercise revealed very little variation in the managers' power as both they and the union considered the managers' influence to be 'a great deal' or 'complete' in all areas of decision-making. In fact, estimates of management influence exceeded that of the union on every decision confirming managements' dominant position in the workplace. The 'frontier of control' may have been relatively well-advanced in coalmining, but our data suggest that management maintained the upper hand. (For a more detailed discussion of this point see Edwards, 1983.)

The managers' evaluations of union influence tended to be less generous overall than the union's estimate of their own influence but the two measures were highly correlated. This high degree of congruence between the two lends confidence to the methodology adopted.[2]

Figure 7.2 shows the mean pattern of the union's estimate of its own 'influence' across the grouped decisions in 1976 and 1981. As with decision-making, it is largely confined to the area of 'job control' with very little influence over strategic decisions. Management–union bargaining, the focus of most workplace research, is largely confined to these job-control issues, and assessments made on observations of this activity alone would tend to produce relatively high estimates of union power. The unions' lack of power over strategic decisions as demonstrated here is rarely taken into account in such assessments.

Despite their lack of influence over strategic decisions, compared with most other industries which have been studied, the union officials' level of influence on job-control issues would appear to be relatively high. This was especially the case where a national agreement gave the NUM a right to be involved. For example, in 1976 over two-thirds of the union officials in the survey said they had complete or a great deal of influence over the distribution of overtime and the distribution of extra payments such as water money. There was, however, considerable variation across the sample, indicating some NUM officials were far more successful in exploiting the opportunities offered by these agreements than others.

The scale of 'influence' is in many respects a rather blunt instrument with which to measure change, but it does pick up increases in influence over work and shift organization, welfare, contractors, and safety. It also identifies an area of decline—long-term planning—which will be discussed later. Thus, the introduction of an element of bargaining over pay did not for the most part mark a withdrawal of union influence over

---

[2] Pearson correlation coefficients averaged 0.7 significant at 1% for each sample, with a range from 0.5–0.9.

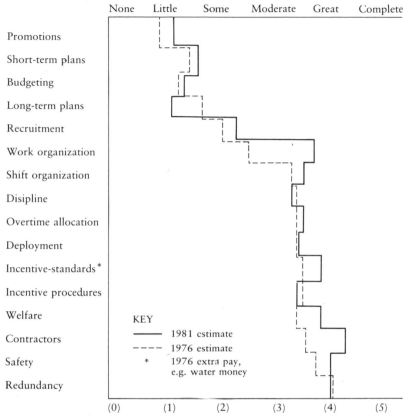

Figure 7.2.   The average of the NUM branch official's estimates of own
influence: 1976 and 1981

non-pay issues. Union influence in fact increased not just over matters of
remuneration but over other matters as well.

Priorities in Deploying Power Resources

Another significant aspect of the power process is the importance each side
attaches to determining decision outcomes. As we have explained earlier,
these priorities may not reflect the 'real' interests of those involved but will
owe more to the influence of the dominant ideology or to a pragmatic
assessment of what is possible within the current structure of constraints.
Nevertheless such preferences affect the degree to which the NUM
officials or management use the resources at their disposal in order to
achieve their objectives.

   The colliery managers and NUM lodge leaders were asked how
important it was for them to get their own way over what happens for

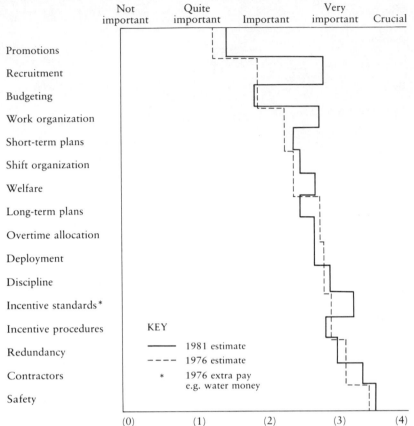

Figure 7.3. The importance of influence: average of NUM officials' views

each of the twenty-seven decisions. Their responses were recorded on a scale:

(5) Crucially important.
(4) Very important.
(3) Important.
(2) Quite important.
(1) Not very important at all.

Figure 7.3 summarizes the NUM responses in the two surveys. Reference to Figure 7.3 reveals that, somewhat unexpectedly, the NUM leaders attach rather lower priority to influencing strategic decisions which have profound consequences for their members than to more routine matters. For example, it can be seen that long-term planning, which affects the employment prospects for the entire colliery, is rated on average as less important than the choice of which old or sick workmen should be allowed to take redundancy.

When a group of NUM officials in feedback sessions were confronted with these findings, however, they explained that their priorities were realistic in terms of what they could hope to achieve. Moreover, both NUM officials and managers pointed out that they are constrained by the need to maintain a working relationship and their priorities reflect what are 'reasonable' objectives for each side to have. Thus, for most NUM officials there is an acceptance of management control over the strategic decision-making process. There were differences between them, however, as to whether this acceptance was merely pragmatic or reflected a genuine acceptance of management's right to manage. A number of union officials appeared to fall into the latter category in that they asserted that it was 'managements' job to manage—to get on with the job of making decisions—and ours to disagree if we don't like what they do'. Others, however, rejected this reactive stance giving many examples of occasions when their exclusion from strategic decision-making had worked to the disadvantage of their members. None the less, even they felt that effective participation would be difficult for 'people like them' because they lacked the expertise and training necessary to take on management as equals (a view, of course, endorsed by many commentators on the subject). A few, however, positively welcomed the prospect of running a colliery and cited numbers of mineworkers who, having taken courses at, for example, Ruskin College, Oxford, could take on management on an equal footing. None, however, held any hope of such participation becoming a reality in the foreseeable future.

When the priorities of both the colliery managers and the union officials in decision-making were examined in detail it was apparent that they mirrored the influence they already had over the decision outcomes. Thus the managers generally placed greater priority on influencing strategic decisions and the NUM on influencing the more routine decisions to do with the job and pay. In terms of day-to-day bargaining, therefore, this left considerable room for compromise—a fact reflected in the relatively low degree of conflict over objectives which is discussed below.

Comparison of the responses for the two surveys in Figure 7.3 suggest that changes in the industrial 'climate' since 1976 were heightening NUM awareness on a number of issues. Recruitment had greatly increased in importance as mineworkers strove to ensure that their sons were given preference at a time of increasing unemployment. Short-term planning and the use of subcontractors were more significant as both could affect incentive earnings, and the level of employment in collieries. Long-term planning, on the other hand, fast becoming a major national issue, actually declined in priority. One explanation put to us was that local union officials were becoming increasingly aware of the uselessness of pursuing such issues at the local level.

Disagreement on Objectives

At the outset of this chapter we rejected a narrow 'zero-sum' definition of power based on the outcomes of conflict.[3] Nevertheless, although there is a growing recognition of the importance of the latent power structure in assessing union power, some writers insist that the study of conflict is an essential element. Kelly (1987) for example, argues that 'to learn about the balance of power we need to know the interests or goals of the parties, we need to establish that they conflict; and we need to establish that the parties do indeed mobilise power resources in pursuit of them' (p. 281). We would concur that areas of disagreement between management and union are of interest. Manifest conflict may not reflect the underlying fundamental divisions of interest between capital and labour but they do none the less indicate the general climate of industrial relations in terms of co-operation and conflict. More significantly, they can identify the points at which the status quo is being challenged by either side. In this section, therefore, we look at the extent to which the objectives of management and union officials are in opposition, and in the next section, we see in whose favour this conflict is resolved.

The managers and NUM leaders were asked to say for each of the representative decisions, 'When decisions of this kind come up how often do their objectives differ. That is the manager wants one thing and the union another?' Their responses were recorded on a scale:

(5) Always.
(4) Very often.
(3) Fairly often.
(2) Sometimes.
(1) Rarely.
(0) Never.

Figure 7.4 shows the mean response for the NUM for 1976 and 1981.

It can be seen that the union officials reported very little disagreement between the two sides on objectives. Furthermore, the managers' estimates of disagreement (not shown) were even lower. This finding might seem surprising to those who view coal-mining as one of the traditional 'battlegrounds' of industrial relations. However, all the colliery managers and union officials interviewed rated their relationship as good in 1976 and the injection of the conflictual issue of incentive pay did little to alter this by 1981.[4] Although colliery managers were slightly

---

[3] Weber's (1947) classic definition of power is 'the probability that one actor within a social relationship will be in a position to carry out his own will despite resistance'.

[4] Diaries kept by colliery managers and branch secretaries of their mutual interactions over a period of a year at 8 collieries and one of the authors' personal observations of bargaining at 4 collieries, confirmed this low level of overt conflict. (See Edwards, 1983).

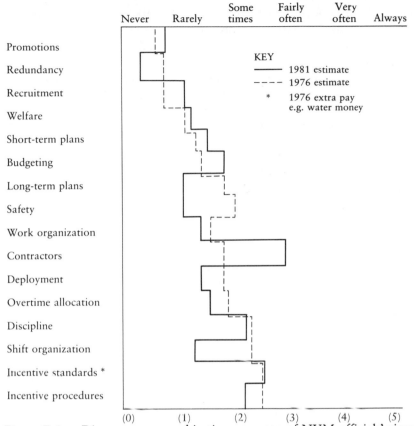

Figure 7.4.   Disagreement on objectives: average of NUM officials' view

less enthusiastic about the relationship in 1981 the overwhelming majority of managers and union officials described their relationship as 'very or quite good', and not one described it as 'bad'. This is not to say that bargaining between the two lacked vigour and often it was very tough indeed. However, at the interpersonal level it was largely conducted in a congenial manner.[5] These conclusions are supported by the relatively low level of local disputes in the industry during both studies (see Chapter 4).

The reasons for this relatively low level of overt conflict lie in the adoption of 'realistic' objectives by both sides, noted earlier, and the fact that over the years mutual understandings were developed as to how problems were to be approached and resolved. Disagreements tended to arise when either side wished to revise the custom and practice or a major

---

[5] Typical of the usually congenial but very tough bargaining relationship was the comment of one branch official who said he had an excellent relationship with his colliery manager but none the less described him as a 'tough bugger' and a 'bit of a bastard at times'.

change had been introduced. By the time the 1981 survey was conducted the initial disruptive effect of the incentive scheme had subsided and most of the issues associated with it had been resolved. Hence, little increase in conflict is apparent.

There were some minor changes between 1976 and 1981. Conflict over subcontracting and recruitment had increased. 'Budgeting' had become slightly more contentious owing to managers' need to control overtime costs more strictly and union pressure to increase the manpower budget to alleviate local unemployment. In other matters, however, a decrease in contention is apparent. One of these, strangely in view of later events, is long-term planning. However, it is important to appreciate here that *local* management and its work-force have always been united in the desire to develop their pit's capacity to its maximum and to prolong its life.

A reduction in disagreement over safety is another area of interest. In 1976 managers had often expressed the view that the union, in the absence of other significant bargaining levers, sometimes used safety 'as a stick to beat management'. One explanation for the reduction, therefore, is that the incentive scheme had provided more effective means of forcing management's hand. It might also be the case that the union's preoccupation with the scheme had reduced the attention given to safety matters—thus realizing a fear frequently expressed by those opposing the introduction of the scheme. A third explanation lies in the introduction of joint union Health and Safety Committees as a result of the Health and Safety at Work Act. This formalized the system of routine inspections made by the NUM, and added representatives of management and NACODS to the teams, thus, perhaps, making safety a more consensual, less conflictual issue. Other reductions in disagreement can be directly attributed to the work-force's responses to incentives. These would include shift and work organization, deployment, and overtime allocation.

Thus, as might be expected from the pattern of priorities identified in the previous section, there is little indication that the union was attempting to push back the 'frontier of control' into the area of strategic decision-making. Union officials mainly appear to be defending the control they already had. Again, these averages mask variations within the samples and there was a small number of union officials who had on occasion challenged managements' domination of strategic decision-making. As we shall see in the next section, however, where they did, they tended to have little success.

The Outcomes of Conflict

The outcomes of conflict over decisions were identified by asking the colliery managers and NUM officials for each decision, 'When your

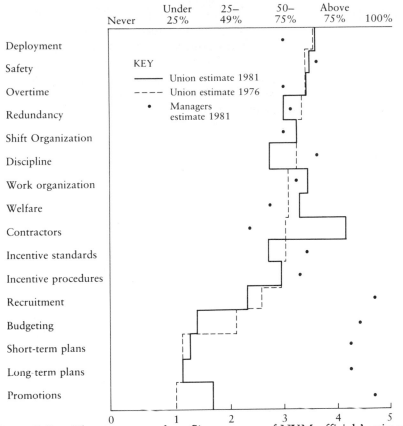

| | Never | Under 25% | 25–49% | 50–75% | Above 75% | 100% |

Deployment

Safety

Overtime

Redundancy

Shift Organization

Discipline

Work organization

Welfare

Contractors

Incentive standards

Incentive procedures

Recruitment

Budgeting

Short-term plans

Long-term plans

Promotions

KEY
——— Union estimate 1981
– – – Union estimate 1976
• Managers estimate 1981

Figure 7.5. The outcomes of conflict: average of NUM officials' estimate of success

objectives differ what percentage of the time do you get your own way?' Their responses were recorded on a scale:

(5) 100 per cent.
(4) Above 75 per cent.
(3) 50–74 per cent.
(2) 25–49 per cent.
(1) Under 25 per cent.
(0) Never.

Figure 7.5 shows the average union responses for 1976 and 1981 and the managers' mean estimate for 1981. Looking at the pattern overall it can be seen that both management and union appear more or less equally successful in contesting routine decisions to do with the job itself, but that conflict over strategic decisions tends to be resolved mainly in management's favour. Again this emphasizes the general inability of the local NUM officials to extend their influence beyond the usual job control issues. There were some instances of minor successes however. For example, one branch had reduced the overtime budget for its colliery by getting its members to observe a strict limit on the amount they worked. Although the NUM officials normally studiously avoid any part in the promotion of their members to supervisors, another branch reported having persuaded a manager to reject an especially unpopular candidate.

The degree of union success remains little changed between 1976 and 1981, despite the increased involvement of the NUM in decision-making, and despite an increase in its influence. This fact, combined with the relatively low level of conflict in 1981, leads us to suggest that although union 'power' increased during this period, it had expanded largely into areas where management was happy for it to go. Even the union's most spectacular increase in success in the case of conflict over the engagement of subcontractors (see Fig. 7.5), can be partly explained by a change of policy by management between 1976 and 1981 on the use of contract labour. The NPLA period was marked by an increased use of outside contractors for tunnelling work and roadway ripping in order to counter an alarming drop in the productivity of development workers. However, the reintroduction of incentives had its largest impact precisely on this group, thus reducing management's need to rely on outside labour (see Chapter 1). Therefore, while the opposition of the NUM to subcontracting had intensified under incentives, management was less determined in the face of union opposition and, consequently less likely to get its own way.

Summary: The Extent of Union Power

Our analysis of the various aspects of the power of the NUM shows its scope to be wide compared with that of shop stewards in many industries, but none the less largely confined to routine, job-related decisions. This finding would support those who have argued that the extent of union power in industry in general may have been exaggerated in the past. Thus, although our study would confirm the expectation that the coal-miners' encroachment into the managerial prerogative was fairly well advanced, it could be argued that the extent of this advance is relatively modest in the context of colliery decision-making as a whole. This is not to say, however, that union power was insignificant from management's point of view. Most managers viewed the NUM branch as a considerable force to be reckoned with and recognized that their job would become almost impossible without the union's active co-operation in the running of the colliery.

Nevertheless, there were differences in the degree of involvement and influence of the union officials across the samples. For example, a summary measure of union power based on the average of the union's

TABLE 7.1   The distribution of union power

| Mean power | Non-incentive decisions % | | Incentive decisions % |
	1976	1981	1981
1.5–2.0	12	3	3
2.1–2.5	24	37	3
2.6–3.0	35	31	11
3.1–3.5	26	26	20
3.6–4.0	3	3	46
4.1–4.2	—	—	17
No. of collieries	35	34	34
No. of decisions	27	20	6

estimate of their own influence over the twenty-seven decisions clearly shows that some union officials were, on average, far more successful than others in their attempts to get their own way in the decision-making process. The distribution of this measure in the 1976 sample, for equivalent decisions in the 1981 sample and for decisions relating to the incentive scheme (1981) are shown in Table 7.1. These not inconsiderable differences in union power between collieries cast doubt on how far it is possible to generalize about its extent in one industry, let alone make statements about union power in the country as a whole. Variation both within as well as between industries, therefore, presents problems for those who wish to pronounce on union power in any general way. No doubt it is this fact, combined with the use of different indices of power, which has produced so many contrasting accounts of the extent of union power in the workplace and of the impact of recession on workplace trade-unionism.

Reference back to Table 7.1 reveals another point of interest. The measures of union power based only on the decisions relating to the incentive scheme yield much higher indices of union power than those based on all decisions. This suggests that measures of union power based solely on matters related to pay would tend to overestimate the power of the union in relation to workplace decision-making as a whole. This again emphasizes the fact that conclusions regarding the nature of union power in the workplace are very much dependent on how 'power' is conceptualized and measured.

Conclusion

In the introduction to this chapter it was reported that research on the power of workplace trade-unionists in Britain has primarily been concerned with isolating the effect of three variables. These are the structure of collective bargaining and, in particular, the extent to which bargaining occurs at the workplace level; the formality of bargaining and the extent to which union participation in the bargaining process is constrained by a framework of written rules and procedures; and, finally, the external economic environment and the support it gives to trade union bargaining activity. The empirical material presented in this chapter has enabled us to investigate the effects of these three variables on the involvement of NUM branches in colliery decision-making. By way of conclusion, we now want to draw together these findings and indicate their significance for the wider debate concerning the influence of trade-union power.

Our findings on the effects of bargaining structure were somewhat contradictory. The research evidence from the 1976 survey, for instance, demonstrates that the centralization of pay-bargaining under NPLA had not served to rob local industrial relations of significant content. Indeed, our data show local bargaining in coal-mining to be as extensive as that found in the 'unregulated and anarchic' engineering workshops studied in the 1960s and 1970s (McCarthy and Parker, 1968; Storey, 1980) despite the difference in bargaining structure. Our research supports the view of several of the managers that we interviewed that NUM officials, deprived of the opportunity to bargain over pay under NPLA, had sought to influence a wider range of issues than they had under piece-work. Safety and welfare issues, subcontracting, work organization, and the remaining means by which pay could be influenced—grading, overtime, and special payments—all became a focus of workplace bargaining.

The 1981 survey, however, did provide evidence that a movement toward decentralized bargaining can stimulate workplace trade-union activity. It revealed that the reintroduction of local pay-bargaining had greatly increased the involvement of NUM officials in initial decision-making; and further analysis demonstrated that in 1981 greater numbers of branch representatives were becoming involved in bargaining with management and the frequency of meetings between union and management had increased. Moreover, the 1981 survey also revealed that the restoration of local pay-bargaining had not led the NUM to abandon the wider bargaining agenda it had developed under the day-wage system. There was some suggestion that safety was used less as a stick to beat management. Other issues, however, such as subcontracting and recruitment had, in fact, become more salient.

Turning to the issue of the formality of industrial relations rules and the power of trade-union representatives, we feel that our research supports Clegg's (1979) contention that formal rules may confer as well as constrain trade-union power. A major finding of our study is that the NUM locally exercises most power over decisions where national agreements give it a right to be involved. National agreements in coal-mining have endowed local NUM officials with rights to consultation and negotiation on a wide range of issues concerning the use and deployment of the work-force. These formal rights have undoubtedly buttressed union power at the colliery level. Since the union's defeat in the 1984/5 strike, though, management has attempted to amend the industry's framework of national agreements and a probable consequence of this will be to weaken the position of local trade-union representatives (see Chapter 8).

A further important point is that formal rules alone cannot guarantee influence for union officials.[6] The variation in union power noted above was found even where a national agreement clearly indicated the degree of union involvement. For example, the National Powerloading Agreement states that face-team selection should be carried out by management in consultation with the NUM. In the 1976 study, however, only half of the colliery managers said that this was a joint decision. Thirty per cent said that the selection was made solely or mainly by management and 15 per cent said that it was made by the union alone. Disparity of this order was found across all decisions covered by national agreements in the 1976 and 1981 surveys. Why some branch organizations are able to amass greater influence than is specified in national agreements, while others even fail to attain what they are formally entitled to, is the subject of our next chapter, which investigates variation in union power across the industry.

The final influence on trade-union power which has concerned scholars is the business cycle and its changing capacity to both support and undercut trade-union bargaining. In recent years a great deal of debate has taken place over the impact of recession and high unemployment on shop-steward organization and activities. Our 1976 and 1981 surveys were conducted at points in time when the economic fortunes of coal and the general economic environment in the country at large were markedly different. Despite this our evidence shows that at the workplace level trade-unionism had been relatively untouched and the power of trade-union representatives remained largely intact. Our research seemingly supports the argument of Batstone that the efficacy of recession in disciplining workers and loosening trade-union control over work organization is rather limited.

However, this point requires some qualification. Our research in 1981 was conducted while public subsidy of the coal industry remained at a high level and was, in fact, interrupted by large-scale unofficial strike action which was successful in forcing the government to withdraw a programme of colliery closures. Since then, the environment within which local industrial relations are conducted has been significantly changed. This

---

[6] The introduction of the 1974 Health and Safety Legislation modelled on the coal industry was not followed by an upsurge in union activity and power in other industries (Dawson *et al.*, 1984). The NUM's effective use of the Health and Safety Legislation in the coal industry has to be explained in terms of the other power resources at their disposal.

process is described fully in Chapters 9 and 10, but its main elements have been a reduction of government subsidy to the industry and the introduction of colliery closures on explicitly financial grounds. Moreover, these changes have occurred in the context of a major defeat for the NUM in a national strike and a division of its ranks. In previous chapters we have described some of the consequences of these events for the conduct of local pay-bargaining. We feel that if a further survey of union influence in colliery decision-making was conducted today then there might well be significant reductions in the estimates of union power compared with those reported here for 1976 and 1981. We do not believe local union power has collapsed in coal-mining and in the following chapter we will expand on this point. We do believe, however, that the scope and depth of union influence has probably been pushed backwards in at least some pits, so that to an even greater degree than in 1981, workplace trade-unionism in mining is focused on a relatively narrow range of job control issues. It is only in the wake of the miners' great defeat of 1985, we believe, that 'recession' has truly arrived within the mining industry.

8

Union Power in the Workplace: Determinants and Consequences

Introduction

Our analysis of the power of the NUM in collieries has revealed a high degree of involvement and influence over job-related issues. However, we have also shown this to be variable between collieries, indicating that some trade-union representatives are far more successful than others in their attempts to determine what happens in the workplace. In this chapter, therefore, we explore the reasons why mineworkers have been able to achieve the power they have in relation to colliery decision-making and attempt to identify the factors accounting for variation in their success. We then conclude our discussion by assessing the impact of changes in the power position of the NUM since the completion of the research.

The Analysis

In order to identify the main factors associated with variation in union power across the sample, general measures of power, based on the managers' and unions' responses across the twenty-seven decisions were calculated. Those reported here are the average of the NUM's estimate of their own influence over (a) the twenty-seven decisions used in the 1976 survey; (b) twenty equivalent decisions from the 1981 survey; and (c) six decisions relating to the operation of the incentive scheme in 1981. (The distribution of these measures across the samples has already been shown in Table 7.1 of the previous chapter.) In this part of the research, therefore, we have selected the union's estimate of their ability to determine what happens in the workplace as our measure of power.

These power measures were related to a wealth of data on colliery structure and performance, payment levels, manpower statistics, and various indices of industrial relations activity, attitudes, and behaviour. Unfortunately there were not identical sets of data for each survey: the 1976 study had the results of a survey of 1,027 workmen and supervisors' attitudes to work, management, and the industry, but resources were not available for a replication in 1981. The 1981 surveys of the managers and NUM officials, however, inlcuded many more questions on the nature of management and union relations in response to changes in the focus of academic debate since 1976.

The Determinants of Power

Power, as we have defined it in this study, is derived from three main sources. First there are resources which provide the *potential* for the exercise of power. Second is the way in which the work-force, through organization and activity, mobilizes resources in pursuit of their interests. Third is the means by which such interests and related goals and objectives are shaped and articulated, i.e. the means by which values or consciousness determine for which ends power is exercised. We start with a consideration of the resources available to the NUM branch officials basing our analysis on the general measure of union power derived from their influence over non-incentive decisions in 1976 and 1981.

Strategic Position and the Control of Uncertainty

Several writers, notably Crozier (1964) and Hickson *et al.* (1971), have suggested that the ability to control uncertainty, in the sense of being able to solve problems associated with non-routine occurrences, bestows power on an individual or group (see also Pettigrew, 1973; Zald, 1962). The main sources of uncertainty or unpredictability in the colliery manager's task are geological conditions, electrical and mechanical failure, and the behaviour of the work-force. Managerial strategy is aimed at minimizing the effects of uncertainty in order to achieve a planned level of production (the annual budgeted output) and, as collieries generally operate with little spare capacity and cannot easily make up production losses, a smooth flow of output. Despite massive technological development and its impact on the organization of work in the industry, colliery management is very much dependent on the effort and skill of the work-force in achieving these goals. As we have argued in Chapter 2, the introduction of the incentive scheme was in itself an admission of this fact. The mineworker's skill may no longer be derived from his ability to wield a pick or pack a stall, but skill based on the knowledge gained from years of working in a difficult, unpredictable, and dangerous environment remains. As one colliery manager explained, 'whether a machine does one or four cuts in a shift depends on how far faceworkers are willing to work with it and for it'. Thus, technology may have reduced the physical labour involved in minework, but it has not diminished management's dependence on the co-operation and special knowledge of the work-force in the uncertain task of extracting coal.

TABLE 8.1 Correlations[a] between measures of union power and uncertainty

Measures of uncertainty	1976 NPLA	1981 Equivalent decisions
Strategic position: task uncertainty	0.32	0.39
Continuity of working environment: rate of face change	− 0.38	− 0.44

[a] Pearson correlation coefficient significant at 1% or less.

The strategic position of mineworkers in the production process and their ability to control uncertainty for management is clearly a significant factor in explaining their power in the industry as a whole. However, not all coal-faces present the same degree of difficulty and unpredictability in their operation so that the opportunities for exploiting this power resource could be expected to vary from colliery to colliery. In order to explore this possibility some kind of standardized measure of the degree of uncertainty inherent in the management task is required.

One important source of uncertainty in coal production is the geological condition of the seam to be worked. An indication of the degree of uncertainty inherent in the system can be obtained by measuring the amount of variability in face outputs. *Ceteris paribus*, a face with fewer unanticipated geological problems can be expected to have a more stable output than one where problems are frequently encountered. Where variability in output is high, the strategic position of the work-force within the production process should be enhanced as it is particularly important for management to have their complete co-operation. Management's dependence is based not only on the need for extra effort but also on the special knowledge of the face and development workers in overcoming production problems. As expected we found measures of task uncertainty, based on variation in face outputs, had a positive correlation with the measure of union power in both surveys. (See Table 8.1.)[1]

Another factor affecting the strategic position of the work-force is the degree to which a flow of production is maintained during the geographical relocation of faces. Terminating and starting up new coal-faces is a standard feature of colliery operations and management attempt to ensure a smooth transfer of work from old to new. A rapid turnover of faces, however, usually indicates unplanned terminations due to unexpected geological problems. Such occurrences might be expected to increase management's dependence on the work-force. None the less, in this situation, the strategic position of the work-force is minimal as there is

[1] The measure of uncertainty was based on the weekly face output of the colliery for the financial year preceding each survey. It was calculated as follows: $U = (S_1/M_1 + S_n/M_n)100$. Where S = standard deviation of face outputs; M = mean output for face; n = number of faces.

little work for them to do and individual face-workers are deployed to odd jobs underground until a new face is developed. The fragmentation of the work-groups, moreover, has an adverse effect on work-force solidarity, and their support for the union. Face changes, especially those not accomplished to plan, may involve breaking up established work-groups and are often accompanied by a deterioration in working conditions and friction between supervisors and workmen. In this situation, the union can rely on little support from the fragmented and alienated work-force. Consequently, measures of the rate of face change had a negative correlation with union power both in 1976 and 1981 as can be seen in Table 8.1.[2]

Occupational Community

The existence of occupational communities in coal-mining has become a widely accepted explanation for coal-miners' militancy, solidarity, and strength (Kerr and Seigal 1954, Lipset, Trow, and Coleman, 1956). However, although the classic features of an occupational community— geographical and social isolation, an integrated set of social relationships, common values, and a common identity—can still be found in some mining villages, the number of miners who both live and work in the same village has been considerably reduced by pit closures and extensive transfers of labour.

None the less, writers such as Salaman (1974) have proposed that job satisfaction and involvement, the ability to use a skill, responsibility, and so on generate an identification with an occupation akin to that based on a common geographical location. Evidence from the 1976 attitude survey clearly reveals the presence in coal-mining of a highly developed occupational community in this second sense. The majority of mineworkers rated their relationship with their fellow workers, supervisors, and managers well and said that they gained intrinsic satisfaction from their work and enjoyed a fairly high degree of autonomy and responsibility. Their evaluations, in addition, were significantly more favourable than those taken from manual workers in light engineering and confectionery firms (see Edwards and Harper, 1976). There was also direct evidence of a fairly high degree of identification with their occupation in that 61 per cent of the mineworkers interviewed agreed with the statement, 'I am a mineworker and I would not think of taking any other job.'

There was variation within the sample however. Thus the significance

---

[2] Another structural feature, size, measured by the number of employees, also had a weak negative relationship with the power measure in 1976 (-0.3, significant at 5%), but this correlation disappeared when rate of face change was held constant.

TABLE 8.2 Work-force attitudes and union power, 1976

	Pearson's correlation coefficient[a] with power measure
Proportion of the work-force who:	
Rate fellow workers well	0.36
Rate supervisors well	0.43
Rate management well	0.40
Say they have job autonomy	0.61
Say they have interesting job	0.50
Say they have satisfaction from job	0.41
Say management take their views into account in making decisions	0.39
Say pit well-managed	0.38
Say they were happier at previous pit	−0.62

Note: n = 21. [a]Significant at 5% or less.

of this work-based occupational community as a power resource might be expected to vary also. There were, in fact, very high correlations between variations in the proportion of mineworkers in a colliery with positive attitudes towards their work, supervisors, and management and the measure of union power. These are shown in Table 8.2.

For example, the higher the proportion of mineworkers in the colliery saying that they found their work interesting, gained satisfaction from the job, had a great deal of 'say' in how they did the job, and rated their workmates well, the higher was the power of the union. Favourable attitudes towards supervision and management, and saying that management and men work together like a team were also positively related to union power. Those mineworkers with *pro* work and management attitudes were also more likely to attend branch meetings.[3]

The findings present a paradox for those who view the employment relationship in mainly conflictual terms. It might be expected that support for the union, and therefore greater union power would be based on dissatisfaction with the job, supervision, and management. However, the 1976 attitude survey, carried out in the wake of the 1972 and 1974 national strikes, revealed surprisingly little antagonism towards local management. It is also the case that a large number of studies in the USA have identified positive relationships between participation in the local union, job satisfaction, and the degree of 'social integration' into the plant (Stagner, 1953; Lipset *et al*, 1956; Spinrad, 1960; Tagliacozza and

[3] Pearson's correlation coefficients between attitudes to work, management and supervision were 0.4, 0.5, 0.5 with branch attendance.

Seidman, 1966; Glick *et al.*, 1977). Thus, 'dual loyalty' (i.e. having favourable attitudes to work, management, and the union), which is a widely noted feature of industrial relations in the USA, was also a characteristic of local industrial relations in the British coal industry at the time of the study.

These findings could be interpreted as an indicator of incorporation, but in our view are entirely consistent with a willingness to take on management in militant industrial action when the need arises. It is the mineworkers' very solid commitment to their job, their work-groups, colliery, community, and to the industry, which can make them such a formidable force when these are threatened.

This is not to claim, however, that occupational communities alone, whether geographically or work based are sufficient to generate union power. Indeed, there are features of such communities which may mitigate against its exercise and development. Moore (1975) and Lummis (1977), for example, suggest that they may act as an integrating mechanism hindering the creation of class consciousness and militancy in terms of 'us' and 'them' views of the relationship between management and work-force. Consider Moore's (1975) proposition that

the miner only developed a consciousness of market interest. Market interest is usually equated with class interest, but we are suggesting that the worker may be conscious of his interest in an economic situation which he believes includes not only his fellow workers but his employers and supervisors also (p. 54).

The geographical and/or social isolation of occupational communities, moreover, can produce an insular and chauvinistic perspective which presents obstacles to the development of organization and collective action on a wider front. For example, in Chapter 4 we have documented the individualistic response of colliery work-forces to the incentive scheme, noting that, with the exception of some collieries in Yorkshire, none were willing to combine their resources in order to bargain collectively over incentive pay with management. The difficulties the mineworkers have experienced over the years, first in creating, and now in maintaining a national union bear further witness to the problem.

The significance of the mining communities in sustaining national action, most clearly demonstrated in the 1984/5 strike, is undeniable,[4] but even direct threats to the existence of these communities do not necessarily provoke widespread organized opposition. Between 1957 and 1968, for example, the NCB was able to carry out the largest programme of redundancy and redeployment ever undertaken by an employer without a major strike (McCormick, 1979). Similar closure programmes in France and Belgium at this time met with a wave of strike activity. In

[4] For accounts see Allen (1979), Samuel *et al.* (1986), Parker (1986), Dolby (1987).

contrast, the British mineworkers' response to the contraction of jobs and loss of their communities was largely one of individual retreat, as miners left the industry in droves.[5] The reason for their acceptance was, according to Allen (1981), a lack of collective consciousness, leadership, and organization.

Occupational communities, therefore, are a potential power resource in that they can generate solidarity, commitment, and a common identity but whether these forces can be translated into collective action in opposition to managements' will depend on other factors. It is to a consideration of some of these that we now turn.

Organization, Leadership, and Consciousness

We have suggested that occupational communities alone are not sufficient to guarantee union power. Similar arguments also apply to the role of strategic position as a source of power. Uncertainty may render management more dependent on the co-operation of the work-force, but it is the effectiveness with which this potential power resource is exploited which will ultimately determine the amount of power. In particular, there is the problem of extending its use to cover issues not directly related to the production process and to serve the interests of groups of mineworkers who are not directly involved at the point of production.

Leadership, organization, and collective consciousness can be seen as the principal means whereby resources are translated into union power. The role of these in mobilizing the resources of the mineworkers nationally has been well documented elsewhere (e.g. Allen, 1981) and is dealt with in more detail in Chapters 9 and 10. Suffice to say that they can be seen as critical factors in the waxing and waning of the fortunes of the NUM in the country as a whole. Variations in these factors at the local level might also be expected to account for differences in workplace union power.

Workplace Organization

Scholars have paid a great deal of attention to union workplace organization and leadership as the main instruments through which power is exercised (Boraston et al., 1975; Batstone et al., 1977). The growth in the development and coverage of steward organizations (in terms of their number, degree of hierarchy, resources, facilities, and formal recognition, etc.) since the 1960s has generally been interpreted as a sign of increasing union strength. However, we would question the

---

[5] During this period some 228,326 jobs were removed through wastage and 89,774 through redundancy, redeployment, and dismissals (McCormick (1979) p. 106).

importance of organization alone as an indicator of union power. Where organizations have been created for the convenience of managements, rather than emerging from grass-root support, for example, they are unlikely to provide effective opposition to management's will. As Edwards (1987) has shown in relation to the railway, such institutions, however well developed, may be empty of any real significance in terms of power if they are not underpinned by the resources and the leadership necessary to exploit them.

None the less, there are features of the NUM's local organization which, in combination with other resources, clearly strengthen their power position. Branch organization is almost always based on the colliery, which not only increases the mineworkers' identification with the branch but also facilitates communication and the management of collective action. As we have seen in Chapter 5 the facilities the union enjoys, the degree of recognition within the formal structure of negotiation and consultation, and, at the time of the study, the near monopoly of manual union membership are all superior to those found in most other industries.

These features of workplace union organization, however, are uniformly well developed in coal-mining, and the small differences between collieries which do exist are unlikely to account for variation in local union power. Certain aspects of leadership, on the other hand, varied considerably between collieries.

Union Consciousness and Leadership

There was a very clear division among the branch officials interviewed in the 1981 sample as to how widely they defined their role as trade unionists. Forty-six per cent took a narrow view of their function, defining it solely in terms of defending or protecting pay and working conditions. Fourteen per cent were also committed to serving the local community, extending their representative role to widows, retired miners, and the overall welfare of their members. Twenty-eight per cent, however, added a third, political, and educative dimension to their role. These differences in levels of 'union consciousness' yielded high correlations with the power measures (Pearson's correlation coefficient 0.51, significant at 0.1 per cent). Thus, the broader the definition of their role and members' interests, the greater their awareness of the need for political action and to raise the level of membership 'consciousness', the more powerful was the NUM branch.

The reasons for this are threefold: firstly, union officials who define their own role and the interests of their membership widely are more likely to attempt to exert influence across the broader range of issues. They are, in addition, more likely to 'educate' or persuade their membership of the need to support action in pursuit of goals other than those related to pay and conditions. Therefore, our data would support Lukes's (1974) proposition that beliefs about what are 'reasonable' or 'proper' demands in a bargaining relationship will affect the power aspirations of subordinate groups. In the case of the NUM officials, it appears that those with less constrained ambitions achieve more. Secondly, those officials with commitments and contacts outside the colliery may be able to draw on external resources in their bargaining with management. They are more likely to have access to expert advice and to have superior channels of information. Personal contacts with the area management or union hierarchy or in the community can also be used to put pressure on local management. Moreover, those who are actively involved in the local council are able, on occasion, to facilitate colliery operations which impinge on the local community, and thus enhance their bargaining position when it comes to settling matters inside the colliery. Finally, there is evidence to suggest that those officials who defined their role broadly also tended to be better prepared for their task. They were more likely to have attended training courses and, furthermore, their political activities gave them ample opportunities to test and perfect their bargaining skills in other contexts.

Leadership Style

Batstone *et al.* (1977) have placed considerable emphasis on leadership style in explaining success in bargaining with management. They were able to show, for example, that shop stewards who lead rather than follow their membership are more likely to establish a strong bargaining relationship with management and to achieve more in substantive terms. Attempts to distinguish different styles of leadership in the 1981 sample of NUM spokesmen yielded very little variation, as all but three adopted a 'leadership' rather than a 'representative' role *vis-à-vis* their membership. For example, virtually all agreed with the statement that 'an NUM spokesman must, on occasion, persuade his members to accept unpopular management decisions for the good of the pit as a whole'.

There was, however, variation in the strength of the bargaining relationship that they had established with management. Where NUM officials had developed a greater degree of 'trust' by management (i.e. the colliery manager felt they would stand by agreements and that he could rely on their information) they tended to be more powerful (Pearson's correlation coefficient 0.30, significant at 5 per cent). Those who dealt with the colliery manager himself rather than his subordinates also tended to be more successful. This latter point, dealing personally with the colliery manager, was not a significant factor under NPLA. However, one important effect of the incentive scheme was that colliery managers tended to centralize decision-making in their efforts to keep strict control on costs. Therefore, the ability to deal directly with the colliery manager rather than his subordinates was a determinant of their power, and no doubt also a reflection of it.

Edwards (1987) found the intensity of steward activity an important correlate of union power on the railway and it is also significant here. Activity, in terms of frequency of contact with administrative staff and under-managers, monitoring installation performance with a view to keeping a record of incentive pay earned, and saying that the incentive scheme had not reduced the time they spent on other issues, all had positive correlations with the power measure (Pearson's correlation coefficients 0.41, 0.37, 0.34 and 0.33 respectively, all significant at 5 per cent or less).

Branch Officials as Informational Gatekeepers

Communication between management and the work-force in collieries presents considerable problems. The work-force is widely dispersed, there is usually a shift system and there is no central meeting point for the dissemination of information. Personal communication between management and work-force, therefore, tends to be sporadic.

Branch officials, on the other hand, tend to have more opportunities for personal contact. They are usually free to move underground visiting mineworkers at their place of work. Most have an office close to the lamp-room so men can drop in before or after a shift. Many are closely involved in the local community and regularly deal with queries outside working hours at the Miners Welfare and in their own homes.

As Pettigrew (1973) has shown, information can be a source of power, especially where individuals or groups act as gatekeepers manipulating the flow for their own purposes. The 1976 survey of mineworkers' attitudes clearly showed that some union officials had been able to develop a gatekeeping role, especially in relation to communication between management and the strategically placed underground workers. For example, whereas 42 per cent of development and 25 per cent of face-workers mentioned the branch officials as a means of finding out what was going on in the pit, only 31 per cent of development and 15 per cent of face-workers mentioned management. As might be expected, there is a relatively high correlation between the power measure and the proportion of the work-force mentioning the branch officials as an information source (Pearson's correlation coefficient 0.48, significant at 1 per cent).

The significance of the NUM officials' control over information was also demonstrated in the 1984/5 strike. Senior management's attempts to communicate directly with the mineworkers ran into difficulties. Some local managers used to relying on union officials, word of mouth, and notices, found they did not even have an up-to-date list of employees' names and addresses from which to work.

TABLE 8.3   Age, branch attendance, membership support, and union power

	Pearson's correlation coefficient with power measure[a]	
	1976 NPLA	1981 Equivalent decisons
Men prepared to support branch on *any* issue	—	0.36
Attendance at branch meetings	0.34	n.s.
% of work-force aged under 40 years	0.43	—

[a] Significant at 5% or less. —means not included in survey. n.s. means not significant.

Membership Support

Effective leadership is ultimately dependent on membership support and as might be expected the few indicators that we have of this are positively correlated with our power measure (see Table 8.3).

The union spokesman's view that the membership were prepared to support the branch on *any* issue (i.e. not just those related to incentive pay) was associated with higher power scores. The proportion of the work-force usually attending branch meetings was also positively related to union power in the 1976 survey, but by 1981 the association had ceased. This is because meetings had largely become a forum to complain about incentive earnings, and, for some mineworkers attendance had become a mark of dissatisfaction with the union rather than one of interest and support.

Finally, in the 1976 study, the percentage of younger mineworkers in a colliery yielded a positive correlation with union power. Branch attendance was also related to union power and to the age profile of the colliery, suggesting that younger mineworkers were even more willing to lend support and to participate in union affairs than their seniors.

The younger workers' greater support for the union might be explained in a number of ways. One explanation is that their most formative years in the industry were during the period of increasing militancy leading to the 1972 and 1974 strikes.[6] The strikes, morcover had clearly demonstrated the benefits to be gained by supporting the union and pursuing their objectives through collective action.

---

[6] Not that older mineworkers were excluded from the process. One from the North East area which had suffered some of the severest contractions during the 1950s and 1960s explained his own 'conversion' to the radical cause in 1971: 'I used to think the worst thing that could happen would be to put the lid on this place, but then I thought that's why we're sunk so low—out of fear . . . before we'd accepted everything was inevitable but then we got up off our knees and fought!'

Explaining Variation in Union Power over the Operation of the Incentive Scheme

Our analysis so far has considered NUM power in relation to non-monetary decisions. In this section we examine the ability of the NUM to determine the outcome of decisions relating specifically to the operation of the incentive scheme.

Table 8.4 shows the main factors correlated with the power measure based on union influence averaged across the six 'incentive' decisions. The amount of leadership activity and a measure of work-force solidarity (the managers' view that face-team members are more critical of poor workers since the introduction of the scheme) are positively associated with power as before, but generally the pattern of relationships which emerges is very different from that explaining union power over non-monetary decisions. For example, high branch attendance and industrial action are now associated with less union power and are evidently indicators of membership frustration over the union's inability to satisfy their aspirations in respect to incentive pay rather than union support. None the less, the *threat* of industrial action apparently enhances union power as it is higher where managers perceive industrial action to be more likely since the introduction of the scheme (see Table 8.4).

By far the strongest relationships are found between various measures of colliery and work-force performance and the power measure as can be

TABLE 8.4   Explaining variation in union power over the operation of the incentive scheme

	Correlation coefficients with power measure[a]
Leadership activity	
More contact with deputy manager than before	0.29
More contact with administration officer than before	0.39
Union monitors performance on installations	0.29
Membership	
Attendance at branch meetings	− 0.34
Manager says men more critical of poor workers	− 0.36
Industrial action	
Manager says unofficial disputes more likely	0.33
Frequency of industrial action [b]	− 0.28

[a] Pearson's correlation coefficient significant at 5% or below.   [b] For fiscal year 1980/1.
n = 34.

seen from Table 8.5. These are particularly strong for statistics indicating an improvement in productivity since the introduction of the scheme, and the manager's perception that work-force motivation has improved. Absolute levels of productivity, particularly profit per ton, also yield relatively high correlations. We would suggest, therefore, that the union is more powerful where there has been a real, or at least a perceived, improvement in productivity, and where performance measures are high. Union power, in this case, is very definitely not associated with poor productivity.[7] These findings would support those who reject the view that union power is necessarily a cause of low labour productivity (see Nichols, 1986; Daniel, 1987).

The reasons underlying the positive relation between union power and colliery performance have already been explored in Chapter 4. Here we argued that the aspirations of the work-force and their representatives are largely based on what they think the pit can afford, rather than what others are getting, or the maximum they could extract through

TABLE 8.5   Union power and performance indicators

	Correlation coefficient[a] with power measure
Improvement in performance indicators since 1976	
Costs per ton reduced	0.53
Output per face man increased	0.35
Productivity per man year increased	0.35
Manager's perception of effect of scheme on effort	
Men more receptive to new methods of work	0.50
Men work more flexibly within team	0.30
Men more interested in planning	0.35
Performance indicators	
Face productivity per man year[b]	0.44
Profit per ton[b]	0.48
Face output per man-shift[b]	0.39
Absenteeism (days lost)[b]	− 0.34
Accident rate (days lost)[b]	0.29
Bonus pay (average p.a.)	0.43

[a] Pearson's R significant at 5% or lower.   [b] For fiscal year 1980/1.

[7] The assumption that work-group or union power is a major cause of Britain's poor record of productivity can be found in the work of economists such as Caves and Crause (1980), or Pratten (1976), as well as the popular press.

industrial action. We attributed the source of these constraints to the tradition of payment by results in the industry which we argued overrides the principle enshrined in the incentive scheme blueprint that bonus pay should reward effort rather than the value of the coal produced. We would suggest, therefore, that the resoluteness with which the branch officials attempt to exercise influence over incentive decisions is largely determined by their perceptions of management's ability to pay.

It could be argued, moreover, that management has the upper hand in defining the level of pay the pit can 'afford' in that measures of productivity, profit, and economic viability are defined and calculated by management, and it is difficult for branch officials to produce alternative estimates. It is also the case that management in the more productive pits would be less likely to resist union attempts to influence incentive-pay decisions as long as these more or less concurred with their own view of how much the 'pit could afford'. Of course, the managers' and unions' definition of the managers' 'ability to pay' will not always agree, and, as we have seen, at the inception of the scheme conflict levels rose as these disagreements were resolved. However, the very strong relationship between productivity and union influence over these decisions demonstrates the fact that, in most (but by no means all) pits, managements' view of what the pit could afford prevailed. Here, we suggest, the mineworkers do not differ from the majority of workers in that as Hyman and Brough (1975) propose 'the general work ethic and the particular conception of a "fair day's work" prevalent among employees are unlikely to diverge radically from managerial expectations' (p. 74). To this general normative or pragmatic acceptance in society of what constitutes a 'reasonable' reward for manual work must be added the effect of the general atmosphere of recession and closure threats in the industry, and in the country as a whole at this time. These no doubt added weight to management's arguments concerning the need to keep incentive pay in line with their definitions of productivity.

It is no doubt for these reasons that the measure of union power over incentive decisions has only a relatively high, but by no means perfect, correlation with the level of bonus pay. Branch officials who were able to influence the operation of the scheme did not necessarily use this influence to maximize earnings but more to ensure a 'reasonable' reward. Other considerations such as fairness in distribution or keeping the level of earnings stable were also important. Nevertheless, there is no evidence to suggest that those branch officials who felt the scheme was unjust,[8] or those who defined their role more widely than merely bargaining over pay (i.e. those with higher levels of 'union consciousness'), were less likely to

[8] Only 26% of NUM officials felt that the principle of incentive payment was just.

influence the operation of the scheme. There is, in fact, no relationship between these measures and that of union power over the incentive decisions.

Power over Incentive and Non-monetary Decisions

Many of the studies which have been made of union power in the workplace have concentrated their attention on the branch officials' or shop stewards' ability to determine pay. However, the assumption that power in relation to earnings is indicative of a general or global power capacity is not borne out by our data. There is only a relatively weak correlation (0.31) between the power measure, based on estimates of influence over incentive decisions and that based on non-monetary decisions. The variables associated with each measure are also for the most part different, suggesting that power over pay and power over other matters are derived from different sources. Thus, we would argue that a narrow focus on levels of earnings may yield a distorted or inaccurate view of a shop steward's power position in relation to the operation of the workplace as a whole.

Managerial Tactics and Union Power

Our discussion so far has paid little attention to managerial tactics in explaining the success or failure of the NUM's attempts to determine colliery affairs. At the time of the 1976 and 1981 surveys a colliery manager was judged on his ability to meet production targets within budget and without industrial unrest. Virtually all the managers we interviewed were aware of their dependence on the co-operation of the work-force and their representatives (the NUM) in achieving this goal. For example, all but two of the thirty-five colliery managers in the 1981 sample agreed that 'when I have to make decisions which might be unpopular with the men it always pays to involve the lodge officials from an early stage' and that 'a strong NUM lodge official is more a help than a hindrance to colliery management'. As we have seen in the previous chapter, moreover, the majority enjoyed good relationships with their NUM officials and there was a fair degree of agreement on objectives in decision-making. Most colliery managers, therefore, viewed the NUM officials as, if not quite a second arm of management, at very least a useful tool which could be used to control the work-force.

The main problems from management's point of view were not caused by overly powerful NUM officials but by weak ones who were unable to deliver work-force co-operation either because of inadequate membership support or because of factionalism within the pit. Very few managers pursued a policy of 'divide and rule' in relation to the work-force. As one explained, it placed 'an intolerable burden on management because you have to negotiate separately with each group . . . and leads to strife and disorder in the pit".

Generally, therefore, local management did not attempt to diminish the power of the NUM at the time of our studies but mainly sought to channel it into acceptable areas. Despite their apparent strength virtually all managers seemed to accept the level of NUM involvement in colliery affairs. In the 1981 survey, in response to the question 'In general, do you feel that representatives from the lodge have too much or too little say over matters at this colliery?' only two of the thirty-five managers replied 'too much' and one actually said it was 'too little'.

This is not to claim, however, that the NUM was the tool of management—we have already dismissed that proposal emphatically in Chapter 6. Nor do we wish to imply that colliery managers were the compliant partners in this bargaining relationship. The evidence presented in the previous chapter clearly demonstrates that despite the relatively advanced levels of union power in the industry management had none the less maintained the upper hand. Colliery managers are recruited only after several years' experience in the industry (including at least two years' face training) and they were usually well prepared to take on the not inconsiderable challenge from the NUM. The colliery manager's bargaining skills derived from experience were clearly important factors as his length of time in post was negatively related to union power over incentive and non-incentive decisions in both surveys.[9] The greater the colliery manager's experience, the less powerful is the union.

The relationship between colliery managers and the branch officials may have been congenial, but as the authors' observed on many occasions the bargaining was usually very tough indeed. As one colliery manager explained to us, 'you need to always keep one step ahead and use every trick in the book!' One of his 'tricks' was to allow NUM officials he favoured who were standing for re-election some obvious bargaining successes to ensure their safe return. We encountered several other managers who used this tactic to try to influence the composition of the branch.

Colliery managers are not entirely free agents in their dealings with the NUM, and senior management could intervene if national agreements or general policy were transgressed. However, in Chapter 4 we have demonstrated the reluctance of senior management to intervene in the management of the incentive scheme, and similar considerations applied to other matters as well. The degree of autonomy enjoyed by colliery

[9] Pearson's correlation coefficients, significant at 1%, -0.41 (1976) -0.43 (1981) for the power measure based on non-monetary decisions, -0.36 for that based on incentive decisions.

managers appeared to run counter to official senior management strategy at that time and reflects the difficulty of centralizing decision-making in the face of a highly uncertain production process. As Lawrence and Lorsch (1967) have pointed out, in this situation decisions need to be made near or at the source of uncertainty in order to optimize performance. This fact enhances the power position of the colliery manager in relation to his superiors—control of uncertainty is as much a source of power for the manager as it is for the NUM. However, such devolution would also enhance the power of the branch officials by expanding the opportunities for involvement and influence at the level of the workplace (see Leijnse, 1980; Edwards, 1987; Donovan Report, 1968). Our data clearly demonstrate this fact. Some colliery managers were allowed more discretion than others, and where they were the union had more power over non-monetary decisions.[10]

Changes in Workplace Union Power since the 1984 – 1985 Strike

In concluding our discussion of workplace power we attempt to assess the impact of the major changes which have taken place in the industry since the completion of our research in 1981. Since an evaluation of the position of the national union is presented in following chapters, we focus our analysis here on the local level.

The most salient event since 1981 has been undoubtedly the 1984/5 strike. Few would deny that the union's conclusive defeat and the aftermath of pit closures have considerably diminished the power of the NUM nationally. At colliery level, the disarray of the national union, the indebtedness of the miners, fear of closure, high levels of unemployment, and the continued existence of the rival union, the Union of Democratic Mineworkers must all have sapped the mineworkers' will to oppose. However, there are some indicators which suggest that the resounding defeat of 1984/5 has not left British Coal with a totally subjugated and compliant workforce. In 1986/7 the ratio of output lost in disputes per man shows an increase of 37.5 per cent over the 1981 figure, earnings in the industry have held up relatively well, and some of British Coal's attempts to change national agreements in their favour have met with unexpectedly widespread opposition. (These trends are discussed in more detail in Chapter 10.)

The power of the NUM, therefore, at least in some pits and areas may be more resilient in the face of adversity than popularly supposed. Clearly a closer examination of the way in which recent events have altered or

---

[10] The Pearson's correlation coefficient between the measure of power based on non-monetary decisions and the colliery managers' estimate of how much freedom of action they have from higher management in agreeing things with the NUM lodge officials was 0.26, significant at 5%.

destroyed the power resources of the mineworkers and their will to use them is required.

The Strategic Position of the Work-force

Since the 1980/1 study, coal-mining capacity has been increasingly concentrated into fewer, more productive collieries. We suggest that this policy could enhance the strategic position of the work-forces in the collieries that survive in three main respects.

First, the contribution of individual collieries to the industry's output is proportionately greater, thus heightening the disruptive impact of industrial action at each colliery. Second, our research clearly demonstrated that union power, at least over pay, was greater in the collieries which were more 'productive' in management's terms. Unions in the surviving collieries, therefore, may be well-placed to continue their involvement and influence over matters relating to pay.

Third, the closure programme has favoured collieries employing the more advanced mining techniques. We have already argued on several occasions that the introduction of advanced mining technologies are unlikely to decrease management's dependence on the work-force in the foreseeable future. In fact management's need to extract maximum performance from its large capital investments may enhance the value of work-force co-operation. The use of retreat mining techniques, moreover, which have increased by 10 per cent since 1981, may actually increase union power. We found that major geological problems leading to unplanned face closures and the break-up of established work-groups had an adverse effect on union solidarity and union power. In retreat mining, however, radical problems of this kind are discovered in the developmental stage of the extraction process, thus ensuring that face-teams once formed remain together for the life of the face.

The Mining Communities

The effect of the strike and closure programme on the geographically or work-based occupational communities, however, may not be so uniformly benign. In contrast with the response to the massive closure programmes of the 1950s and 1960s many mineworkers in 1984 were willing to strike in defence of their jobs and local communities. Clearly those communities and collieries which stayed solid throughout the strike experienced a strengthening of their commitment to each other and to their work (Dolby, 1987; Parker, 1986). Other pits and villages, however, with proportions of working miners, or those who gave up the struggle early, were rent asunder (Samuel et al, 1986). Moreover, the post-strike closure programme claimed many of the most solid, geographically based mining communities as its victims.

As far as the work-based community is concerned a number of factors have probably increased the mineworkers' commitment to work. Mineworkers who remain in the industry have rejected redundancy terms which are generous compared with those offered in other industries, and it could be surmised that those who have stayed have done so either because there is no alternative or because they are committed to the job. It is also the case that those collieries which have survived the closure programme exhibit more of the characteristics associated with job satisfaction and social integration at work, i.e. the characteristics of a strong occupational community which we found to be positively associated with union power.

However, it should be noted that the very aspect of community which sustained the NUM in their opposition to British Coal probably also served to sustain the working miners in their opposition to the NUM. This again underlines the fact that the ties of solidarity generated by work or locality are not necessarily mobilized in united opposition to management.

Union Consciousness

The single-mindedness with which British Coal have pursued their closure policy, rejecting any pleas for survival on social grounds, has no doubt facilitated management's attempts to keep expectations with regard to incentive pay in line with its definitions of productivity. This must be particularly the case where the economic viability of the colliery is in question. However, how far this has affected the mineworkers' expectations in relation to other matters is difficult to assess. On the one hand, the experience of the strike may have sharpened the awareness of ordinary mineworkers and their officials of the broader social and political issues shaping their fate, thus raising their 'union consciousness'. On the other hand, however, defeat has also demonstrated their inability to achieve such broader objectives in the economic and political climate of the 1980s.

So far, the mineworkers' response to British Coal's intended assault on some of their most hallowed national agreements has been variable. For example, when British Coal announced plans to introduce six-day working, thus breaching the five-day-week agreement, the reputedly militant Welsh miners, faced with what they perceived to be a choice between compliance and possible extinction, voted to accept. Miners at Frickley Colliery in South Yorkshire, on the other hand, struck over the implementation of a new disciplinary code in July 1987.

Criticism of Arthur Scargill's leadership and policies, widely reported in the press, suggest a mood of pragmatic compliance on the part of a number of mineworkers. However, such compliance may be a temporary affair and British Coal may have much to do in order to win positive support, as opposed to reluctant obedience, for its new policies.

Leadership and Organization

Given the resounding defeat in 1985, leaving the union exposed to the full impact of recession, some 'roll-back' in union organization may have been expected in the industry. None the less, the local union organization and 100 per cent union membership remain intact. Local unions have not emerged totally unscathed from the conflict, many branches have lost their most experienced officials by transfer, closures, or redundancy, and there was a disproportionate number of union officials among the mineworkers who were sacked during the strike and who have yet to be reinstated. However, they may have been replaced by younger, more radical mineworkers drawn into union activity and militant action through the strike.

The presence of the UDM in some collieries clearly weakens the position of local leaders, but there is little evidence to suggest much further expansion of the UDM beyond the collieries it claimed during the strike. In fact the potential for factions forming around groups of transferees from closed collieries, who bring with them a different set of expectations for action and leadership, may pose more of a threat to the solidarity of the work-force.

These difficulties, added to low morale amongst the membership, may have made the task of local leaderhip much harder. Such problems could adversely affect the strength of their bargaining relationship with management in that they may not be able to secure the co-operation of the membership to the same degree as before. However, the other critical factor is how far colliery managers are themselves willing to return to the strong bargaining relationships which existed prior to the strike.

Management Tactics since the 1984–1985 Strike

It is uncertain how many colliery managers have succeeded in capitalizing on the NUM's national defeat in order to diminish the influence and involvement of the NUM branch in colliery affairs, or indeed how many have sought to do so. There were some press reports of 'macho' colliery managers proposing a 'roll-back' of union control in the wake of the strike. Take, for example, a colliery manager quoted in the *Financial Times* (1 March 1985): 'Management in the past have conceded too much and built up problems for the future . . . the pendulum is now swinging the other way.' It is true that some colliery managers have been resolutely opposed to the reinstatement of branch officials sacked during the strike, but evidence of other 'anti-union' tactics is hard to find. There is, however, much stronger and more determined backing from senior management for those colliery managers who wish to take on their work-forces over particular issues. Nevertheless, as we have argued earlier, the colliery managers' dependence on the co-operation of the work-force remains and has probably increased since the strike. Where branch officials are able to deliver that co-operation management will no doubt be anxious to re-establish a strong bargaining relationship. It is also unlikely that colliery managers would encourage the development of the UDM in their pits, unless it already had majority support, if the net result would be two competing groups with conflicting objectives, each demanding their quota of managerial time. Finally, the generally congenial relationship between local managers and miners must be recalled, and it is apposite to question how many colliery managers would willingly exchange their largely comfortable relationship with the NUM for one of confrontation.

Senior management, on the other hand, is clearly willing to risk what it would expect to be a temporary deterioration in local relations in order to push home its advantage on a number of fronts. As one board member commented in interview, 'perhaps colliery industrial relations have been too cosy in the past'.

As we have seen, British Coal have targeted some national agreements such as the five-day week and the disciplinary code, which they feel impede productivity, for complete revision. They are also seeking an 'updating' of the Health and Safety Legislation to deal with modern mining methods. The proposed revisions would allow colliery managers greater flexibility in applying the rules. Should British Coal be successful, the NUM would find their opportunities for exploiting this power resource severely diminished.

How far British Coal will succeed in obtaining these revisions of national agreements has yet to be seen. Our research, moreover, has shown that national agreements may be one thing, but their implementation another. Even if they are revised, there is potentially a second battle to be fought in applying these revisions to particular pits. Despite this reservation, any weakening of the protective umbrella of national agreements must ultimately diminish the power of the local union. National agreements set the agenda for discussion, the standards to which, to a greater or lesser extent, participants conform. For the local union, they represent a power resource which, depending on their power position, they can exploit to the advantage of their members. (See also Batstone and Gourlay, 1986.) National agreements reframed to the advantage of management will present problems even for the strongest local union and those collieries with few resources may find themselves hopelessly exposed.

There is yet another aspect of British Coal's post-strike strategy which has the potential to diminish the power of the local union. This is a policy of developing means of direct communication with the work-force. Some of the ways in which British Coal has attempted to improve its channels of communication have already been described in Chapter 1—the introduction of briefing groups in some coalfields, the use of videos and other media to drive home the industry's need for continued productivity improvement, and the introduction of training in employee involvement for colliery managers. Another example is the change in the use of *Coal News*, the industry's newspaper. Ian MacGregor instituted the direct mailing of *Coal News* to the homes of the industry's employees and it is now used much more deliberately as a means of influencing work-force opinion. Although methods of this kind are primarily directed towards increased worker involvement and towards improving management's control of work, they also serve to weaken the centrality of the unions as a channel both of representation and of communication. They are particularly aimed at displacing the union with management as the 'natural' representative of British miners. Should they succeed, the NUM branches' role as an informational gatekeeper, which we identified as a major source of their power, could be severely eroded.

Finally, there is a policy which in contrast to most other developments, might actually increase the power of the local union branch. That is the weakening of central control in the industry and proposals for greater autonomy and responsibility for colliery management. Such a development could enhance the power of the NUM officials by bringing many more decisions within their sphere of potential influence. Whether the NUM, however, will have sufficient strength to exploit this advantage has yet to be seen.

Conclusion

In our discussion we have rejected the view that national defeat has necessarily left the local union organization defenceless in the face of an all-powerful management. We have, in contrast, identified a number of factors—their strategic position in the production process, the strengthening of ties of solidarity, and the devolution of decision-making in the industry—which allow the NUM, in some collieries at least, the potential for power. However, several aspects of British Coal's policy since the strike present very real threats to local union power, especially for those in less 'productive' pits. The most salient of these policies are the assault on national agreements, the erosion of the NUM's monopoly of communication with the work-force, the recognition of the UDM, and perhaps, most salient of all, the continued threat of closures.

These factors, we suggest, will result in greater variability in union power across the coalfields as each local union organization is thrown upon its own resources in its bargaining with management. This could in turn make it much more difficult to achieve the wider collective action necessary to resist British Coal's policies which are responsible for such a trend. The national strikes of 1972 and 1974, therefore, may prove to be the sole examples of unified action in a long history of division within the NUM.

PART V   National Industrial Relations

9
The Return to Decline:
National Industrial Relations in Coal-mining
1974–1985

Introduction

So far in this book we have provided detailed accounts of the management of mining labour at the workplace. In this chapter and the next we want to switch our attention to the national level, to examine the evolving pattern of industrial relations within the industry as a whole. The theme which will guide this examination is the changing capacity of the NUM to exercise influence over the coal industry's strategic development. Our starting-point is the settlement secured by the union in the wake of the successful national strikes of 1972 and 1974 and the return of Labour to government. Under the terms of this settlement certain of the NUM's interests were incorporated as basic objectives of the industry. The Wilson Government gave the union effective commitments that coal would become Britain's primary source of energy, that production and investment would be expanded, that the union would become a partner in the management of coal, and that the miners would remain at the top of the industrial wages league. These assurances were to set the parameters within which the NCB was to operate.

Our finishing-point, in Chapter 10, is the settlement imposed on the union in the wake of the 1984/5 miners' strike. The essential feature of this is the removal of the last vestiges of NUM influence over the industry's strategic direction. The Conservative Government has successfully insisted that the most appropriate guides to management action in the coal industry are the commercial pressures emanating from the world energy market. Union influence which prevented the NCB responding in an unambiguous manner to these signals has been pushed backwards. The government has insisted that the coal industry must bend to the forces of the market. This has required a restructuring of labour relations in the industry and a diminution in the role of the NUM.

Our first aim in these chapters, therefore, is to describe and typify these two 'settlements'. Our second aim is to describe the process of transition from one to the other. In our view the key feature of the first settlement was that it was founded on the disruptive power of the NUM which had been revealed in the 1972 and 1974 strikes. Our account of the process of change, therefore, concentrates on the decline in the NUM's ability to compel government to treat with it and give it central consideration in the running of the industry. Much of our attention is directed toward explaining the defeat of the NUM in the 1984/5 strike. The strike must be seen as a critical turning-point in the industry's development. Before it occurred the 1974 settlement had been subject to considerable erosion. Under Norman Siddall's chairmanship, for example, the pace of colliery closure was substantially quickened. In the aftermath of the strike, though, with the NUM financially crippled and with the miners divided, management has had a much freer hand to redraw the industry. Change has been initiated at a pace and on a scale which would not have been possible if the union had not lost the pit-closure dispute.

Sectoral Corporatism: The 1974 Settlement

At the heart of the 1974 settlement was a 'political exchange' (Pizzorno, 1978) between the state and the NUM, in which the latter undertook to refrain from using its immense capacity to disrupt the economy in return for a number of procedural and substantive benefits. These included participation in tripartite deliberations over the future of the industry, an extension of the NCB's system of joint consultation, state commitment to high wages for miners, and an expansion of production by 42 million tonnes over the next decade.

The most significant procedural concession to the union was the negotiation of a tripartite agreement to determine the future of the industry. The NUM was a signatory both to the 1974 *Plan for Coal*, which established ambitious output targets for the industry, and to its later revision in 1977. Its involvement in tripartism, moreover, extended beyond the coal industry itself to embrace the entire energy sector. The union was given representation on the albeit rather ineffective Energy Commission established by Labour in 1976. Supplementing these opportunities to influence the setting of corporate objectives was a widening of consultative arrangements designed to draw the union more fully into the running of the industry. From 1972 Derek Ezra, the Board's chairman, set about extending the industry's consultative machinery. The colliery review procedure was established, giving the union the opportunity to discuss and contest pit closures. Area review meetings were later added to discuss the prospects of all pits and not simply those with difficulties. And, at national level, the National Consultative Council, introduced with nationalization, was supplemented by the setting up of a

Joint Policy Advisory Committee to discuss wider business issues such as marketing and research.[1]

The principal substantive concession to the NUM after the strikes of the early 1970s was the restoration of its external differential over other industrial workers. The Wilberforce Inquiry, called to resolve the 1972 strike, acknowledged that the miners were a special case and recommended a substantial pay award. The miners settled at a point slightly above the Inquiry's recommendation. The 1974 strike was called to re-establish the position achieved in 1972, which had been eroded by inflation and incomes policy. In its wake the miners leapt to front position in the manual workers' wages league (they had been lying thirteenth in 1971) and achieved gross earnings standing at 125 per cent of average manufacturing earnings (Lloyd, 1985, p. 5). This favourable position was maintained well into the 1980s, though it required the introduction of incentive payments in 1978 to rescue the miners' differential once more from the effects of incomes policy. According to the Report of the Monopolies and Mergers Commission (MMC, 1983, p. 275) the 'percentage relativity for 1982 [was] probably at an all-time post-nationalization high point'.

The other main substantive concession to the union was the slowing of the industry's decline. The oil crisis had transformed the coal industry's prospects and the miners were assured that the relentless abandoning of pits and exodus of labour which had characterized the 1960s were at an end. The 1974 *Plan for Coal* envisaged raising the then deep-mined output level of 113 million tonnes to 150 million tonnes by 1985. In 1977 this target was revised downwards, in a new tripartite statement *Coal for the Future*, to 135 million tonnes. The highest output figures reached in the post-1974 era, however, were 116.9 million tonnes deep-mined output and 127.2 million tonnes total output in 1974/5.

Some of the concrete effects of these commitments can be seen in Table 9.1. The first and most critical thing this shows is that the drastic run-down in the industry's manpower and number of production units was halted. Between April 1966 and April 1972 the industry closed 40 per cent of its collieries and shed 38 per cent of its labour-force. Between April 1974 and April 1979 the comparable figures were 13 per cent and 7 per cent. Thereafter, as economic and political pressure on the industry increased, the pace of colliery closure and job loss again speeded up. Between April 1979 and April 1984, 24 per cent of the industry's pits were

[1] The extension of the NUM's formal rights to participation in the management of the NCB was complemented by a closer informal integration of the union's leadership. The 1970s witnessed the growth of a strong and co-operative bargaining relationship between Joe Gormley and Derek Ezra, what was reputedly known in Whitehall as the 'Derek and Joe' show (Adeney and Lloyd, 1986, p. 74). It should also be noted that the strengthening of union participation at national level was supplemented by a strengthening of union representation in the pits. As we have seen, for example, there was an increase in paid time off work for branch officials in this period.

TABLE 9.1   Trends in coal industry manpower and number of collieries
1965–1984

	Number of collieries	Manpower 000s
1965/6	483	455.7
1971/2	289	281.5
1972/3	281	268.0
1973/4	259	252.0
1974/5	246	246.0
1975/6	241	247.1
1976/7	238	242.0
1977/8	231	240.5
1978/9	223	234.9
1979/80	219	232.5
1980/1	211	229.8
1981/2	200	218.5
1982/3	191	207.6
1983/4	170	191.5

Source: NCB 1986.

closed and 18 per cent of its labour-force shed. Much of this reduction occurred in the final year of the period when the industry was entering the crisis which produced the year-long closure dispute.

What the NUM obtained in the 1974 settlement, therefore, was a shift from a rapid to a moderate reduction in the scale of the industry. There was no cessation of pit closures even in the mid 1970s. Some were bound to occur because mining is an extractive industry. However, pits closed in this period for economic and not purely geological reasons. Langwith Colliery was closed in Derbyshire in 1976 and Teversal Colliery was closed in Nottinghamshire in 1979, for example, despite official union opposition and claims that workable reserves existed (Allen, 1981, p. 303). It must also be stressed that neither the 1974 nor the 1977 tripartite agreements on output gave the union cast-iron assurances that closures on grounds other than exhaustion would cease (Lloyd, 1985, p. 14).

It was the case, however, that the NCB operated a sensitive closure policy in the 1970s. The 1974 *Plan for Coal* envisaged the loss of about 2 million tonnes of capacity per year, to be replaced by new investment.According to Adeney and Lloyd (1986, p. 18), actual performance fell well short of this target. In part this was because new investment initiated under the *Plan for Coal* expansion programme did not produce benefits of the scale anticipated. In part, too, it was because of the industry's poor productivity record before and even after the introduction of the incentive scheme. High-cost capacity had to be kept open to meet market demand. It was also due, however, to pressure from the NUM. In its evidence to the Monopolies and Mergers Commission in 1982, the NCB reported that high-cost capacity had not been closed due to 'the necessity of maintaining good industrial relations' (MMC, 1983, p. 175). The same verdict has been given by Adeney and Lloyd (1986, p. 18), who cite the reprieve of Deep Duffryn Colliery in South Wales in 1979 as an example of union ability to influence the closure issue.

The clearest example of such influence was the strike against closures in several areas in February 1981. This forced the withdrawal of a new government target for reducing capacity by 4 million tonnes a year, and led to the release of subsidies to stockpile coal. This exertion of strength by the union produced the final and rather limited affirmation of the 1974 settlement by the British Government.

The 1974 settlement, therefore, gave the NUM greater access to management and government decision-making, and assurances about high pay and investment in greater output. There was no firm guarantee given to the union that its own policy of opposition to all pit closures on economic grounds would be adopted by the industry, but the 1970s did see a significant slowing down of the pace of closure. One reason why an assurance on pit closures was possibly not given, was that the issue was not of pressing concern at the time the 1974 settlement was reached. Although the optimistic output targets of *Plan for Coal* were never attained, the post-1974 period was one of relative buoyancy for the industry. A large investment programme had been initiated, involving the development of new pits, such as those at Selby in Yorkshire, and the updating of many existing pits. Compared to the previous decade, the prospects for coal looked good and both management and government appeared wedded to the continued provision of secure, well-paid employment in the mining industry.

The exchange with government which the NUM secured in 1974, we believe, can be accurately described as a venture in sectoral corporatism. According to Goldthorpe (1985, p. 133) the key element in the concept of corporatism, and what differentiates it from pluralism, is that private interest groups are not only 'accorded a role in the formation of public policy in areas that are of central concern to them, but are then required to assume a responsibility for the effective implementation of policies with which they have become associated'. Of particular importance here is the requirement to guarantee 'the appropriate conduct of their own memberships'.

What guarantees of membership conduct was the NUM required to give in 1974? The most important has already been mentioned. It was to refrain from using its members' collective strength in return for the recognition of its interests as legitimate objectives of the industry. In concrete terms, this meant that the NUM president, Joe Gormley, was required to control the union's powerful left wing and block its attempts to use militancy to wrest further concessions from the government. Gormley's battles with the left, however, were inextricably linked with two further requirements the government placed on the union. The first of these was that it would co-operate in raising the industry's productivity.

The second was that it would comply with the Social Contract incomes policy. Both requirements led to pressure on the union to accept the reintroduction of incentives. Management felt an incentive scheme was necessary if adequate use was to be made of capital equipment and if the ambitious output targets of *Plan for Coal* were to be seriously pursued. Incentives had been recommended by the Wilberforce Inquiry in 1972, by the Pay Board in its recommendations following the 1974 dispute, and were urged too by the tripartite authors of *Plan for Coal*. The NCB continued to urge the union to accept incentives until the successful introduction of the area incentive schemes in 1978. By that time the introduction of a self-financing productivity scheme was the only way in which the miners could continue to comply with the government's policy of wage restraint and simultaneously remain at the top of the industrial workers' earnings table at the same time. Gormley's acceptance of the area incentive schemes, therefore, was vital if the union was to fulfil its side of the 1974 settlement. Securing membership acceptance of incentives involved simultaneous delivery of union co-operation in raising productivity and with incomes policy. Indeed, it also involved compliance with the requirement to deliver industrial peace as acceptance of incentives partly fragmented the interests of miners in different pits and so reduced the chances of further national strikes over pay.

For the left opposition to Gormley such 'payments' for the 1974 settlement were intolerable. In its view a 'political exchange' with government and state managers was necessarily debilitating, involving the incorporation of the union into management and the shortening of its objectives. Throughout the period of the 1974 settlement the left urged the extension of the union's demands and continually advocated the use of industrial action to force the government into further concessions. Its starting-point was the unsatisfactory nature of the agreements achieved as a result of the 1972 and 1974 strikes. These had to be extended. Indeed, even in the 1984/5 strike, which was a primarily defensive action to retain the remnants of the 1974 settlement, Arthur Scargill continued to propose ambitious demands. His insistence, for example, that government concede that no colliery should close on grounds other than exhaustion was an enlargement of the guarantees given in 1974 and 1977.

The NUM left opposed the 1974 settlement, in the first instance, therefore, because the procedural and substantive benefits it gave to the union were too modest. One section of the left, headed by Peter Heathfield, for example, was keen to transform the industry's consultative machinery into an ambitious system of industrial democracy. It was urged that this should be based on the election of a colliery management team by all employees at the pit and that this body should have the power to appoint the colliery management, to plan production and manpower, to market output, and to set the annual budget. Although some on the left, such as Scargill, rejected the proposals as simply a more sophisticated tool of incorporation they clearly would have represented a significant shift from consultation to co-determination if they had been implemented. The scheme would have constituted the most extensive formal invasion of managerial prerogative in British industry.

The left was also critical of the substantive components of the 1974 settlement, and on this issue it spoke in unison. Throughout the 1970s the left-wing areas submitted motions calling for large increases in basic wage-rates to the union's annual conference (Allen, 1981, pp. 269–71). The left opposed the leadership's acceptance of wage restraint and advocated free collective bargaining. It also urged an expansion of the industry beyond the targets set in *Plan for Coal*. In 1974, for example, the Scottish area launched *The Miners New Charter*, a critique of *Plan for Coal*, which called for a 200 million tonne industry (Allen, 1981, pp. 285–7). The demands contained in this document became the focus of left-wing attempts to extend the 1974 settlement. In addition, the left adopted an increasingly militant line on pit closures, urging that closures on economic grounds be opposed through strike action.

The other facet of the NUM left's scepticism toward the 1974 settlement was a belief that the costs of the 'political exchange' were too high. This was illustrated clearly in its opposition to the incentive scheme. The left refused to concede that the maintenance of the Labour Government's incomes policy or the improvement of the coal industry's productivity were legitimate concerns of the union. The former threatened the miners' position in the industrial wages league, the principal fruit of the 1972 and 1974 strikes, and higher productivity was perceived either as a matter simply for management or as a threat to the work-force through its possible adverse effects on mine safety. At the core of the left's opposition to incentives, however, was the belief that the reintroduction of pit-head wage-bargaining would fragment the unity of the miners. It was believed that the union was being asked to surrender the industrial strength which had restored its fortunes and which was seen as vital for both the preservation and the extension of the 1974 settlement. The left had a keen appreciation that the union's recent gains had been extracted through industrial action and did not want to jeopardize its main source of strength. It was sceptical of the value of mutual accommodation with either management or the state. It effectively rejected a 'political exchange' with government, in which the union traded costs and benefits, in favour of the imposition of its demands through the continued use or threat of industrial action. For the NUM left the furtherance of the union's procedural and substantive interests was to be achieved not through issuing guarantees as to membership conduct but through nurturing and preserving the membership's ability to take collective action.

In the first years of the 1974 settlement, therefore, the principal threat to the accord between government, management, and union came from within the latter. The NUM left, strengthened after the strikes of the early 1970s, was committed to pressing for further concessions from the other parties to the exchange and was committed, too, to reducing the costs of exchange for the union. Tensions within the NUM, the possibility that the union's leadership would cease to be able to deliver membership acquiesence, posed the major threat to the continuance of sectoral corporatism in mining. In the 1970s this threat was contained. Joe Gormley retained a fairly tight grip over union policy, and the crucial issue of the period, the reintroduction of incentives, was resolved against the wishes of the left. By the time Gormley had been replaced as president by Arthur Scargill in 1982 and the left's control of the union was at last secured, a new threat to the 1974 settlement had emerged, one which would eventually destroy it. From 1979 the Conservative Government under Margaret Thatcher began to develop a new strategy for coal. At the heart of this strategy was a conviction that the political exchange granted by Labour to the NUM was too costly. In the 1980s it was the government which assessed the costs and benefits of the 1974 settlement negatively and it was the government's attempts to withdraw from the settlement which eventually produced the year-long strike over pit closures.

Conservative Strategy for the Mining Industry

Conservative strategy towards the coal industry has been motivated, in the first instance, by a desire to alter the relative contributions of nationalized and private sectors to the economy. Within the ideological frame of 'liberal conservatism' the NCB and its fellow public corporations are viewed as, at best, necessary evils imposing a heavy burden on the private 'productive' sector of the economy. Where state firms have been in receipt of public subsidy the Thatcher Government has sought to progressively eliminate this support until they become self-financing.[2] It has wanted a coal industry no larger than the energy market will support. It was frustrated in its first attempt to achieve this by the successful miners' strike of 1981 which led to the withdrawal of the target of a self-financing

[2] Much of this view was shared by the Labour administration of the 1970s. In 1975, for example, Tony Benn, the Energy Secretary, told the House of Commons that the government wanted to phase out subsidies to the coal industry (Lloyd, 1985, p. 14), and in 1978 Labour established the external financing limit (EFL), a ceiling on the amount each nationalized industry could borrow. The Conservatives, however, have tried to enforce a much more thoroughgoing imposition of the 'commercial paradigm' on the nationalized industries. Their concern to reduce inflation by holding down public sector borrowing has led them to elevate the EFL as 'the dominant mechanism' for controlling state firms (Heald and Steel, 1981) at the expense of longer-term economic objectives or of social objectives such as the provision of employment in depressed regions. They have also developed the 'final solution' for the nationalized industries, privatization.

industry by 1983/4. This retreat was only temporary, however, and the same target was readopted. It was the government's insistence that the NCB should stand free of state support by the end of the 1986/7 financial year that propelled the Board into a further conflict with the NUM.

A second element in Conservative strategy towards the nationalized industries arises from a deep conviction that they are repositories of inefficiency. Because state firms are frequently monopolies and because they are subsidized from the public purse, it is held that they are slow to innovate. In the view of the government, the nationalized industries in the past have not been subject to sufficient external discipline. It has attempted to rectify this situation by exposing them to market forces and to market proxies such as tight external financing limits. Measures such as these, it is hoped, will stimulate an internal process of rationalization. The same measures which have been used to reduce the burden of the state sector on the private economy are also intended to have a beneficial, though abrasive, effect on the nationalized industries themselves.

Exposure to market forces has been supplemented by two other devices designed to stimulate greater efficiency. One has been the replacement of existing nationalized industry managers, men of the stamp of Derek Exra, with figures more sympathetic to government strategy and possessed of experience in the allegedly more entrepreneurial environment of the private sector. The other has been the granting of powers to the Monopolies and Mergers Commission (MMC) to investigate nationalized industries. Both of these devices came together in the months immediately preceding the 1984/5 miners' strike, when Ian McGregor was appointed chairman of the NCB in September 1983 and declared himself committed to implementing the MMC's recommendations for the industry published three months earlier. Most prominent among these was the need for the industry to shed its tail of high-cost pits.

In Conservative eyes the major beneficiaries of shelter from competition for the nationalized industries have been powerful public-sector unions like the NUM. The burden imposed on the private sector and the inefficiencies of state firms have been traced to the coercive power of unions and their ability to insist on job security, high wages, and restrictive practices. Weak public-sector managers too often, it is felt, have acquiesced in this aggrandisement. Achieving a new balance between public and private sectors and rationalizing the nationalized industries, therefore, have been seen to require a prior challenge to the public-sector unions. The Thatcher Government had displayed a determination to roll back the influence of such groups. The 1984/5 miners' strike was only the most bitter of a series of showdowns with workers in nationalized industries, among them steelworkers, waterworkers, railway workers, and post-office workers.

This aggressive commitment to reduce union influence and establish a more unitary form of management in the nationalized industries represents a major break with previous state policy in this sector. In the past the nationalized industries have been used to demonstrate to the private sector the value of management by agreement. State firms have been required by statute to consult with representatives of their employees and have been expected to act as 'good' employers. They have been pivotal to government attempts to extend collective bargaining as the dominant form of employment regulation within Britain and, partly as a result, they have high levels of unionization and relatively formalized collective-bargaining and joint-consultation procedures.

The Thatcher government has been completely opposed to such a policy. There are two significant ironies, however, associated with its alternative of releasing the managerial prerogative from union restriction. The first is that, although the stated aim of Conservative policy is to make state industries operate more like private-sector businesses, there is some evidence that large private companies have not made use of the recession to engage in the kind of sustained assault on union influence seen in the public sector (Batstone, 1984, pp. 308–16). Indeed, there are indications that increasing numbers of private-sector firms have adopted joint consultation, a technique once primarily associated with the nationalized industries, in an attempt to foster greater internal consensus (Edwards, 1985).

The second irony is that it is government subsidy of the nationalized industries which has permitted the assault on union influence and generated the new division in labour relations between public and private sectors. The very thing which was said to encourage excessive indulgence towards labour has allowed a strong assertion of the managerial prerogative. The 1984/5 miners' strike could only be sustained by the state's ability to underwrite the costs. During the course of the dispute the Chancellor declared the colossal expense of the strike a 'worthwhile investment'. Where the costs of industrial conflict cannot be readily transferred, however, employers are likely to remain rather more cautious in their dealings with trade unions.

The Conservative Government, then, has operated with three strategic objectives towards the nationalized industries. It has attempted to eliminate public subsidy of their activities; it has attempted to stimulate a more cost-effective use of resources; and it has attempted to reduce trade-union influence over their management. Applied to the coal industry these objectives necessitated the withdrawal of the procedural and substantive concessions to the NUM which constituted the 1974 settlement.

The first objective, rapid progress toward a self-supporting and competitive industry, most obviously required the abandoning of the ambitious output targets of the *Plan for Coal* era. More significantly, however, it required the speeding up of the rate of colliery closure. This

TABLE 9.2   Coal production and consumption 1979–1983

	Production			Consumption
	Deep-mined	Open-cast	Total[a]	
1979	106.9	12.9	122.4	129.4
1980	112.4	15.8	130.1	123.5
1981	110.5	14.8	127.5	118.4
1982	106.2	15.3	124.7	110.0
1983	101.7	14.7	119.3	111.5

[a] Includes production from licenses mines.

Source: Department of Energy, 1985 Digest of UK Energy Statistics.

was so firstly because the industry in the early 1980s was facing a serious problem of over-capacity. The onset of recession in 1980 had cut the demand for electricity and hence coal. Table 9.2 shows a transition in that year from a situation where domestic production fell short of consumption to one where it exceeded it by a considerable degree. The effect of this was to swell the industry's deficit, which by 1983 stood officially at £1.3bn. (Curwen, 1986, p. 149). The problem in the government's eyes, however, was not simply one of over-production. A second reason why the requirement to achieve financial independence necessitated closures was that a large proportion of the industry's output was considered 'uneconomic'.[3] The implication of this was that imports of cheaper coal or other fuels should replace home-produced coal in supplying the domestic energy market.

The adoption of the Conservatives' first objective not only required the abandoning of the promise of expansion and practice of moderate decline, it also required wage restraint for the industry's work-force and a threat to the miners' external relativity. One of the principal purposes of tight external financing limits for the nationalized industries, according to Curwen (1986), is to restrain incomes. The report of the MMC on the industry in 1983 questioned the magnitude of miners' earnings relative to those of other workers and urged that more be done to control labour costs. Later in the year this advice was heeded by the NCB. The overtime ban which preceded the pit-closure dispute was triggered by the NUM's rejection of a 5.2 per cent pay offer which the Board refused to improve.

The application of the government's second objective, the quest for

[3] There has, of course, been considerable debate among economists over what constitutes an 'uneconomic' pit, with some contributors denying the phenomenon exists and others placing a varying proportion of the industry's production units within that category. For a useful summary of the debate see Curwen (1986). For our purposes it seems fair to assume that the Conservative Government has operated with a definition of 'uneconomic' which is unfavourable to the mining unions.

greater efficiency, also threatened the substantive concessions at the heart of the 1974 settlement. It effectively required the Board to meet its declining demand from low-cost production. The Board was encouraged to maximize output from a core of high-productivity collieries, and to close 'peripheral' pits with lower productivity. This, in turn, involved the abandoning of the practice of gradually phasing out high-cost capacity and an explicit rejection of the argument that mineable reserves should be exhausted before collieries are closed.

The final objective of the government, the reduction of union influence over the management of the nationalized industries, required the weakening of the procedural guarantees given to the NUM in 1974. Although the semblance of tripartism continued under the Conservatives, the NUM was progressively excluded from deliberations over coal's strategic direction. The 1981 industrial action by the NUM was prompted by an announcement by Derek Ezra that production had to be cut back and between twenty-five and fifty pits closed over a two-year period. The 1984/5 action was prompted, firstly, by the announcement by the South Yorkshire area of the NCB on 6 March that Cortonwood colliery should be closed on economic grounds, and, secondly, by Ian McGregor's announcement five days later that there would be a 4 million tonne cut in the planned output for 1984/5. For the NUM all three of these statements constituted unilateral withdrawals by management from the agreements inscribed in *Plan for Coal*. They represented the abandoning of the joint regulation of the industry's size and development, which had been at the heart of the 1974 settlement.

In summary, therefore, we have argued that the government, and through it NCB management, replaced the NUM left as the principal threat to the 1974 settlement in the 1980s. In part this was because the costs of that settlement had been vastly inflated by the decline in the demand for coal. It was also due to the ideological cast of the British Government with its scepticism towards the value of public enterprise and its antipathy towards trade unions. We have argued, however, that the base on which the 1974 settlement was built was the industrial power of the NUM, and it was this power which stood as the major obstacle to the Conservatives' attempts to refashion the mining industry. This was demonstrated by the government's temporary withdrawal in the face of the 1981 industrial action. Eventually, though, the government was successful in radically restructuring the industry. In 1984 the NUM was not possessed of sufficient resources of strength to compel the government to reaffirm the substantive and procedural guarantees of the previous decade. Its defeat in the strike permitted its own influence over the industry to be replaced with harsher, more strictly commercial guides to management action. It is to an attempt to explain that defeat, and the collapse of NUM strength which it embodied, that we now turn.

The 1984–1985 Strike: The Collapse of the 1974 Settlement

A useful framework for the analysis of trade-union power has been developed by Erik Olin Wright (1984). He argues that bargaining power, and strike effectiveness, can be understood as the product of two interrelated variables. The first of these he defines as 'positional power', the 'capacity to generate systemic disruption if a strike were to occur'. The second variable he calls 'organizational power'. In order for workers to exploit a strategic position within the economy they must develop effective collective organization. A position of strength, however, itself encourages this development. As Wright himself puts it, 'the disruptive potential of workers constitutes a basic determinant of the cost benefit trade offs they face in attempting to organise, form unions and engage in collective action' (p. 422). There are other independent influences on organizational capacity, however, apart from strategic position. Among the most important are the structure of collective bargaining within an industry, the structure of the trade-union movement and the ideological dispositions of trade-union leaders and their members. The miners' dispute of 1984/5 revealed a collapse in the strike effectiveness of the NUM since the triumphs of the 1970s and even since the limited victory of 1981. Wright's framework can guide an analysis of this collapse by directing examination towards changes in both the 'positional' and the 'organizational' power of the NUM.

Change in the 'Positional Power' of the NUM

The capacity of the NUM to 'generate systemic disruption' can be viewed as a function of three things: the 'centrality' of coal-mining to the national economy, the 'immediacy' with which a strike could cause disruption, and the degree of 'substitutability' of those who work within the industry

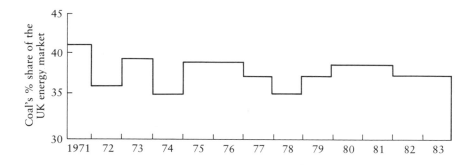

Figure 9.1.   Coal's share of the UK energy market 1971–1983

TABLE 9.3   Changes in the level of coal stocks

| Date | Coal stocks 1,000 tonnes | | | |
	NCB stocks	Consumer stocks	Total	Coal stocks as % of total inland coal consumption
Dec. 1971	10.4	21.2	31.6	22.4
Dec. 1973	10.9	17.0	27.9	21.0
Dec. 1980	17.3	20.4	37.7	31.0
Dec. 1983	23.5	34.0	57.5	52.0

Source: Department of Energy (1985), Digest of UK Energy Statistics.

(Hickson *et al.*, 1971). Figure 9.1 shows that from the early 1970s up to the 1984/5 strike the 'centrality' of coal remained more or less unchanged. The industry throughout this period supplied the economy with just over a third of its energy requirements. Indeed, the oil-price rise of 1979 led to a strengthening of coal's position relative to that of its main rival (NCB, 1984).

However, although coal remained a basic supply industry there had been a significant diminution in the 'immediacy' with which the miners could inflict disruption on the economy. Table 9.3 shows the level of coal stocks before each of the union's major confrontations with the Board in recent years.It also gives coal stocks expressed as a percentage of coal consumption in the previous year. It shows that, even without the split in the NUM ranks, the 1984/5 strike was bound to be a prolonged struggle, with the miners incurring substantial costs themselves before they could seriously damage the economy. The 'immediacy' of the miners' strength was further reduced by the fact that the strike commenced in March, when demand for energy was beginning to fall. MacGregor's decision to cut capacity and the South Yorkshire areas's announcement of the closure of Cortonwood occurred when the Board was in a very strong position to withstand a strike.

However, although the Board occupied a position of strength, the length of the strike meant that the miners could only be defeated by reducing the economy's dependence on coal. It was the ability of the Central Electricity Generating Board (CEGB), and other coal users, to switch to alternative sources of energy which led ultimately to the failure of the strike. Since the early 1970s there had clearly been an increase in the 'substitutability' of the miners, not in the sense that they themselves could be replaced but that their function within the economy could be assumed by other industries for prolonged periods.

During the strike coal was replaced as the basic fuel for electricity generation by, largely imported, oil (Wilsher *et al.*, 1985, p. 217). Oil's share of the UK energy market leapt from 33.9 per cent in 1983 to 43.3 per cent in 1984. Imported coal was also important, particularly in supplying the industrial market. Coal imports increased from 5.1 million tonnes in 1983/4 to 10.9 million tonnes in 1984/5 (NCB, 1985). Other fuels such as gas and nuclear power did not increase their share of the total energy market by great amounts during the strike itself. However, their market shares had grown significantly since 1970, and even since 1981, and so they were important to the longer-term erosion of the miners' 'positional power'.

The switch from coal- to oil-fired electricity generation was only possible because the CEGB possessed considerable excess capacity. During the strike coal-burning power stations in the heart of the striking areas simply ticked over, preserving their stocks of coal for surges in demand. Their place was taken by large, previously little used, oil-burning stations in the south, which were run at full tilt throughout the strike. The existence of such excess capacity was partly fortuitous; the recession had led to an overall reduction in the demand for electricity. However, it was also the result of deliberate planning. The CEGB had been actively discouraged from shedding its high-cost capacity by the Conservative Government because this would have increased the economy's dependence on coal. In 1982 a row with Nigel Lawson, then Energy Minister, over who would pay for the buildup of coal stocks and the maintenance of heavily uneconomic oil-burning capacity, led to the departure of Glyn England, the CEGB's chairman (Wilsher *et al.*, 1985, p. 218). He was replaced by Walter Marshall, an enthusiast for nuclear power, who shared the government's concern at 'the monopoly power of the miners' (Beynon and McMylor, 1985, p. 37). Realizing that their strategy for the mining industry threatened the NUM, the Conservatives assiduously prepared for conflict by attempting to reduce their vulnerability to strike action.

Developments in the UK energy sector, therefore, encouraged and supplemented by state contingency planning, served to erode the strength of the NUM, the main foundation upon which the 1974 settlement rested. Although the 'centrality' of coal's contribution to the national economy remained comparable to what it had been in 1974, there had been significant changes in the other determinants of the union's 'positional power'. The 'immediacy' with which the miners could effect disruption had been reduced by the buildup of coal stocks, and their 'substitutability' had been increased through the presence of spare capacity in the electricity supply industry and the ability of the CEGB to use alternative fuels for electricity generation. The significance of these developments was revealed when the long months of the pit-closure dispute failed to produce significant cuts in electricity supply.

Change in the 'Organizational Power' of the NUM

In the financial year 1984/5 the NCB produced 27.6 million tonnes of deep-mined output. Much of this was extracted by the working miners during the strike. Coal from Nottinghamshire and working pits in other areas provided the CEBG with 30 per cent of its energy requirements throughout the dispute (Wilsher *et al.*, 1985, p. 218). The coal produced by the working miners further reduced the disruptive impact of the strike and played a vital part in the NUM's defeat.

In the national strikes of the 1970s the traditionally moderate Nottinghamshire miners 'were in some respects even more uncompromising and aggressive than those of Scotland and South Wales' (Allen, 1981, p. 186). The reason for this was that the Nottinghamshire miners had suffered particularly severely from the abandonment of piece-work under the National Powerloading Agreement of 1966. Previously the industry's highest paid workers, along with the Kent miners, they had experienced a sharp erosion of earnings with the establishment of the national day-wage system. National bargaining, however, meant they could only rectify this situation through the pursuit of an industry-wide wage increase in unison with the rest of the NUM. The change in the structure of collective bargaining, initiated in 1966, attached Nottinghamshire, and other right-wing areas, securely to the national union. It greatly enhanced the NUM's 'organizational power' and permitted the cohesive actions of 1972 and 1974.

Since then there has been a return to a more fragmented system of collective bargaining with the introduction of the incentive scheme. This has been blamed for the split in the union during the 1984/5 strike by the NUM left. However, although the scheme may have frustrated the left's attempts to build a national campaign over wages in the years following its introduction, the issue in 1984 was colliery closures. The threat of closure is necessarily experienced more acutely by some groups of workers than others. It seems unnecessary to point to the decentralization of an element of pay negotiation as a source of union division when the issue at the heart of the strike itself divided miners' interests. Closure acts in a manner akin to the fragmentation of collective bargaining, though possibly the incentive scheme had a supplementary effect, weakening miners' attachment to the national union in the period before the closure issue came to a head.

Although closure split the interests of *groups* of workers in different pits and areas, there were other potent sources of division which served to detach the interests of *individuals* from those of their fellow workers. The state had provided relatively generous severance payments for those wishing to leave the industry and the NCB had committed itself to finding alternative work for those who wished to remain. There were to be no compulsory redundancies. For miners with considerable service colliery closure could be interpreted as being in their immediate interest.

In 1984, therefore, the NUM was faced with a considerable task of mobilization. Its members were aware of the relatively weak position of the union when the closure programme was announced and they were threatened by it to a variable degree. The union was asking many of them to behave altruistically, to take solidaristic action to defend the interests of other workers and distant communities. It was making this request, however, when it was already apparent that a sizeable bloc of, largely leaderless, members were alarmed at the potential costs of the left's strategy (Campbell and Warner, 1985). The narrow victory of Peter Heathfield in the election for general secretary in February 1984, for example, was achieved over a relatively unknown right-winger, John Walsh, who fought his campaign on the issue of the national union's overtime ban. It was the recognition of this dissatisfaction which guided the union's tactical choices at the beginning of the strike and led to the failure to hold a national ballot. As Jack Taylor of Yorkshire told the Nottinghamshire delegation at the Special Conference of 19 April, 'I will tell you what worries me about ballots, and I do not want to be offensive to anyone because we have got enough problems. I will tell you what is up. We don't really trust you. We don't really trust you' (Crick, 1985, p. 102).

Suspicion of the moderate areas, then, led the union leadership to decide against calling a national ballot under Rule 43 and rely instead upon a series of official area strikes under Rule 41. Areas which were not prepared to fall in with this tactic were to be picketed out by miners from those areas that were. This course of action was justified on the grounds that a ballot permitted miners in the industry's core, who were less threatened by the closure programme, to effectively vote miners in the peripheral coalfields out of a job. Underlying the decision was also a conviction that once the strike had started the 'educative' effects of conflict would come into play. A ballot would not reflect the heightened consciousness of the miners, which could only come into being through participation in the strike. If the miners could only be mobilized then they would swing behind the leadership. Mobilization, therefore, and attempts to 'picket out' the moderate areas, became the first requirement once Yorkshire had begun the strike.

This tactic failed dismally. South Wales was successfully picketed out after the majority of its pits had voted not to strike and remained the most solid area till the dispute's end, but miners in Nottinghamshire and other moderate areas were antagonized by the presence of pickets from elsewhere. The decision to spread the dispute by picketing and to dispense with a national ballot exacerbated the deep division in the union.

Balloting in the past had served as a means of resolving such divisions (Undy and Martin, 1984, p. 131). The NUM, since its foundation, had remained a federation of different areas each jealous of its autonomy. The national ballot provided a means of overcoming the fragmentation inherent in the union's structure and of binding the areas to a common policy. Because the leadership chose to dispense with the ballot in 1984 it enabled its opponents to question the legitimacy of the strike and provided them with a justification for not showing solidarity. In the first weeks of the dispute miners in Nottinghamshire and other moderate coalfields had participated in area ballots which produced votes against strike action. They were then instructed by the national leadership and by their area officials to strike nevertheless in support of other areas, such as Yorkshire, which had not held a ballot on the closure issue for three years. Considerations of self-interest rather than democratic principle may have been uppermost in the minds of those miners who continued working, but the union's tactics provided them with a powerful and principled defence.

In the course of the dispute an alternative leadership emerged to articulate the working miners' case. This was composed of previously inactive members, of experienced right-wing branch officials and of some more senior right-wingers such as Roy Lynk of Nottinghamshire. Its main challenge to the national union during the strike was through the courts. In a series of favourable hearings it obtained rulings which minimized the powers of the union's executive and conference and emphasized the rights of individual members and constituent areas (Lloyd, 1985, p. 32). The most spectacular of these was the declaration by Mr Justice Nicholls in September 1984 that the strike was 'unconstitutional'. This led to the fining of the NUM for contempt when it refused to accept the court's decision, and eventually to the sequestration of its assets. The effect of this on the actual conduct of the strike, however, was limited. The strike was not sustained by national union funds and the proclamations of judges were unlikely to dissuade committed strikers from their loyalty to the union (Harper and Wintour, 1985).

Another result of the court actions was the holding of branch and area elections in Nottinghamshire in defiance of the national leadership's instructions. This proved extremely important because it enabled the 'new right' to establish a secure hold on a vital part of the union's machinery. Having displaced the pro-strike leadership of the area the working miners were in a position to extend their rebellion. Before the strike had ended Nottinghamshire had deleted that portion of its rulebook which gave the national union the final say in disputes between them and had thus taken a considerable step towards complete independence. The failure to hold a national ballot, therefore, made it easier for those miners unwilling to incur the cost of industrial action to avoid doing so. It remains true, however, that it was only members in certain pits and areas who chose to exploit the tactical errors of the leadership and the federal structure of the

TABLE 9.4   Job loss in striking and working areas 1981–1984

| | Employment (000s) | | Absolute change % | |
	1981	1984	1981	1984
Striking areas				
Scottish	19.8	13.1	− 6.7	− 33.8
North-East	32.0	22.9	− 9.1	− 28.4
North Yorkshire	15.1	12.9	− 2.2	− 14.6
Doncaster	16.2	13.4	− 2.8	− 17.3
Barnsley	15.3	13.7	− 1.6	− 10.5
South Yorkshire	16.7	14.0	− 2.7	− 16.2
South Wales	25.3	20.2	− 5.1	− 20.6
Areas with considerable numbers of working miners				
North Derbyshire	12.2	10.5	− 1.7	− 8.4
North Notts.	18.1	16.7	− 1.4	− 7.7
South Notts.	15.5	12.6	− 2.9	− 18.7
South Midlands	16.4	12.9	− 3.5	− 21.3
Western	22.2	18.5	− 3.7	− 16.7

Source: Hudson and Sadler (1985).

union. Large numbers of miners who were not directly threatened by the Board's closure programme remained loyal to the union. Although the NCB's strategy had widened the gap between core and peripheral coalfields, this was not mirrored exactly in the division between striking and working areas. This is indicated by Table 9.4 which shows the level of job loss in the years preceding the strike in the NCB's twelve administrative units. These are divided, somewhat crudely, into those where the work-force generally supported the strike and those where there were substantial numbers of working miners.

There was strong support for the strike in three areas which had suffered relatively high job loss and which can thus be allocated to the industry's periphery, the Scottish, North-East, and South Wales Areas. There was also strong support, however, in the four Yorkshire Areas, two of which, North Yorkshire and Barnsley, had suffered relatively moderate job loss in the period before the strike. Among the 'working' areas it is perhaps not surprising that North Nottinghamshire failed to join the strike or that the drift back to work first developed in North Derbyshire. South Midlands, though, which according to the indicator is more 'peripheral' than South Wales, contained large pockets of working miners in Leicestershire, South Derbyshire, and Warwickshire. Only the militant Kent pits which were attached to this area reacted strongly to the prospect of further rationalization. South Nottinghamshire had also suffered heavy job loss and faced the prospect of further closures but its miners reacted no differently to their colleagues in the north of the county.

The areas in the first section of the table are those with traditions of left-wing leadership. Only the North-East constitutes an exception and in recent years there has been a swing to the left in a number of its pits. Among the 'working' areas the left-led North Derbyshire miners and the highly militant Kent section of the South Midlands provided most support for the strike. Clearly the ideological traditions of different areas exercised considerable influence on their propensity to join the dispute. The left areas were far more successful in persuading their members that the costs of industrial action should not be assessed instrumentally. In some cases generations of left leaders had forged a potent 'collective identity' for the membership which demanded loyalty to the union and sacrifice in the interest of solidarity. The left's conception of leadership and its style, with its emphasis on mobilization, increased its own 'organizational power'. In the right-wing areas, where the leadership has emphasized accommodation and the pursuit of limited goals through negotiation, the union proved less able to appeal to the altruism of its members. Indeed, leaders failed to mobilize men in pits directly threatened with closure.

In assessing the decline in the NUM's 'organizational power' since 1974, therefore, we have emphasized three factors. In the first place, the nature of the issue at the heart of the 1984 dispute, pit closures, served to divide the interests of workers in different pits. We do not believe the reintroduction of local incentive pay-bargaining was critical as the union's leadership has argued, but note that the issue of closure acted in a manner identical to a shift in the level of bargaining in fragmenting miners' interests. In the second place, we have emphasized the structure of the NUM, the fact that it is a federation whose constituent areas both in practice and in law retain considerable autonomy. It was the tactical choice of the NUM leadership, however, not to hold a national strike ballot, which permitted the union's federal divisions to find expression in the course of the dispute. The third factor, which we believe, was important was the tradition of union leadership in the different coalfields. Some area and branch leaders were more successful than others in persuading their members not to assess the costs of industrial action in purely instrumental terms: they had accumulated a greater reserve of membership loyalty upon which they could draw. However, what factors lie, in turn, beneath these differing leadership traditions we are not in a position to say. It could be due to differences in community structure. Marsden, for example, has put this forward as a reason to explain the dogged solidarity of the South Wales miners (1986, p. 79). It could also be due to different histories of work organization in the various coalfields, a factor emphasized by Krieger (1984). We are conscious, therefore, that our own attempt to explain the decline of the NUM's 'organizational power' is both limited and partial.

Failure to Borrow the 'Positional' and 'Organizational' Power of Other Unions

Since the 1970s, therefore, there has been a decline in both the 'positional' and the 'organizational' power of the NUM. For this reason the union was particularly dependent in 1984 on its ability to generalize its conflict with the state and draw on the resources of other groups of workers. Its leadership, however, was extremely jealous of the union's autonomy and so attempted to prevent the involvement of the Trades Union Congress (TUC). Mindful of the TUC's role in bringing recent rail and printing disputes to a close, and mindful too of its role in the General Strike, Scargill preferred to rely on assistance from individual, left-wing allies. After six months of the strike the NUM was at last driven to seek help from the TUC; before then it had relied primarily on the support of the left-led transport unions.

These did lend assistance. The seamen's union, the rail unions and the Transport and General Workers Union (TGWU), all refused to handle coal. Such action reached a peak with the calling of a two-week dock strike in July 1984 over the use of non-registered labour at Immingham. The 'positional power' of these unions, however, also proved insufficient to sway the conflict decisively in the NUM's favour. The work of their members was as replaceable as that of the striking miners. Coal and oil were carried to Britain in foreign-crewed ships for unloading at small, poorly organized ports. The output of the working coalfields was ferried to the power-stations in convoys of lorries which neutralized the secondary action on the railways.

Though the transport unions did provide industrial support, sections of their membership refused to comply with the instruction to support the miners. The 'organizational power' of the NUM's allies had also declined since 1972 and 1974. The ban on the movement of coal by rail was never absolute and large numbers of TGWU drivers participated in the movement of coal by road. The national dock strike effectively ended with a repudiation of the action by dockers at Dover and a second dock strike, called in August, met with an extremely patchy response.

The inability of union leaders sympathetic to the NUM to deliver support became most apparent after the TUC conference in September 1984. This voted by ten to one to give financial support for the miners and to urge all unions not to handle coal or coke or oil substituted for coal. Financial support was forthcoming and was important in sustaining the NUM's picketing operation and the strikers' families. The offer of practical assistance, however, proved hollow. There was no significant increase in secondary action after the TUC decision. Partly this was due to opposition to the policy from the leaders of the Electrical, Electronic Telecommunication, and Plumbing Union and the Engineers' and Managers' Association who organize powerful groups of workers in electricity supply. The main reason, though, was that rank-and-file members were unwilling to translate the declarations of their leaders into effective action.

This, in turn, was largely due to the failure of the NUM's 'organizational power'. It is customary for workers only to take secondary, supportive action when they are presented with a strong justification for their doing so. A strong moral argument has to outweigh the costs of giving support. It is usual, for instance, for support to be withheld if the group requesting it is divided (Kahn et al., 1983, p. 57). Not only was the NUM divided, it had failed to remain true to its own tradition and hold a national strike ballot. It was not in a strong position to argue for support. Its inability to get all of its own members out on strike provided an opportunity for other groups of workers to escape from the demand for solidarity. It was also important that the costs for many workers, from whom the NUM did request support, were by no means insignificant. Lorry-drivers moving Nottingham coal faced the prospect of losing large wage-packets; railway workers faced discipline and suspension; while steelworkers feared the further contraction of their own industry. Recession had induced caution in the rank and file.

A final influence which reduced the NUM's ability to borrow the strength of others was the tactical finesse of its opponent. The government encouraged the employers of possible allies of the miners not to do anything which might provoke secondary action. It intervened on several occasions to ensure the isolation of strikers. In the first weeks of the strike it prevailed upon Ian McGregor not to use its own trade-union legislation and proceed with an action against the NUM's Yorkshire Area (Wilsher et al., 1985, pp. 68–9). The government was concerned lest this strengthen the NUM's moral case for support both from its own members and from other unions. The government also ensured that relatively favourable settlements were given to workers who threatened to make common cause with the miners. At its insistence British Rail increased its 1984 pay offer to head off the challenge of a rail strike, and the dock strikes ended with at least the reaffirmation of the Dock Labour Scheme. Most significant, however, was the NACODS dispute in October 1984. When the NACODS membership voted by 80 per cent to take strike action, the NCB, under strong government pressure, withdrew its threat to discipline supervisors who failed to cross NUM picket lines and agreed to negotiate a modified colliery review procedure.

'Solidarity through Force'

Given the inability of the NUM to induce solidarity from all but its most loyal supporters, it turned to what Allen has described as 'solidarity through force' (1981, p. 194). The union attempted to use force of numbers to blockade working pits and other key installations to prevent the entrance of both labour and materials. Mass picketing was directed first of all at working collieries, particularly in Nottinghamshire. After some early successes it proved ineffective and the pickets were then directed primarily at the steel industry. The union saw choking off the supply of steel to the economy as the best means of achieving a rapid conclusion to the dispute. Again, it was unsuccessful. The steel industry actually exceeded its output target during the strike and the union's failure was illustrated graphically by the police rout of pickets at Orgreave. In the final months of the dispute mass picketing was directed chiefly at the strikers' own pits in a largely futile attempt to stem the flow back to work.

The reason for these repeated failures was the massive police operation mounted to counter picketing. The scale and effectiveness of this operation clearly took the NUM by surprise. Jack Taylor admitted in March 1984 that 'the establishment has learned more since the 1972 and 1974 strikes. The criticism you can hold against the union is that we did not learn enough. If you asked me three weeks ago if the police would behave in the numbers and manner in which they have I would have laughed' (Harper and Wintour, 1985).

The miners were the victims of their own history. The romance of Saltley Gates, the belief that mass picketing could overwhelm the forces of the state, led them to rely on the methods which had gained victory in the 1970s. Since then, however, police tactics for the maintenance of public order have altered considerably. Two developments proved most significant. The first was greater co-ordination between police forces. This was achieved through the National Reporting Centre (NRC). Set up as a direct response to Saltley, the NRC was able to mobilize large numbers of police from virtually every force in the country and direct them to points vulnerable to picketing. The second was the militarization of police tactics and training which had been intensified after the 1981 inner-city riots. This was intended to raise the capability of the police to maintain order without recourse to military aid (Kahn et al., 1983, pp. 76–7). Its result was seen in the use of cavalry charges, riot gear, and snatch squads to control pickets. Other significant developments were the widespread use of road-blocks to prevent pickets reaching working collieries and the issuing of highly restrictive bail conditions to thousands of arrested miners to prevent them rejoining the picket lines. The actions of the police, and of the criminal courts, were ruthless and occasionally brutal and provided ample evidence of the Thatcher Government's preparedness to rely on forceful solutions to social conflict; and that the emergence of a strong state has been integral to the attempt to 'liberalize' the British economy.

In the 1972 and 1974 strikes the NUM had waged a successful 'war of movement'. The union's own considerable 'positional power' had been supplemented by the effective use of flying pickets to halt the movement of coal, oil, and other strategic industrial materials. The miners had carried their dispute out of the coalfields and into the economy at large. In 1984, however, when the union's positional and organizational weakness rendered it even more dependent on this tactic, the state had developed the ability to neutralize picketing. The pickets were contained and eventually forced back to the coalfields and the strike developed into a war of attrition. It was sustained, on the union side, by funds from other unions, by public donations, and by the mobilization of the coalfield communities behind the strikers. Without industrial strength, however, the fortitude and sacrifice were bound to be in vain.

10

The Post-strike Settlement: Industrial Relations in Coal-mining 1985–1988

Introduction

Since the 1984/5 strike British Coal has moved rapidly to restructure the industry. With the strength of the NUM in ruins there have been few barriers to management effecting the implementation of much of the Conservative Government's strategy for the industry. In this final chapter we want to describe the main elements of the new settlement between management and unions which has emerged in the wake of the dispute. Where the key feature of the 1974 settlement was 'sectoral corporatism', the inclusion of the NUM in a great deal of management decision-making, the defining characteristic of the post-strike settlement has been the exclusion of the union from influence. At all levels there has been a reduction of union participation in the process of decision-making, though the decline has been most marked at the strategic, national level.

The End of Tripartism

In 1974 the power of the NUM had permitted it to obtain tripartite agreements on output and the overall size of the industry. The collapse of its power has permitted government and management to dispense with this form of regulation and set new, explicitly financial objectives for the industry without prior consultation with the union. Coal's intermediate target has been set by the Coal Industry Act of 1986 which has charged the industry with breaking even by 1989. This external financial pressure has been translated into rigorous internal financial targets. Since the strike, British Coal has adopted a new set of 'management rules' to guide manpower and investment decisions. Its reformulated objectives are now expressed in terms of production costs per gigajoule, a metric measure of heat value which takes account of the differing qualities of coal produced. All collieries have been required to reduce their operating costs to a level below £1.65 per gigajoule in 1985 money values. Those failing to do so have become candidates for closure. The NUM were informed of the adoption of these new 'management rules' at a Joint Policy Advisory

Committee on 15 October 1985. They were also informed that the new framework of objectives would not be a matter for negotiation.

The demise of tripartite regulation of the industry's objectives has been accompanied by the withdrawal of other procedural concessions to the NUM. In the latter part of Ian MacGregor's chairmanship, for instance, the process of national consultation with the unions was effectively suspended. Sir Robert Haslam, MacGregor's successor, has reversed this decision and inaugurated his period as chairman by meeting the full executive of the NUM. The close ties between management and union which existed in the 1970s, however, appear to be at an end. In addition, the NUM's monopoly of representation of the industry's manual workers in its consultative and conciliation machinery has been broken. In May 1986 the Board unilaterally withdrew the industry's existing negotiation and conciliation machinery, which had been in place since nationalization. It proposed in its stead separate pay negotiations for the NUM and UDM at national level and a new joint consultative machinery which would embrace both unions. In addition the Coal Industry Act of 1986 provided the UDM with rights to representation on the national joint committees which oversee the industry's social welfare, benevolent, and pension funds.

In one area, however, the 1984/5 strike ostensibly led to a strengthening of the provisional rights of the NUM and of the other coal industry unions. The only collective agreement to result from the dispute was the amendment to the Colliery Review Procedure, negotiated with NACODS in the autumn of 1984. NACODS' intention was to strengthen the formal capacity of the industry's unions to contest pit closures by establishing an independent appeal body as the final stage of the Colliery Review Procedure. As the strike had arisen over the Coal Board's insistence that management must have the freedom to restructure the industry in accordance with political and economic imperatives this appeared to be a significant compromise. If the NUM had joined with NACODS in accepting this agreement in October 1984, before its defeat, then a revised procedure might well have proved an effective brake on the closure programme. Without the NUM's industrial muscle to back it up, however, British Coal has been able to escape from the implications of the NACODS deal. In the immediate aftermath of the strike, for instance, the Board closed several pits without recourse to the review procedure on the grounds that they had suffered such deterioration during the dispute that no useful production could take place. It withdrew from this position under the threat of an overtime ban from NACODS but it did not agree the form of the independent appeal body with the unions until October 1985 and attempted to narrow its terms of reference so as to exclude from consideration the social costs of pit closure. When the independent appeal body has recommended that pits be kept open on social grounds, as happened for example with Cadeby Colliery near Doncaster, British Coal

TABLE 10.1   Trends in coal industry manpower and number of collieries
1981–1987

	Number of collieries	Men on colliery books (000s)
1981/2	200	218.5
1982/3	191	207.6
1983/4	170	191.5
1984/5	169	175.4
1985/6	133	154.5
1986/7	110	125.4
1987/8	94	104.4

Source: British Coal (1988).

has disregarded its advice, arguing that management must retain the final decision as to whether or not a pit should be closed.

Closures and Reductions in Output

Overall, therefore, there has been a considerable curtailing of the NUM's rights to participate in the industry's management at national level. This, in turn, has been associated with the withdrawal of several substantive concessions at the heart of the 1974 settlement. The most significant of these has been the abandoning of any explicit output target. Output has been allowed to decline sharply to achieve a more even balance with demand and to bring the industry closer to its break-even objective. Deep-mined output fell from 104.9m. tonnes in 1982/3 to 82.4m. tonnes in 1987/8 (British Coal Corporation 1988). This has been achieved principally through pit closures and has been accompanied by large-scale redundancies. Moreover, both of these trends have been intensified by the sharp increase in productivity in the industry since the strike, which has permitted demand to be satisfied from fewer pits. Table 10.1 shows the steep decline in the number of pits and the number of employees since the strike's end.

The table clearly shows a return to the accelerated decline of the industry which marked the 1960s and the abandoning of the state's commitment to preserve mining employment. The adoption of the costs per gigajoule target is particularly significant in this regard because it recognizes that colliery closure should be decided on explicitly economic grounds. In the years since the strike the industry has largely lost its tail of high-cost pits, with seventy-five collieries being closed, 44 per cent of the 1984/5 total. The equivalent figures for manpower were a loss of 71,000 or 40 per cent. In its evidence to the Parliamentary Select Committee on Energy the NCB expressed its hope that the worst of the closure and redundancy programmes was over and that the industry could look forward to a less traumatic period of change. The Committee, however, felt this was unduly optimistic; that financial pressure, the replacement of old with new capacity, and the introduction of new technology could well lead to additional closures and heavy job losses. Coal's downward spiral away from the expansionist vision of 1974 may therefore continue into the 1990s.

Changes in Wage-bargaining

The other major substantive concession of the 1974 settlement concerned miners' wages. It was accepted by the state that, owing to the dangers and economic importance of miners' work, they be treated as a special case and remain pre-eminent in the table of manual workers' earnings. Face-workers have retained this position. The 1986 New Earnings Survey revealed that in the year following the strike coal-miners remained the highest paid group of non-supervisory male manual workers. Despite this fact there have been significant changes since the strike in the wages settlements given to the miners. The annual increase in basic rates for both the NUM and the UDM has been modest, below 5 per cent in 1985, 1986, and 1987. The proportionate increase in the standard incentive payment has been greater, however, and there has also been the introduction of attendance and 'conciliation' bonuses. Partly as a result of this the proportion of miners' pay composed of incentive earnings has increased and according to New Earnings Survey data reached its highest level since the reintroduction of incentives in 1986.

Increased reliance on incentive payments to maintain the external relativity of face-workers is likely to have two further consequences. Firstly, it will continue to produce variation in face-workers' earnings between pits and areas though the closure of low productivity collieries which tended to provide lower incentive payments has probably acted to contain differentiation in the pay of face-workers. Secondly, it will produce a widening of internal differentials within collieries as existing incentive agreements are primarily designed to reward the direct labour force at the coal-face. At the time of the 1974 settlement in mining the NUM was successfully operating a solidaristic wages policy in which standard day-wage rates existed for each grade of mineworker and in which differentials between the coal-face and other groups remained limited. This solidaristic policy suffered its first setback with the introduction of the incentive scheme in 1977/8. In the wake of the miners' strike it has all but collapsed. Face-workers continue to be well paid in many pits but British Coal is moving deliberately towards a more differentiated pay structure. Direct production workers, who remain crucial to the industry's economic success, are being rewarded relatively generously, while those whose contributions are more peripheral are experiencing a decline in relative income.

However, not only has the structure of miners' wages been altered as a result of the strike, there has also been a significant shift in the manner in which wage settlements have been arrived at. This has been most apparent in the Board's dealings with the NUM. In the first place management has attempted to tie the annual wage increase to the yielding of significant concessions by the union. Since the strike British Coal has attempted to link the annual wage increases for NUM members to an acceptance by the union that incentives should form a larger component of pay, to an agreement that strikers should incur a loss of pension benefits, to the introduction of new negotiating machinery which would include the UDM, and to the acceptance of the Board's new disciplinary code. The second change in the manner in which pay settlements have been concluded has been a readiness on the part of management to impose its proposals without agreement. The NUM has not negotiated an annual wage settlement with the Board since 1982, and in the years since the strike British Coal has unilaterally extended settlements agreed with the UDM to cover NUM members.

Even in the area of pay, therefore, where miners have retained some of the achievements of the 1970s, there have been significant changes since the end of the pit closure strike. Substantively there has been a reinforcement of the trend to payment by results which will widen existing differentials in miners' earnings. And in procedural terms there has been a considerable hardening of the Board's negotiation stance with a determination on its part to link annual pay settlements to the yielding of concessions by the unions and a preparedness to dispense with negotiation if these are not forthcoming.

Weakening Mining Trade-unionism

The effective abandoning by the state and by British Coal management of the last vestiges of the 1974 settlement has been one feature of the new industrial relations in coal.[1] In large part this has amounted to the removal of NUM influence over the strategic direction of the industry. A second feature of the post-strike settlement in coal has been an attempt by management to ensure that the NUM should find it difficult to reacquire such

---

[1] This process may not stop with the abandoning of the 1974 settlement but may also extend to the abandoning of the 1947 settlement in mining which transferred the pits into public ownership very largely at the miners' insistence. Since the end of the pit strike there have been repeated calls for the privatization of British Coal. These have been endorsed by Sir Robert Haslam, the company's chairman, and by Sir Peter Walker, the Energy Secretary, while the Tory-dominated Parliamentary Select Committee on Energy has recommended the expansion of private mining and urged British Coal to develop joint investment projects with the private sector.

influence. As union influence over the industry in the 1970s was built on the disruptive potential of strike action by the miners this has led British Coal management to consciously attempt to reduce the 'organizational power' of mining trade-unionism. In the past sixteen years the coal industry has experienced three national strikes together with a near national strike in 1981. Particularly in the period of Arthur Scargill's presidency the militant stance of the NUM has meant that major industrial action has been a contingency that management has had continually to be prepared for. Even since the defeat of the NUM in the 1984/5 dispute its leadership has continued to urge strike action against closures and over pay and flexible shifts, and between September 1987 and March 1988 a rather ineffective national overtime ban was instituted in response to the Board's introduction of the new disciplinary code. Given this situation, attempting to reduce the ability of the NUM to mount effective strike action has not surprisingly been a major consideration of management policy.

The most significant decision management has taken with respect to weakening mining trade-unionism has been the recognition of the UDM. This has confirmed the division in mining unionism which appeared in 1984. In the region of 30,000 mineworkers are now members of a recognized trade union which was formed out of a deliberate repudiation of Scargill's militancy. The UDM has adopted a constitution which makes the initiation and continuance of official industrial action difficult and a major theme of statements by its leadership has been the need to develop more stable industrial relations in coal. It has reassured its own membership that it will not lightly ask them to absorb the costs of collective action and has expressed a kind of 'war-weariness' among mineworkers, a rejection of the uncertainties of the period of Scargill's leadership of the national union with its incessant appeals for mobilization against the Board. The new union, therefore, has offered management the prospect of developing more predictable industrial relations in which continual challenge to management would be eschewed in favour of stability. It has also offered management a potential strike-breaking force in the event of Scargill successfully persuading the NUM to reopen the fight against pit closures.[2]

---

[2] The UDM has offered management more than a division of the national union. In the first flush of its existence some believed it offered the prospect of replacing the NUM, with its militant tradition, with a moderate alternative. The idea that the breakaway could ever replace the national union, as the dominant force within the industry though, was surely based on an underestimation of the depth of the loyalty many miners offer to the NUM. After all, the majority of British miners had faithfully stuck by the union's leadership throughout the longest strike in its history; and while some disillusion with that leadership has been evidenced since the union's defeat, the idea that miners would flock to a new union endorsed by the very managers and politicians they had been striking against was never very credible. Those who believed the UDM could overhaul the national union have committed a classic unitarist error in discussion of industrial conflict—they have seen strike action as the work simply of a minority of activists, who successfully cajoled or bullied a moderate and loyal work-force into following the militant path.

A further means through which British Coal has attempted to reduce the 'organizational power' of mining trade-unionism has been the encouragement of a more decentralized pattern of industrial relations. Since the miners' strike there have been several moves to reduce the importance of national negotiations in favour of local agreements. This can be viewed as an extension of the trend towards more decentralized collective bargaining which first emerged with the negotiation of the Area Incentive Schemes in 1977/8. The recognition of the UDM, with its consequent removal of large numbers of miners from the coverage of agreements negotiated by the national union, is itself one example of this development. Another is the introduction of new, local incentive schemes in Yorkshire and the Midlands, which was discussed in Chapter 4. A third example is the attempt by the Board to break existing national agreements on hours of work, which was revealed most clearly in the stipulation that Margam Colliery in South Wales would only be developed if the South Wales NUM agreed to six-day working.

The encouragement of more decentralized industrial relations springs from several motives. Making it more difficult for the NUM to achieve broad support among miners for national strike action, however, is arguably one of the most important. Local agreements which produce variation in miners' conditions of employment create differences of interest among union members, while local negotiations which multiply the points of access to management decision-making create alternative means for realizing objectives to reliance on the national union. There have already been significant instances of the more decentralized pattern of industrial relations in coal frustrating attempts by the NUM's national leadership to co-ordinate opposition to management policies. For example, the attempt to preserve the forty-year-old five-day-week agreement in the face of management proposals for six-day working ran into difficulty when the South Wales area agreed to comply with management's conditions for the development of Margam. British Coal's offer of local negotiations was crucial in this case.

While the movement towards more decentralized industrial relations is important in fragmenting the interests of miners' representatives, it can also hinder NUM attempts to reacquire influence over the industry in another way. If collective bargaining is increasingly confined to pit and area level then this will serve to exclude the union from access to those senior managers controlling the overall direction of the industry. The decentralization of collective bargaining can, therefore, be seen as the obverse of management's and government's attempts to reduce the procedural rights of the union at the industry's centre. British Coal appears to have deliberately altered the structure of collective bargaining in order to marginalize the unions, to confine their role to the negotiation of wages and conditions within the context of an overall business strategy devised by the government and by management itself.

Although the recognition of the UDM and other moves to decentralize industrial relations have been the main methods used to reduce the 'organizational power' of mining trade-unionism, there have been other methods. One of these has been the introduction of financial penalties for striking. Members of the NUM who strike for more than two weeks are now required to make up lost contributions to the miners' pension scheme or else incur reduced benefits. In addition, as a result of the Board's 1986 wage awards for both the UDM and the NUM, all miners are now entitled to quarterly 'conciliation' bonuses of £25 provided they do not go on strike. This is particularly intended to discourage small, unofficial walkouts which management claims have an adverse effect on productivity and customer confidence. The industry's new disciplinary code, which strengthens the disciplinary powers of the colliery manager, is intended to have a similar effect. All of these measures are designed to raise significantly the costs of industrial action for individual mineworkers and so reduce the propensity to follow leadership calls for collective action. Just as the decentralization of collective bargaining is intended to fragment the interests of *groups* of miners in different pits and coalfields, so these measures are designed to fragment the interests of *individual* miners.

The final, and perhaps the crudest way in which management has tried to reduce the 'organizational power' of mining trade-unionism has been through altering the character of union leadership. There have been several attempts to replace union militants with leaders less committed to mobilizing the work-force against management's policies. The support given to working miners during the 1984/5 strike and to the breakaway union in its aftermath is one example of this. Another has been the sacking of union activists for their actions during the pit-closure dispute. In the Board's Scottish area, where the toughest line on sackings was adopted by management, it has been estimated that two-thirds of those sacked were NUM branch officials (Sutherland, 1985). A third example of this kind has been initiated by the Conservative Government and has as its target the NUM's national leadership. The 1988 Employment Act has changed the law to require all members of union national executives to stand for re-election every five years. This means that non-voting executive members, like Arthur Scargill, who were exempt from previous legislation, will have to put themselves to the test of a membership ballot. The government's motive in changing the law seems to arise from a belief that union members will repudiate militant leaders of Scargill's stamp if they are given the opportunity to do so. To pre-empt the legislation Scargill stood for re-election in January 1988 and was returned to office, though with a smaller majority than when he was elected NUM president. The Employment Act has been so framed, however, that he will have to stand for election a third time before he retires.

Flexibility and Decentralization of Collective Bargaining

So far we have discussed the post-strike settlement in terms of the exclusion of the NUM from strategic influence over the industry's development and in terms of management and government attempts to confirm that exclusion. Management's post-strike policy has been described as an attempt to confine union access to decision-making at lower levels of the industry and to decisions covering only the traditional, limited agenda of collective bargaining. A further element of the post-strike settlement, however, has concerned this traditional, limited area of miners' pay and conditions. Since the strike British Coal has initiated a number of changes in the system of collective agreements and legal regulations which govern the use of mining labour. The purpose in all cases has been to release management from constraints on the flexible deployment of the work-force. It has been argued at several points in this book that concern about low productivity and the insufficient exploitation of existing capital investment have been among the principal guides of management's industrial relations policy over the past two decades. The defeat of the NUM in the pit-closure dispute has been viewed by management as an opportunity to improve performance by pushing back some of the controls on the use of labour which the union has secured in the past. Such 'deregulation', it is hoped, will secure better use of capital equipment and hence a more cost-effective industry.

Since the end of the strike there have been a number of instances of management attempting to rewrite, replace, or subvert existing collective agreements regulating the use of labour. One example, has been the amending of the 1978 incentive scheme in several coalfields in order to provide a sharper incentive for face and development workers. There have also been the proposals for six-day, twenty-four-hour working at Margam and other new developments. This would involve abandoning the industry's national, five-day-week agreement. Another area of change has been flexible working. Without seeking the formal agreement of the mining unions British Coal introduced a programme of multi-skill training for craft trainees at the industry's ten regional workshops in 1986. The Board has expressed an intention to extend this venture into flexible working into the pits. There are likely to be moves towards the introduction of multi-skilled craftworkers underground and the devolution of some routine maintenance functions to face-workers. Ultimately, changes on these lines would involve the revision of existing agreements on training and on the industry's grade structure.

In addition to seeking the relaxation of collective agreements management has also experessed a desire to have the legal regulations governing the use of labour in mining altered. The introduction of more intensive twenty-four-hour mining, for instance, would require the lengthening of miners' shifts and the repeal of those parts of the 1908 Mines Act which limit the period miners spend underground to seven and a half hours. The Board has also petitioned the Health and Safety Executive to back changes in the regulations governing the industry. It has proposed a rewriting of the 1954 Mines and Quarries Act which would reduce the volume of regulations governing mine safety and permit greater flexibility in the deployment of the work-force underground.

An important feature of several of these changes in miners' employment conditions has been a drive to replace existing national agreements either with new local agreements more suited to management's purposes or with less precise national regulations which provide greater scope for local adaptation. One reason for this preference for change through decentralization is that the national leadership of the NUM has proved a reluctant negotiating partner. It has reacted with hostility to most of the Board's proposed changes. Arthur Scargill, for instance, has remained committed to abolishing payment by results, has advocated a retention of the five-day-week agreement, and has condemned the proposed alterations in mine safety. Given this policy British Coal has bypassed the national union and negotiated local agreements with the UDM and with individual NUM areas and branches. For a variety of reasons these alternative bargaining partners have looked more favourably on the Board's proposals to achieve greater flexibility in the use of labour. The Nottinghamshire and South Derbyshire coalfields, for instance, the main bases of the UDM, have long been supporters of piece-work, and the breakaway union has continued this tradition in showing its preparedness to accept an increase in the incentive element of its members' wages. Within Yorkshire and North Derbyshire, despite official policies of opposition to payment by results, local NUM representatives have also been prepared to countenance the negotiation of new incentive schemes. One reason for this was undoubtedly fear of competition from the breakaway union in the first year of its existence. Another reason, though, was suggested to us by a senior industrial relations manager at Hobart House. He said that local NUM officials in the wake of the return to work were 'grateful for any negotiations at all', and were prepared to concede to the requests of managers for changes in the incentive scheme.

Similar feelings of insecurity prompted the leadership of the South Wales NUM to accept the principle of six-day working at Margam. The union here was faced with the choice of negotiating a local agreement on management's terms or seeing the possible withdrawal of the Margam project with its promise of 800 mining jobs and the creation of other employment in the depressed South Wales economy. There was also the possibility of another union agreeing to provide labour for the new pit if the NUM refused to co-operate.

A feature of the Margam case has been conflict between the national union leadership and the South Wales area, not just over the content of union policy but over the respective rights of each level to concede major changes in miners' terms and conditions. The South Wales area has contended that Margam is a local issue while the national leadership has argued that departures from the five-day-week agreement affect all mineworkers and so must be negotiated centrally. Divisions of this kind must be seen as an inevitable consequence of the Board's attempt to change the locus of collective bargaining and will probably continue to occur.

While bypassing the national leadership of the NUM has been an important tactical reason for British Coal seeking to achieve flexibility through local agreements, there is a further and more fundamental reason. This is that the move towards more decentralized industrial relations form part of a broader policy of devolving the managerial power of decision in the industry. The structure of industrial relations has been altered as part of a more general refashioning of the structure of management. This was originated before the outbreak of the pit-closure dispute by Ian MacGregor, who instituted a process of divisionalization in the industry, reducing the size of the headquarters staff and encouraging the industry's geographical areas to operate to a greater extent as separate businesses. In the aftermath of the dispute this trend has continued with a further devolution of responsibility to individual colliery managers. One reason for this was that it was felt colliery managers had to be given a wide degree of discretion to try and restore production in the wake of the strike. A second reason was the introduction of the new system of financial control for the industry. This strengthened and simplified the industry's system of management objectives, by replacing a number of different performance criteria for colliery managers with one, principal financial objective, controlling costs per gigajoule. In pursuing this objective it was considered that colliery managers should exercise as much control as possible over the determinants of colliery financial performance and this, in turn, was recognized to require a widening of their field of decision-making.

This increase in the scope of colliery managers' decision-making has included industrial relations. It has been recognized by senior management that the industry's framework of national agreements and legal regulations can restrict local managers in achieving a more effective use of the labour force. Accordingly, both colliery and area managers have been permitted to negotiate new agreements which are tailored to local conditions and which can facilitate flexible working. Sir Robert Haslam speaking of the Board's policy on incentives, for example, has said, 'We want to give areas the flexibility to introduce a whole range of incentives tailored to the needs of pits, units within pits and individuals' (*Financial Times*, 7 Oct. 1986). The weakness of the NUM, in particular, has largely ensured that such local departures from the national framework have occurred on terms favourable to management.

There has been a shift, therefore, from a situation in which local managers were largely responsible for applying existing agreements to one in which they have been granted the freedom to negotiate new agreements which increase management's ability to direct the labour force and facilitate low-cost production. The introduction of new local incentive schemes is one example of this shift. Another is the interest of several British Coal areas in negotiating local agreements on hours of work which would match shift patterns more closely to the requirements of production in particular coalfields. A third is management's proposal for new safety procedures which would enable colliery managers to devise their own set of safety regulations provided these complied with broad principles set out by the Health and Safety Commission.

Just as the switch to more local bargaining has had ramifications for the internal politics of the unions, so it has affected the internal organization of management. It has been associated with a downgrading of the role of specialist industrial relations managers in British Coal and a concentration of the managerial power of decision in this area in the hands of line management. One example of this change was given in Chapter 4. The central monitoring of local pay-bargaining has been abandoned. Another example is that the right of the industrial relations department to attend formal accountability meetings for area directors, and other line managers, has been withdrawn. A third example is that where new incentive schemes have been negotiated this has been done by colliery managers, not by industrial relations staff, and the final agreements have been authorized by line managers at area level. Although it would be wrong to overemphasize the centrality of the industrial relations function in the period of the 1974 settlement (Heery, 1985), there has clearly been a decline in recent years. This was readily acknowledged by those industrial relations managers we interviewed in 1987. The decentralization of collective bargaining in the industry since the miners' strike has involved the relegation of industrial relations staff to a reduced and more definitely advisory role.

Restoring 'Normal' Industrial Relations

Although the dominant features of the post-strike settlement in mining have been the rolling back of union influence over the industry and the conscious redrawing of its pattern of industrial relations by management, we would not like to exaggerate either of these trends. The unions in coal have not been utterly supine since the end of the 1984/5 strike and management's actions have been subject to a degree of contestation. The final element of the post-strike settlement that we want to discuss is based on an appreciation of these facts by management itself. Particularly since Sir Robert Haslam was appointed chairman there has been a conscious attempt to rebuild 'normal' industrial relations in coal. This has had two components. In the first place there has been an attempt to resolve those legacies of the miners' strike which continue to cause rancour and disruption in the industry's industrial relations. In the second place there has been an attempt to induce acceptance by the NUM of the new coal industry which has emerged since the strike and of its own place within it. The final element of the post-strike settlement, therefore, has been a deliberate attempt on management's part to stabilize the industry after the turmoil of the mid 1980s.

The legacy of the strike which has perhaps caused most bitterness is the issue of sacked miners. Since the end of the dispute the NUM has continued to campaign for the reinstatement of those men who lost their jobs during the dispute, and there has been sporadic industrial action over the issue. The response of British Coal has been to offer to re-employ, not reinstate, those miners who had been dismissed for relatively minor offences. Of an estimated 1,014 men dismissed for strike-related actions, about two-thirds have been offered re-employment in an attempt to restore the Board's reputation with its work-force as a fair and reasonable employer. This has failed to satisfy the NUM, however, which has continued to demand the reinstatement of all sacked miners.

A second disruptive legacy of the miners' strike which British Coal has attempted to resolve has been inter-union competition resulting from the recognition of the UDM. On this issue there has been a notable difference between the approach of Ian MacGregor with his partisan support for the breakaway union and the more even-handed approach of Sir Robert Haslam. The latter's statements indicate that within British Coal there has been increasing recognition that the division of mining trade-unionism against itself has not worked unambiguously in management's interest. There has been a growing appreciation within management of the disadvantages usually associated with breakaway unionism, its tendency to promote discord and instability in collective bargaining. Both the UDM and the NUM have involved the Board in court cases intended to preserve or extend their negotiating rights, and competition between the two has continued to have a serious disruptive effect at pits where both have members. At a time when the virtues of single unionism have been widely trumpeted the Board, which has long had the advantage of this form of employee representation, has found itself moving in the opposite direction.

As the removal of either union has not been a credible possibility for British Coal, its reponse to this situation has been to try and minimize the disruptive consequences of inter-union competition. One way this has been attempted has been through pressuring the NUM and the UDM into accepting that the other union should enjoy sole rights to representation at any pit where it has a majority of the work-force in membership and that both unions should have rights to representation in the industry's negotiating and consultative machinery. This has been conceded by the UDM but the national union has continued to reject any limitation of the representative monopoly it was granted when the industry was nationalized. Associated with this attempt to stabilize the pattern of union representation has been a second tactic of offering both unions broadly similar pay and conditions awards. The intention behind this has been to try and prevent management being drawn too deeply into the rivalry between the two unions and to prevent any 'favouritism' towards the UDM blocking the restoration of 'normal' relations with the national union.

The NUM Response

It was stated above that British Coal's motives in attempting to settle the disruptive legacies of the miners' strike included a desire to stabilize the industry's industrial relations and to induce acceptance of the new settlement prevailing in coal within the NUM. If the statements of Arthur Scargill are taken as a guide to the successful realization of the latter ambition then it has clearly been abjectly disappointed. The NUM president has denounced all of the Board's proposals for restructuring the industry since the end of the strike and the pages of the NUM newspaper, The Miner, have been filled with articles affirming Scargill's advocacy of total opposition. In the period since the return to work, however, there has been a growth of criticism of Scargill within the union's leadership. The most significant feature of NUM internal politics since the miners' strike has been that the previously solid block of the NUM left has split. Influential left-wing leaders such as Michael McGahey of Scotland and Des Dutfield of South Wales have openly criticized Scargill for his lack of 'realism'. The major difference between Scargill and his critics is that they are prepared to adjust the policies and tactics of the union to the constraints of the new settlement which has emerged in mining. They have expressed an ambition to regulate the changes occurring in the industry through collective bargaining, instead of urging a resumption of national strike action to roll back the changes which have taken place and to prevent any further changes being attempted. Sir Robert Haslam's efforts to induce acceptance of the post-strike settlement, therefore, have found an echo within the NUM leadership, though the significance of this for the union's future policy will depend on the extent to which Arthur Scargill's authority as president is further eroded.

There have been a number of significant instances to date of NUM leaders urging a return to less fraught industrial relations in mining, each of which has implied criticism of Scargill's leadership. In the post-strike context the national executive of the union has exhibited greater independence towards the president and has voted several times against his advice and in favour of the resumption of 'normal' collective bargaining with British Coal. The most notable examples of this to date have been the acceptance by the executive of changes to the mineworkers' pension scheme, so that strikers will incur a loss of benefits, and the abandoning of the national overtime ban against the Board's new disciplinary procedure in March 1988. Both these changes were seen as necessary preludes to the resumption of collective bargaining over pay. Another example of a move towards 'normal' relations was the acceptance in principle of new shift patterns at Margam by the South Wales NUM. This was founded on an explicit argument that negotiation and the preservation of joint regulation, albeit largely on management's terms, was preferable to largely impotent defiance. In endorsing the South Wales miners' approach Michael McGahey told their conference in May 1987 that 'I always question those who tell me they stand firm and never move. That only demonstrates you are a monument—not a movement' (*Financial Times*, 7 May 1987).

Pressure on the union's leadership to restore normality in relations with the Board has been associated with moves to restore 'normality' in two other directions. In the summer of 1986, for example, the leaders of the Scottish miners initiated a campaign within the union for *rapprochment* with the UDM. This conflicted with the union's official policy of refusing to recognize the breakaway and was predicated on the belief that the split only served to weaken mining trade-unionism in a context of rapid change. A second significant step towards 'normality' was taken in 1985, when the executive of the NUM instructed Scargill to purge the union's contempt of the High Court and regain control of its assets sequestrated during the miners' strike. This amounted to recognition that the period of mobilization against the government's closure programme was at an end.

It was said above that the NUM left was the principal threat to the tripartite settlement in coal in the 1970s. Arthur Scargill and his allies have remained wedded to the tactics and perspectives of that period, and that segment of the left led by Scargill constitutes the main force of opposition to the post-strike settlement of the 1980s. Scargill has spoken repeatedly since the return to work in 1985 of reopening the campaign against closures and has also advocated industrial action on pay, flexible working, discipline, and the plight of the sacked miners. There must be serious doubt, however, whether this threat carries any real weight. The 1987 national overtime ban over the disciplinary code, for instance, failed to halt the improvement in the industry's performance and failed to escalate into a general challenge to the restructuring of the industry, as Scargill appeared to intend. Although mining remains a dispute-prone industry, and sectional militancy remains deeply embedded within its pattern of industrial relations, we believe that the prospect of such militancy being elevated into a united challenge by British miners to the post-strike settlement appears very remote.

Recognition of the decline in the 'organizational power' of the union has been the point from which Scargill's critics in the NUM have started. There has been a growing realization even on the left of the union that it can no longer base its strategy on the militant appetites of the miners. Accordingly in the wake of the 1984/5 strike there has been a casting around for other resources which the union can use to pursue its objectives. It has been variously suggested that the union should look beyond its own ranks and attempt to win greater public support for its policies, or achieve a closer understanding with other energy-sector unions, or seek the commitment of the Labour Party to a new tripartite plan for coal. In the immediate context of defeat and faced with a newly assertive employer, however, the dominant response of those disillusioned with the left's traditional militancy has been to seek compromise with management. In order to ensure a continued significant role for the union in the industry there has been a preparedness to accede to a great deal of the changes management has insisted must be introduced. On the union side, as well as on the side of British Coal, strong pressures have emerged for a new stability in the industrial relations of the mining industry.

Conclusion

In these final chapters we have sketched the changing pattern of national industrial relations in coal-mining, taking as our theme the shifting capacity of the NUM to exercise strategic influence over the industry's development. In Chapter 9 we described the national industrial relations settlement which emerged in mining in the aftermath of the 1972 and 1974 strikes and typified the NUM's political exchange with the state in the 1970s as a venture in 'sectoral corporatism'. The reasons for this were that, as in models of 'societal' corporatism, it embraced government, trade-union leadership, and management and it extended the range of union influence to encompass strategic decisions in return for co-operation in attempts to modernize the industry, improve productivity, and control wage costs. The new settlement in coal which emerged in the wake of the 1984/5 miners' strike we have typified in terms of the exclusion of the union from strategic influence. This again borrows from general interpretations of state and trade-union relations. Crouch (1985) has described the actions of the Conservative Government in the field of industrial relations in terms of the displacement of corporatism with a policy of 'contestation'. The defining feature of this is that it is considered 'feasible to exclude organised labour entirely from all important decision-making and try to marginalise it within society'. It amounts to a policy of 'labour exclusion'. Much of what has happened in coal since 1984 can be understood in these terms. There have been the withdrawal of tripartite regulation of the industry, moves to slacken collective and legal controls over management's use of labour, and attempts to confirm the collapse of the NUM's 'organizational power'. Even in coal, however, the cockpit of the Thatcherite transformation of British industrial relations, there have been limits to the exclusion of labour. In earlier chapters we have pointed to the continuance of a vigorous workplace trade-unionism and of effective sectional militancy. In this chapter we have described the attempts by Sir Robert Haslam to stabilize industrial relations and restore 'normality' in British Coal's relations with the NUM. Although the union has been weakened and its influence rolled back, it is accepted that it will continue to play a critical role in the management of British miners.

Conclusion

In this book we have analysed the processes involved in the management of British coal-miners. Each chapter has examined the dynamics of labour management at a different level of the British coal industry. Thus, in Chapters 1 and 2 we investigated the management of mining work and attempted to assess the effectiveness of two strategies employed by management to control activities at the point of coal extraction. These were the strategies of 'direct control', initiated in 1966 with the signing of the National Powerloading Agreement, and reliance on group incentives, initiated with the signing of the Area Incentive Scheme in 1977/8. We argued in these chapters that management was driven to reintroduce payment by results in the industry because of the failure of NPLA to raise output and productivity. Management attempts to reduce dependence on labour co-operation through methods of direct control were displaced by an attempt to forge a new identity of interests with the work-force through reforming the payment system.

In Chapters 3 and 4 the focus on incentives was maintained. In these chapters we examined the attempts by management to prevent the reintroduction of local negotiations over incentives in the late 1970s, producing an upward spiral in wage-costs. Much of this effort on the part of management involved the deployment of techniques which have been seen as central elements in the reform of British industrial relations since the publication of the Donovan Report. Our chapters, indeed, were used to test several of the predictions of the consequences of more formalized workplace industrial relations which are contained in the literature on industrial relations reform. The chapters provided detailed insights into the operation of management techniques associated with reform, such as work study, attempts to restrict the industrial relations role of supervisors, and the supervision of local bargaining by specialist industrial relations managers. Our conclusions were that reform notwithstanding, 'disorder' and informality remained key attributes of workplace industrial relations, at least in coal-mining, and that this had produced an escalation in the costs of the incentive scheme.

In Chapters 5 and 6 the focus of attention shifted to the study of the workplace union and the extent to which it can be used by management to instil discipline in the work-force. We argued that although co-operative bargaining relationships between management and union are typical of colliery industrial relations, radical writers have tended to exaggerate the extent to which sophisticated shop-steward organizations, of the kind found in mining, can be employed as a management resource. In our view the role of the workplace union in mining, despite hierarchy and despite management sponsorship of its role, provides little support for those who have claimed to detect a bureaucratization of the rank and file. Specifically, we argued, *contra* this view, that the workplace leadership in mining is subject to considerable membership scrutiny and control; that a central interest of the leadership, which is neglected by the theorists of bureaucratization, is the preservation of a unified and effective workplace organization; and that although the leadership disciplines the membership for management it does so in return for substantial concessions.

Chapters 7 and 8 served as something of a summary to the investigation of workplace employment relations in coal-mining contained in the previous chapters. They presented the results of two surveys of trade-union influence within British collieries and provided a detailed delineation of the 'frontier of control' in the mining industry. On the one hand they emphasized the exclusion of the union from much management decision-making, even in this bastion of the labour movement, while on the other hand they noted the depth of union influence over the 'traditional' meat and drink issues of industrial relations. These chapters also demonstrated that much union influence within pits is exercised in conjunction with management and is not a product of industrial conflict. Finally, Chapter 8 sought to account for variation in the influence exercised by trade-union branches across the industry and identified a number of sources of trade-union power.

In all eight chapters dealing with the management of miners in the workplace attention was paid to recent developments in the industry which have occurred in the wake of the 1984/5 miners' strike. In our view the strike was a key event propelling the industry into a new sequence of its development, though of course many continuities with the pre-strike industry remain. In Chapter 8, for instance, we provided reasons for suggesting that the days of relatively strong work-place trade-unionism in the British coal-mining industry are not at an end.

In our final chapters the questions of change and the impact of the miners' defeat in the great strike were treated more centrally. In Chapters 9 and 10 our focus was directed above the work-place level towards the evolution of national industrial relations in coal-mining. This section fell into three main parts. In the first we examined the 1974 'settlement' in coal-mining which was characterized by a wide-reaching exchange between government, management, and the NUM, which was founded on the union's victories in the national miners' strikes of 1972 and 1974 and which we typified as a venture in 'sectoral corporatism'. In the middle section we catalogued the demise of this settlement, firstly, through the election of a Conservative Government less prepared to propitiate the industrial strength of the NUM and, secondly, through the 1984/5 strike itself, in which the inability of the union to maintain its favourable political exchange with government was revealed. In Chapter 10 the new post-strike settlement in coal was analysed, the key feature of which was said to be the distancing of the unions from the industry's strategic core and the weakening of their influence over its strategic management. In the mining industry of today, relative to that of the 1970s, it was argued, there has been a notable movement towards 'labour exclusion'.

Management Strategy in the Mining Industry

Each of the chapters presented in this book has attempted to relate empirical findings from the mining industry to specific bodies of theoretical literature. To conclude our study of the management of British miners we want to relate our research findings as a whole to one of the central theoretical controversies within contemporary writing on employment relations. This concerns the use of the concept of 'management strategy' as a tool for organizing discussion of the processes of labour management. At various points in the book we have used the term 'management strategy' without offering a definition or defending its use. We now want to rectify that omission and demonstrate how our findings from the mining industry can inform some of the theoretical debates which have coalesced around the concept of management strategy in recent years. These debates have focused on three issues: the definition and identification of management strategies, their determination, and the problems associated with their implementation. By way of conclusion we want to show how our research on mining can assist in the clarification of these three areas of debate.

Definition and Identification

It is a frequent complaint of writers who question the value of the notion of management strategy in labour relations that the term is usually ill-defined (Hyman, 1987, pp. 27–8). This is a justifiable criticism but hardly warrants abandoning the term. In our view management strategy in the field of labour relations consists in the first place in the identification of particular problems in the organization's relationship with its work-force by a group of managers with the power to make significant innovations in this field. A second element is the development of preferred solutions to these problems, the development of reasonably coherent objectives in the field of labour management. The third element is the adoption of specific policies or techniques of labour management designed to realize these objectives.

In the coal industry in the period reviewed in this book several such strategies containing these elements are clearly identifiable. In the 1960s, for example, management decided that the mechanization of the industry had provided it with the opportunity of dispensing with piece-work, with its associated disadvantages of 'disorderly' and fragmented pit-head bargaining and a large number of short, unofficial strikes. Management at this time formulated a clear objective of achieving greater directive control over operations at the coal-face and attempted to pursue this objective through policies such as an increase in supervision and the negotiation of the National Powerloading Agreement, with its provisions for the use of work study and the flexible deployment of mineworkers between tasks.

In the 1970s, when it had become apparent that 'direct control' had not been achieved, the industry's management initiated a new strategic turn. NPLA was itself identified as the source of two major problems. Its removal of payment by results was felt to be a brake on productivity and the centralization of wage negotiations was recognized as having given the NUM the capacity to mount national industrial action over pay. The solution to both these problems was believed to be the reintroduction of incentive payments. This would simultaneously induce mineworkers to make greater use of capital equipment and divide the economic interests of men in different collieries, thus making it harder for the union to mobilize its membership in united action behind ambitious wage demands. The pursuit of both of these objectives assumed concrete form in the introduction of the area incentive schemes in 1977/8 which restored an element of local bargaining over pay. It was also recognized, however, that the reintroduction of incentives itself carried risks for management and the schemes were designed so as to contain local union bargaining pressure.

Since then the industry has come under increased pressure from government to reduce its costs and meet rigorous financial targets. In the field of labour relations the response to this pressure has involved the imposition of large-scale redundancies and renewed efforts to raise productivity. British Coal has been required to develop a smaller, more streamlined industry in which production is concentrated in pits where good geology and the intensive use of modern technology permit the attainment of very high productivity levels. In moving towards this objective a number of policies have been enacted. The tripartite regulation of the industry's size and output has been repudiated at the cost of a long and very bitter industrial dispute; miners have been induced to leave the industry through relatively generous redundancy payments; and there has been a series of attempts to slacken trade-union and legal controls over the remuneration and deployment of mining labour.

In coal in the three decades covered by our study, therefore, management strategies in the field of labour relations are readily identifiable. Managers at senior levels of the organization have identified major problems in relations with the work-force, have formulated solutions to these problems, and have attempted to implement these solutions through a set of industrial relations policies. Our evidence, therefore, suggests that management action in this field may not be as haphazard as some contributors to the debate on strategy have argued. Rose and Jones, for example, on the basis of studies of work reorganization in manufacturing, have argued that 'much management policy making and execution . . . is piecemeal, unco-ordinated and empiricist' (1985, p. 99). This judgement does not appear to be valid for the mining industry. A principal finding of our study, we feel, is that strategic thinking and strategic action form part of the labour management process in coal.

There may be reasons, though, why strategic action has been a feature of labour management in the coal industry. First there is the fact that the actions of managers in nationalized industries are generally subject to more scrutiny and outside intervention than those of managers operating in the private sector. Accountability to the public purse, therefore, may have prompted a more precise articulation and review of industrial relations policies and practice, especially in recent years. Second, labour relations in coal-mining probably constitute a far larger and more problematic component of the management task than is usual in many other industries. Throughout the earlier chapters in this book we have emphasized the high degree of dependence of management on labour in the production process. The strength of the NUM both nationally and in collieries has also been amply demonstrated. The development of unified and coherent labour strategies, therefore, can be seen as a response to this significant 'challenge from below'. Finally, the nationalized coal industry in most of the period covered in this book has operated with a relatively centralized and integrated management. Since Vesting Day, standardization, regulation, and centralization have been elements of its organizational practice and have embraced the area of labour relations. The industry has also supported sizeable complements of industrial relations managers capable of reviewing labour management problems and developing responses. The management organization in coal, therefore, has been endowed with a *strategic capacity*.

Current developments in the industry, however, may diminish this capacity in the near future. Chapter 10 described how there has been a decentralization of labour-management decision-making in recent years. This could lead to greater divergence in labour relations practice between different British Coal areas. It was also reported in Chapter 10 that there has been a lowering in the status of specialist industrial relations staff. This could also weaken the industry's capacity to develop reasonably consistent labour relations strategies.

The Determinants of Management Strategy

A second concern of the debate on management strategy has been the determinants or influences on management action in the sphere of labour relations. A major issue here has been the relative validity of structural and of more voluntarist accounts (Streeck, 1987). The former attempt to trace management actions to the influence of particular environmental 'contingencies' such as technology or the state of product markets, or else, in Marxist versions, to the incessant pressures of the capitalist mode of production and the need for managers to ensure the expropriation of surplus value. More voluntarist accounts, in contrast, emphasize management's ability to make 'strategic choices' in labour relations and also tend to stress the roles of organizational and national cultures in influencing management action (Lane, 1987).

A study of the kind presented in this volume, confined to a single industry and to a single organization, cannot hope to intervene decisively in the contest between these two approaches. However, we do possess longitudinal information on the factors associated with the emergence of successive phases in labour management in the coal industry. This leads us to reject at least a strong version of the structural account of the determination of management action. Significant innovations in labour management in the coal industry do not appear to be related to changes in those environmental contingencies most favoured by structuralist writers. With reference to the influence of technology, for example, it was shown in Chapters 1 and 2 that the period of powerloading was associated with two broad approaches to the management of mining labour. Powerloading coexisted both with attempts to achieve 'direct control' over labour and with attempts to align management and worker interests through the use of incentives. It was also shown in Chapter 2 that current attempts to achieve a much fuller automation of mining operations have been associated with a reaffirmation of the strategy of incentives introduced before microprocessor-controlled equipment became widely available to the industry. There does not seem to be a simple one-to-one fit, therefore, between major developments in technique and major innovations in labour relations strategy. Either some other contingency exercises greater influence over management strategy than technology or else management decision-making in labour relations possesses a relative autonomy.

One possible alternative structural influence is the state of the product market. The role of this factor has been emphasized in Friedman's (1977) theory of management control over labour. Friedman argues that managements in monopoly firms, which are able to partially control their environments and so operate in relatively buoyant product markets, tend to adopt a strategy of 'responsible autonomy' in managing their work-forces. This typically consists of attempts to align worker and management interests through generous wage settlements, 'enlightened' personnel policies, and the integration of trade unions. In peripheral firms, in contrast, which are closer to the competitive edge of the economy, managements are more likely to adopt policies of 'direct control', of strict discipline and direction of labour.

Does this type of account fare better than one based on the influence of technology when placed alongside the evidence from the mining industry? The answer must be, only slightly. Although the Coal Board is a near monopoly, it has been subject to three major shifts in its product market in the period covered by our study. From the late 1950s till the early 1970s, the industry's product market was subject to a sharp contraction as cheap oil replaced coal in many markets and forced the closure of many pits. This period did witness a major management experiment with 'direct control' in the British coal industry, manifested in the National Powerloading Agreement. In the early 1970s the economic fortunes of the industry improved as oil prices rose sharply and the government made a new commitment to coal. Again, management strategy adapted in the manner predicted by Friedman. The 1970s were marked by attempts to foster greater worker participation and greater union involvement in operations, in order to facilitate the solution of production problems. They were also marked, as we have stressed several times above, by an abandonment of direct control in favour of stimulating worker motivation through incentives. In the 1980s British Coal has re-entered recession as the decline of smokestack industries, the emergence of new fuels, and the availability of cheap steam coal from abroad have reduced its markets. The evidence of a return to 'direct control', however, is not readily apparent. True, there have been attempts, documented in Chapter 10, to release the managerial prerogative from joint regulation. Standing alongside measures of this kind, though, are increased reliance on incentives, with continued commitment to high wages for production workers, and renewed interest in experiments with worker involvement. Whereas in the 1970s 'responsible autonomy' was seen as a means of ensuring worker co-operation in the satisfaction of an expanding demand, in the 1980s it has been seen as a means of ensuring worker co-operation with a decline in demand, with ensuring coal is produced as economically as possible from a limited number of pits.

Once again, therefore, the evidence from our study does not provide support for a strong statement of a contingency thesis. The content of management strategy did match developments in the product market in the 1960s and 1970s in the manner predicted by Friedman. However, in the 1980s the pattern broke down. Comparison of the 1970s and 1980s, indeed, suggests that identical or very similar labour management techniques may be used to respond to very different product market situations.

Although we feel our evidence on the origins and content of management strategies in coal-mining does not provide support for strong versions of contingency theory, we do believe it is compatible with weaker versions. Clearly, major changes in technology or product market can create problems or opportunities for management in the field of labour relations to which responses must be developed. Much of Chapters 9 and 10, for instance, was concerned with the implications for labour management of a transition to a less favourable economic environment, though it must be emphasized that this transition was refracted through stringent government policies towards the industry.

In our view management, in most cases, has the capacity to respond to challenges of this kind in a number of ways. There is scope for strategic choice. The precise way in which management does respond is likely to be influenced by a range of factors, such as the values and ideologies of those managers responsible for developing strategy, the traditions of the industry, the quality of relations with trade unions, and pressure from government and other external agencies with an interest in influencing management action. The management response to financial pressure on the coal industry in the 1980s, for example, has built upon the long tradition of reliance on payment by results in the industry. It has also been shaped by government pressure to reduce the role of trade unions in the nationalized industries and has been influenced, too, by a perception that the NUM under Arthur Scargill's leadership is committed to opposing change and cannot be readily incorporated into its negotiation. The value of the concept of management strategy, we believe therefore, is that it directs attention both to the element of choice in management's response to environmental pressures and to the influences underlying those choices which are eventually made. It directs attention to the political process through which strategies are selected, to the influence of values, and to the force of tradition.

A particularly interesting feature of the strategic choices made by managers in the coal industry over the past three decades is that in each phase they have conformed to current textbook recommendations on labour relations. There is and has been an undeniable trendiness to labour management in the coal industry. In the 1960s, for example, the National Powerloading Agreement formed part of a wave of experimentation in British industry with measured day-work and productivity bargaining. In Chapter 2 we demonstrated that in the 1970s the industry participated in the reform of work-place industrial relations. It also embraced industrial democracy and sought to extend trade-union involvement in the running of the industry. In the present decade attention to fashion has continued. British Coal has followed the current vogue for direct communication with the work-force, has developed an interest in 'flexibility', and has also participated in the trend towards tying wages and conditions much more closely to the financial performance of individual operating units.

Although the existence of such trends or waves of innovation in labour relations has been described many times by scholars (e.g. Fogarty and Brooks, 1986), the process of diffusion throughout the economy and the reasons for individual organizations following a trend have not. In our view there are two reasons for the 'up-to-date' nature of labour management in British Coal. The first has already been referred to and described as the 'strategic capacity' of the industry's management. The Coal Board has carried a substantial number of specialist managers with responsibility for labour relations. Included in the responsibilities of such managers have been the review of developments in labour relations practice in the economy at large and particularly in other large industrial concerns. The existence of a corps of industrial relations and other specialists, therefore, provides a conduit through which current thinking and current notions of best practice in employment relations can flow into the coal industry.

The second reason is proximity to government. As a large public industry British Coal has been subject to influence from the government of the day and from other state agencies. Several of the innovations in labour relations described above have been actively encouraged by government. In the 1960s, for example, the state promoted the eradication of 'disorder' in the workplace through payment system reform and productivity bargaining. In the following decade this encouragement of reform was continued through the Commission on Industrial Relations and was extended to embrace experiments with industrial democracy. Finally, in the 1980s, the Conservative Government has urged that union power be reduced within the nationalized industries. The Report of the Monopolies and Mergers Commission, published in 1983, recommended that the joint regulation of the coal industry's output be discontinued and that the Board should move to a more decentralized, market-based system for the determination of miners' wages and conditions. These recommendations paralleled those made for other state industries which fell under the Commission's scrutiny.

The Determination of Management Strategy in the State Enterprise

The impact of political decisions on the business and labour-relations strategies of state firms has been emphasized in several publications by Batstone, Ferner, and Terry (Batstone *et al.*, 1984; Ferner, 1985, 1987). In studies of the Post Office and of British Rail these authors have explored the specific determinants of labour relations in the state enterprise and have argued that managers in state-owned industries are faced with an additional 'political contingency' which renders the task of management peculiarly complex. The fact that state firms are frequently dependent on government for a substantial proportion of their finance and that their senior managers are accountable to ministers means that they are subject to recurrent political control. Such firms can be used by governments as instruments of policy, and as such are likely to experience attempts by politicians to shape their objectives and activities. This is likely to be the case, argue Batstone and his colleagues, even where politicians are committed to a rhetoric of independence for the nationalized industries and where financial controls have been introduced to permit an arm's-length relationship (Batstone *et al.*, 1984, p. 276).

The working of the 'political contingency', these writers argue, affects the conduct of labour relations in state firms both directly and indirectly. Direct influence can occur where the government uses its leverage to encourage management to pursue a specific labour-relations policy. Ferner (1985) has provided an example from British Rail where the Conservative Government tied approval for investment 'formally and openly' to management action to force union acceptance of flexible rostering. Possibly more important than influence of this kind, however, is indirect influence over labour relations. This is exerted through the setting of general business objectives for state firms, which have major implications for the conduct of labour management. The issuing of new objectives to the nationalized industries can have an effect akin to the emergence of a new technology or a change in product markets, in that it can push management into a review of labour relations and lead to the formulation of a new strategy.

Both types of influence are readily discernible in the evolution of labour relations in the coal industry. The two national industrial relations settlements which we examined in Chapters 9 and 10, for example, were marked by both direct and indirect attempts by government to influence the conduct of labour management. Under the 1974 settlement the Labour Government initiated the tripartite regulation of the industry's size and output, while its commitment to sustained investment in the industry provided the basis for the generally co-operative relations between union and management which characterized the 1970s. The post-strike settlement of the late 1980s was also very largely the product of management responses to the 'political contingency'. Direct government influence in this case was exhibited in actions such as the appointment of Ian MacGregor as chairman, with its consequent raising of the industrial relations temperature, in the government's preparedness to subsidize the industry's dispute with the NUM over pit closures, and in its support for the Union of Democratic Mineworkers, which led it to issue new legislation in 1986 to secure the procedural rights of the UDM within the industry's consultative machinery. The post-strike settlement was also shaped by less direct forms of intervention. As was pointed out in Chapter 9, the Board was driven to the repudiation of tripartism and to the reduction of union influence over the industry by the issuing of stricter financial targets by the Conservative Government.

Our research on mining, therefore, supports the argument of Batstone, Ferner, and Terry that the conduct of labour relations in state firms is structured by the operation of the 'political contingency'. There are other elements in their argument, however, which do not fit the experience of coal. Apart from establishing the general point that management in state firms is usually open to political influence, Batstone and his colleagues are concerned with the consequences for labour relations of a growing 'commercialism' in the management of state firms. In their study of the Post Office, for instance, they trace the partial displacement of management's traditional concern with maintaining adequate postal and telecommunications services with a growing emphasis on the costs of service and the earning of revenue. This new 'commercial paradigm', they argue, has had a disruptive effect on established and largely co-operative relations with trade unions. It is shown to be associated with an attempt to obtain workers' co-operation, less through joint regulation and the accommodation of trade-union ideals of fairness, and more through the linking of rewards to performance against financial targets.

How do developments in the coal industry diverge from this interpretation of the dynamics of labour relations in the nationalized industries in recent years? The major difference is that developments in coal have not been driven by the displacement of 'service' with more 'commercial' objectives at the industry's centre. The coal industry since nationalization has never been operated as a service industry, though sections of the NUM have repeatedly urged that it should be, and throughout its history it has been subject to commercial discipline. After all, in the 1960s the industry underwent a restructuring as drastic as that which has occurred in the past few years, as a result of cheap oil undercutting the price of coal.

It is the case, however, that the coal industry has been subject to a tighter commercial discipline in the 1980s as a result of the policy of the Conservative Government, and a major concern of this book has been with tracing the consequences of this pressure for industrial relations. In our view, the objectives which have been displaced by this tighter commercial discipline are, firstly, the provision of well-paid employment in mining areas, and, secondly, the maintenance of a large, domestic coal industry as an economic buffer against fluctuations in the price and supply of oil. It is not the partial abandonment of an ethic of service which has driven developments in management strategy in coal, therefore, but the abandonment of these two rather different objectives.

Batstone, Ferner, and Terry present the emergence of 'commercialism' in the nationalized industries as part of a wide-ranging attempt on the part of government to grapple with the problem of escalating public expenditure. This applies equally to the coal industry as it does to British Rail and the Post Office. The Conservative Government's abandoning of earlier objectives for the industry, for instance, was motivated in the first instance by a desire to cut the NCB's mounting financial losses. We also believe, however, that this policy was motivated by explicitly industrial relations considerations. The pursuit of the two objectives described above had the effect of strengthening the National Union of Mineworkers and of increasing national dependence on what had proved to be a powerful and militant group of workers. Under the Conservatives an alternative strategic calculation has influenced policy towards the industry. There has been a rejection of the argument that coal should be protected from market forces because this has the effect of increasing the economy's vulnerability to a national miners' strike. The movement to tighter commercial discipline in mining, therefore, and the abandoning of earlier objectives, has been motivated by a desire to escape dependence on the NUM.

The Implementation of Labour Relations Strategy

The third and final aspect of labour management strategy that we want to consider is the process of implementation. A dominant theme in the recent literature on management strategy is that of the difficulties which can be encountered in implementation. Writers on organizations have taken pains to emphasize that management initiatives frequently collapse because of insufficient pre-planning, because they run counter to existing elements of organizational practice, or because they are resisted either by groups within management or else by trade unions. Indeed, Rose and Jones (1985) have questioned the value of the concept of management strategy because it can close the minds of researchers to the 'open-ended' nature of change within organizations. In their view management in general, and labour management in particular, is an irretrievably disorderly process with the policies formulated by senior managers being deflected and twisted out of shape as they descend through 'the social structure of the firm'.

Our research on coal-mining leads us to have considerable sympathy with this view. Two things which stand out from the earlier discussion, for example, are that labour management in mining is characterized by division between different functions and levels within the management team, and that it is invariably accompanied by conflict with the direct work-force. Our evidence indicates the political nature of labour-management processes and provides ample documentation of the contested or negotiated character of change.

To take intra-management conflict first, our discussion of the control of local pay-bargaining in Chapters 3 and 4 focused on the division between line managers, particularly those located at the workplace, and area industrial relations managers. It was pointed out in this discussion that a key feature of the design of the 1977/8 incentive scheme was the restriction of local pay-bargaining to a centrally set agenda in order to minimize the risks of 'decay'. The responsibility for monitoring local bargaining and ensuring it did not seep beyond its allotted sphere was assigned to industrial relations staff. The exercise of this responsibility, however, led industrial relations managers into conflict with colliery managers who were keen to maximize their own control over the payment system in order to develop strong bargaining relations with local NUM officials. The experience of implementing a centrally devised industrial relations policy, therefore, was marked by competition between two groups of managers who had different perspectives on how the incentive scheme should function. The outcome of this competition was the extension of line management control over the payment system, the development of informal bargaining within collieries and the acceptance by industrial relations staff of a less than rigorous application of collective agreements.

As well as instances of intra-management competition our work on mining also provides examples of management strategy running into work-force opposition. In the first part of the book, for instance, we described how management attempts to secure 'direct control' over coal-face operations were frustrated by the resistance of work-teams. Management responded to this situation by reintroducing payment by results in order to broaden its common interests with the work-force and to stimulate greater engagement at the point of production. This new strategy, however, also generated conflict as workers tried to deploy their bargaining power to secure favourable incentive agreements at pit level. The evidence from our study, therefore, reveals the element of antagonism in the employment relationship continually reappearing, like a cork bobbing to the surface. It suggests that management strategy will almost invariably be contested.

In coal-mining, then, the empirical material indicates that the process of implementing labour relations strategy is 'open-ended', as Rose and Jones suggest. However, we do not believe this invalidates use of the term 'strategy' as they and other writers imply (Hyman, 1987; Nolan and Edwards, 1984). There is a marked tendency in the work of these authors to contrast a view of management action as highly rational and purposive, which they associate with the term 'strategy', with one in which it is seen as both inherently political and inherently disorderly. Rose and Jones, for instance, insist that discussions of management strategy often display a 'teleological element' (1985, p. 99); and Nolan and Edwards (1984,

p. 214) speak of the 'dangers of investing employers with impossible amounts of knowledge, cunning and foresight'. Underlying these warnings is an appreciation that the informal life of organizations is frequently as important, and is certainly more interesting to social scientists, than formal procedures and activities designed by senior management.

In our opinion, however, such warnings can slip too easily into declarations of the impossibility of strategic management. They can encourage an excessively chaotic view of management processes in which all action becomes unplanned and unpredictable and is seen solely as the product of conflict between groups of managers and between management and workforce. We are particularly suspicious of ritualistic invocations of the powers of 'class struggle' to deflect management initiatives in the field of labour relations, which have become such a feature of the labour process debate.

To conclude our discussion of the implementation of management strategy, therefore, we want to present some ideas on how the useful concept of strategy can be integrated with a recognition of the informal life of large organizations. We want to chart a middle course between an overemphasis on the 'rationality' of the management process and an exaggeration of the difficulties managers can face in controlling their organizations.

Our first point is that strategic initiatives can set the agenda for conflicts both within management and between management and labour. They can establish the terrain within which disorder occurs. Our discussion of the control of local pay-bargaining, for example, showed how the return to incentives and the desire to minimize the risks of payment-scheme decay, led both to conflict between line and industrial relations managers over who would control the incentive scheme and to conflict between management and work-force over the use of those techniques designed to contain bargaining pressures. In this case a train of conflicts was set in motion by a particular strategic initiative.

Our second point is that such initiatives need not inevitably fail. Of course they may do so. They may be blocked by powerful groups within the organization or they may have unforeseen consequences which negate their initial purpose. However, these results cannot be assumed and it seems wiser to us to try and establish the conditions under which successful strategy implementation can occur rather than to reject the concept of strategy because of the possibility of failure. Earlier in this conclusion we spoke of management organizations having differential capacities to develop labour-relations strategies. It is also possible to speak of different organizations having a greater or lesser capacity to implement strategic decisions.

In part such a capacity is dependent on the existence of appropriate 'organizational technology'. There must be effective procedures for implementing senior management directives and adequate lines of communication so that the process of implementation can be monitored and reviewed. However, the existence of 'organizational technology', though important, may not be sufficient to ensure success. In Chapter 4, for example, we demonstrated that the computerization of the NCB's incentive scheme and the use of a computerized monitoring process were not sufficient to prevent the growth of informal bargaining at pit level.

This example suggests that another important influence on the degree of successful implementation is the content of strategy itself and the extent to which it challenges the interests of powerful groups within the organization. Attempting to supervise local pay-bargaining in the mining industry, for instance, was viewed as an unwarranted intrusion into their sphere of autonomy by many colliery managers. Moreover, the control by colliery managers of the production process and support from other line managers located higher in the organization enabled them successfully to resist central supervision of local bargaining.

However, if this example is illustrative of the difficulties which can occur in implementing labour-relations strategy it can also point to some of the conditions of success. It indicates that successful strategies will require the support of powerful groups within the management team and that they must be congruent with the interests of these groups. The content of strategy must run with the managerial grain. In the coal industry since the 1984/5 miners' strike, for example, British Coal has embarked on a seemingly successful policy of further decentralizing industrial relations decision-making. This has formed part of a more general attempt to simplify the management structure and to give greater discretion to those managers directly involved in running operations. Unlike the attempts to restrict local pay-bargaining introduced in the 1970s this new development builds upon and acknowledges the powers of the colliery manager.

This argument that labour-relations strategies can generate more or less conflict within management can also be applied to relations between management and work-force. It was stated above that it is frequently claimed in discussions of management strategy that the 'basic contradiction' between capital and labour will inevitably serve to frustrate management initiatives. Hyman (1987, p. 30), for example, has remarked that the 'key to any credible treatment of strategy within a Marxist analysis is surely an emphasis on *contradiction*', and then goes on to argue that management strategy can best be conceptualized as '*the programmatic choice among alternatives none of which can prove satisfactory*'. We accept that conflict is an irremovable element in the employment relationship. However, so too is co-operation. We also believe that it is important to establish that some management strategies are more effective in minimizing conflict and maximizing co-operation than are others. He would qualify Hyman's statement, therefore, by suggesting that different strategies will prove satisfactory to management to different degrees.

In our discussion of the control of work, for instance, evidence was presented which showed that the return to payment by results in 1977/8 was successful in building management–worker co-operation at the point of production. The result of this was an improvement in the industry's productivity. Compared to the day-wage system, therefore, reliance on incentives was more satisfactory or more successful in realizing a central management objective. Moreover, although the return to payment by results increased conflict over pay at workplace level, it was a near universal judgement among the managers we interviewed that this was an acceptable price for higher productivity.

A further simple, but nevertheless important, point is that management may well be able to override work-force opposition to its strategy and impose change. In most organizations the resources at management's disposal greatly outweigh those which can be deployed by the work-force. Given this disparity in power we believe it is equally mistaken to overemphasize workers' capacity to resist management initiatives as it is to pretend such resistance will never or only rarely occur. Again, our evidence from the coal industry supports this argument. In Chapter 7, for instance, it was demonstrated that management influence over workplace decision-making far exceeds that of the union on most issues, and that where conflict does occur it is more usual for management to prevail. Furthermore, in Chapters 9 and 10 it was demonstrated that the transition from the corporatist industrial relations settlement of the 1970s to a new settlement in mining, founded on reduced union influence, was achieved by the breaking of the union's power by the government. This provides a particularly graphic example, we believe, of the greater resources of an employer permitting the imposition of a new strategy for labour relations.

Summary

In this conclusion to our study of managing British miners we have attempted to relate our research findings as a whole to the debate over management strategy. Three main points stand out from this discussion. Firstly, management strategies, in the sense of policies designed to resolve perceived problems in the organization's relations with its work-force, are clearly discernible in the coal industry and form an important component of its labour relations. However, we acknowledge that this may not be the case in other organizations and have argued that the structure and size of the management organization in coal endow it with a 'strategic capacity'.

Secondly, we have argued that management strategies cannot be viewed as the direct or unmediated products of environmental pressures or contingencies. We believe our work provides support for the view that managers possess an element of strategic choice in the development of labour relations policies. However, we also accept the argument of Batstone, Ferner, and Terry that labour relations in state enterprises are unusually subject to political influence of both direct and indirect kinds. Participation in the process of strategic choice within such firms embraces the political controllers of the organization as well as its own management.

Finally, we have suggested, in line with a number of other writers, that the process of implementing strategy is invariably disorderly and 'open-ended'. Labour-relations strategies are likely to encounter conflict from sections of the work-force and may well be contested by groups within the management team. However, we feel that recognition of this fact should not lead to a rejection of the term 'strategy' or to a conclusion that strategic action is impossible. An important issue for future research in this area, we believe, is establishing the conditions of the successful strategic management of labour.

References

Abercrombie, N., Hill, S., and Turner, B. (1980) *The Dominant Ideology Thesis*, London: Allen and Unwin.

Adeney, M., and Lloyd, J. (1986), *The Miners' Strike: Loss Without Limit*, London: Routledge & Kegan Paul.

Allen, V. (1981), *The Militancy of British Miners*, Shipley: The Moor Press.

Armstrong, P., and Goodman, J. (1979), 'Managerial Custom and Practice', *Industrial Relations Journal*, 10/3.

Bachrach, P., and Baratz, M. S. (1962), 'The Two Faces of Power' *American Political Science Review*, 56.

——(1970), *Power and Poverty: Theory and Practice*, Oxford University Press.

Baldamus, W. (1961), *Efficiency and Effort*, London: Tavistock.

Batstone, E. (1984), *Working Order*, Oxford: Basil Blackwell.

——Boraston, I., and Frenkel, S. (1977), *Shop Stewards in Action*, Oxford: Basil Blackwell.

——Boraston, I. and Frenkel, S. (1978) *The Social Organisation of Industrial Conflict*, Oxford: Basil Blackwell.

——Ferner, A., and Terry, M. (1984), *Consent and Efficiency: Labour Relations and Management Strategy in the State Enterprise*, Oxford: Basil Blackwell.

——and Gourlay, S. (1986), *Unions, Unemployment and Innovation*, Oxford: Basil Blackwell.

Beecham, D. (1984) 'How Far has Rank and File Organisation been Weakened and Incorporated?' *International Socialism*, 2/23.

Berry, D. A., Capps, T., Cooper, D., Happer, T., and Lowe, E. A. (1986), 'Evidence' *House of Commons Energy Committee, Session 1985–1986, The Coal Industry*, London: HMSO.

Beynon, H. (1984), *Working for Ford* (2nd edn.), Harmondsworth: Penguin.

——(ed.) (1985), *Digging Deeper: Issues in the Miners' Strike*, London: Verso.

——and McMylor, P. (1985), 'Decisive Power: The New Tory State against the Miners', in H. Beynon (ed.), *Digging Deeper: Issues in the Miners' Strike*, London: Verso.

Blauner, R. (1960), 'Work Satisfaction and Industrial Trends in Modern Society' in W. Galenson and S. M. Lipset (eds.), *Labour Trends and Unionism*, New York: Wiley.

Boraston, I., Clegg, H., and Rimmer, M. (1975), *Workplace and Union: A Study of Local Relationships in Fourteen Unions*, London: Heinemann.

Bowey, A., and Thorpe, R., with Hellier, P. (1986), *Payment Systems and Productivity*, Basingstoke: Macmillan.

Braverman, H. (1974), *Labour and Monopoly Capital* , New York: Monthly Review Press.

British Coal (1987, 1988), *Report and Accounts*, London: British Coal.

Brown, G., (1977), *Sabotage*, Nottingham: Spokesman.

Brown, W. (1973), *Piecework Bargaining* London: Heinemann.

——(1980), 'The Structure of Pay Bargaining in Britain', in F. Blackaby (ed.), *The Future of Pay Bargaining*, London: Heinemann.

——(1981), *The Changing Contours of British Industrial Relations*, Oxford: Basil Blackwell.

——and Sisson, K. (1983), 'Industrial Relations in the Private Sector: Donovan Revisited', in G. S. Bain, (ed.), *Industrial Relations in Britain*, Oxford: Basil Blackwell.

Bullock Report (1977) *Report of the Committee of Inquiry on Industrial Democracy*, London: HMSO.

Burns, A., Feickert, D., Newby, M., and Winterton, J. (1983), 'The Miners and New Technology' *Industrial Relations Journal*, 14/4.

——Newby, M., and Winterton, J. (1985) 'The Restructuring of the British Coal Industry', *Cambridge Journal of Economics*, 9.

Campbell, A., and Warner, M. (1985), 'Changes in the Balance of Power in the British Mineworkers' Union: An Analysis of National Top-Office Elections, 1974–84', *British Journal of Industrial Relations*, 23/1.

Caves, R. E., and Crause, L. B. (eds.) (1980), *Britain's Economic Performance*, Washington DC: The Brookings Institute.

Child, J. (1985), 'Managerial Strategies, New Technology and the Labour Process' in D. Knights, D. Collinson, and H. Willmott (eds.), *Job Redesign: Organisation and Control of the Labour Process*, Aldershot: Gower.

Clarke, T. G. (1977), 'Introduction: The Raison D Être of Trade Unionism', in T. Clarke, and L. Clements, (eds.), *Trade Unions under Capitalism*, London: Fontana.

Clegg, H. (1976), *Trade Unionism under Collective Bargaining*, Oxford: Basil Blackwell.

——(1979), *The Changing System of Industrial Relations in Great Britain*, Oxford: Basil Blackwell.

Cliff, T. (1970), *The Employers' Offensive*, London: Pluto Press.

Crick, M. (1985), *Scargill and the Miners*, Harmondsworth: Penguin.

Crouch, C. (1982), *Trade Unions: The Logic of Collective Action*, London: Fontana.

——(1985), 'Conservative Industrial Relations Policy: Towards Labour Exclusion' in O. Jacobi, B. Jessop, H. Kastendiek, and M. Regini (eds.), *Economic Crisis, Trade Unions and the State*, London: Croom Helm.

Crozier, M. (1964), *The Bureaucratic Phenomenon*, Chicago: University of Chicago Press.

Cunnison, S. (1966), *Wages and Work Allocation*, London: Tavistock.

Curwen, P. (1986), *Public Enterprise: A Modern Approach*, Brighton: Harvester.

Daniel, W. W. (1987), *Workplace Industrial Relations and Technical Change*, London: Francis Pinter.

——and Millward, N. (1983), *Workplace Industrial Relations in Britain: The DE/PSI/SSRC Survey*, London: Heinemann.

Dawson, S., Poynter, P., and Stevens, D. (1984), 'Safety Specialists in Industry: Roles, Constraints and Opportunities', *Journal of Occupational Behaviour*, 5.

Dolby, N. (1987), *Norma Dolby's Diary: An Account of the Great Miners' Strike'*, London: Verso.

Donovan Report (1968), *Report, Royal Commission on Trade Unions and Employers Associations 1965–1968*, London: HMSO.

Dyer, L., Lipsky, D. B., and Kochan, T. A. (1977), 'Union Attitudes Towards Management Co-operation' *Industrial Relations*, 16/2.

Edelstein, T., and Warner, M. (1975), *Comparative Union Democracy*, London: George Allen and Unwin.

Edwards, C. (1978), 'Measuring Union Power: A Comparison of Two Methods Applied to the Study of Local Union Power in the Coal Industry', *British Journal of Industrial Relations*, 16/1.

——(1983), 'Power and Decision Making in the Workplace: A Study in the Coalmining Industry', *Industrial Relations Journal*, 14/1.

——(1987), 'Formal Industrial Relations and Workplace Power: A Study on the Railway', *Journal of Management Studies*, 24/1.

——and Harper, D. (1975), 'Bargaining at the Trade Union and Management Interface' in P. Abell (ed.), *Organisations as Bargaining and Influence Systems*, London: Heinemann.

——(1976), 'A Study of Attitudes to Work in the Mining Industry', Imperial College of Science and Technology.

Edwards, P. (1985), 'Managing Labour Relations through the Recession', *Employee Relations*, 7/2.

——(1987), 'Does PBR Cause Strikes?', *Industrial Relations Journal*, 18/3.

Farningham, A. I. (1972), 'The Electricity Supply Industry Work Study Data Bank', *Industrial Relations Journal*, 3/1.

Ferner, A. (1985), 'Political Constraints and Management Strategies: The Case of Work Practices in British Rail', *British Journal of Industrial Relations*, 23/1.

Fogarty, M. with Brooks, D. (1986), *Trade Unions and British Industrial Development*, London: Policy Studies Institute.

Fox, A. (1973), 'Industrial Relations: A Social Critique of Pluralist Ideology', in J. Child (ed.), *Man and Organisation: The Search for Explanation and Social Relevance*, London: Allen and Unwin.

——(1974), *Beyond Contract: Work, Power and Trust Relations*, London: Faber and Faber.

——and Flanders, A. (1969). 'The Reform of Collective Bargaining: from Donovan to Durkheim', *British Journal of Industrial Relations*, 7/2.

Friedman, A. (1977), *Industry and Labour*, London: Macmillan.

Gidwell, D. (1977), 'Wage Payment Systems in the British Coalmining Industry', *Industrial Relations Journal*, 8/2.

Gill, C. (1985), *Work, Unemployment and New Technology*, Cambridge: Polity Press.

Glick, G., Mirvis, P., and Harper, D. (1977), 'Union Satisfaction and Participation' *Industrial Relations*, 16/2.

Goldthorpe, J. H. (1985), 'The End of Convergence: Corporatist and Dualist Tendencies in Modern Western Societies' in B. Roberts, R. Finnegan, and D. Gallie (eds.), *New Approaches to Economic Life* Manchester: Manchester University Press.

Goodman, J. F. B., Armstrong, E. G. A., Davis, J. E., and Wagner, A. (1977), *Rule Making and Industrial Peace*, London: Croom Helm.

Griffin, A. R. (1972), 'Consultation and Conciliation in the Mining Industry: The Need for a New Approach' *Industrial Relations Journal*, 3/3.

Handy, L. (1981), *Wages Policy in the British Coalmining Industry*, Cambridge: Cambridge University Press.

Harper, K., and Wintour, P. (1985), 'The Bitter Battle that Ended an Era', *Guardian*, 5 Mar.

Heald, D., and Steel, D. (1981), 'Nationalised Industries: The Search for Control', *Public Money*, 1/1.

Heery, E. (1984), 'Group Incentives and the Mining Supervisor: The Effect of a Change in Payment System on the First Line of Management', *British Journal of Industrial Relations*, 22/3.

——(1985), 'Computers and the Industrial Relations Manager: A Case Study of the Mining Industry' *Personnel Review*, 14/4.

Hickson, D. J., Hinings, C. R., Lee, C. A., Schneck, R. E., and Pennings, J. M. (1971), 'A Strategic Contingencies Theory of Intra-Organisational Power' *Administrative Science Quarterly*, 6/2.

Hill, S. (1981), *Competition and Control at Work*, London: Heinemann.

Hindess, B. (1982), 'Power, Interests and the Outcomes of Struggles', *Sociology*, 16/4.

House of Commons Select Committee on Energy (1987), *The Coal Industry*, London: HMSO.

Hudson, R., and Sadler, D. (1985), 'Coal and Dole: Employment Policies in the Coalfields' in H. Beynon (ed.), *Digging Deeper: Issues in The Miners' Strike*, London: Verso.

Hyman, R. (1971), *Marxism and the Sociology of Trade Unionism*, London: Pluto Press.

——(1975), *Industrial Relations: A Marxist Introduction*, London: Macmillan.

——(1979), 'The Politics of Workplace Trade Unionism', *Capital and Class*, 8.

——(1980), 'British Trade Unionism: Post War Trends and Future Prospects'. *International Socialism*, 2/8.

——(1983), 'Trade Unions: Structure, Policies and Politics' in G. S. Bain, (ed.) *Industrial Relations in Britain*, Oxford: Basil Blackwell.

——(1984), *Strikes*, London: Fontana.

——(1987), 'Strategy or Structure: Capital, Labour and Control', *Work, Employment and Society*, 1/1.

——and Brough, I. (1975), 'Social Values and Industrial Relations: A Study of Fairness and Inequality', Oxford: Basil Blackwell.

——and Elger, T. (1981), 'Job Control: the Employers' Offensive and Alternative Strategies', *Capital and Class*, 15.

Jay, T. (1981), *Time Study*, Poole: Blandford.

Kahn, P. (1985), 'The New Politics of Coal', *New Socialist*, 30.

——Lewis, N., and Wiles, P. (1983), *Picketing, Industrial Disputes, Tactics and the Law*, London: Routledge & Kegan Paul.

Kelly, J., Basset, P., Edwards, P., Brown, W. (1987), 'Symposium: British Workplace Industrial Relations 1980–84', *British Journal of Industrial Relations*, 25/2.

Kerr, C., and Siegal, A. J. (1954), 'The Inter-Industry Propensity to Strike' in Kornhauser *et al.* (eds.), *Industrial Conflict*, New York: McGraw-Hill.

Krieger, J. (1984), *Undermining Capitalism*, London. Pluto Press.

Lane, C. (1987), 'Capitalism or Culture'? *Work Employment and Society*, 1/1.

——Lane, T. (1974), *The Union Makes Us Strong*. London: Arrow.

——(1982), 'The Unions: Caught on the Ebb Tide', *Marxism Today*.

Lash, S., and Urry, J. (1984), 'The New Marxism of Collective Action: A Critical Analysis', *Sociology*, 18/1.

Lawrence, P. R., and Lorsch, J. W. (1967), *Organisation and Environment*, Cambridge, Mass: Harvard University Press.

Legge, K. (1978), *Power, Innovation and Problem-Solving in Personnel Management*, London: McGraw-Hill.

Leijinse, F. (1980), 'Workplace Bargaining and Trade Union Power', *Industrial Relations Journal*, 11/2.

Lindop, E. (1979), 'Workplace Bargaining: The End of an Era', *Industrial Relations Journal*, 10/1.

Lipset, S. M., Trow, M., and Coleman, S. (1956), *Union Democracy*, Chicago: Free Press.

Littler, C. (1983), *The Development of the Labour Process in Capitalist Societies*, London: Heinemann.

Lloyd, J. (1985), *Understanding the Miners' Strike*, London: Fabian Society.

Lukes, S. (1974), *Power: A Radical View*, London: Macmillan.

Lummis, T. (1977), 'The Occupational Community of the East Anglian Fishermen' *British Journal of Sociology*, 28.

McCarthy, W. E. J., and Parker, S. R. (1968), *Shop Stewards and Working Relations*, Research Paper No. 10, London: HMSO.

McCleery, R. (1960), 'Communications Patterns as a Basis of Systems of Authority and Power' in 'Theoretical Studies in Social Organisations of the Prison' in *New York Social Science Council Pamphlet 15*.

McCormick, B. (1979), *Industrial Relations in the Coal Industry*, London: Macmillan.

Mainwaring, T., and Wood, S. (1985), 'The Ghost in the Labour Process' in D.

Knights, H. Willmott, and D. Collinson (eds.), *Job Redesign: Organisation and Control of the Labour Process*, Aldershot: Gower.

Marchington, M. (1979), 'Shop Floor Control and Industrial Relations', in J. Purcell and R. Smith (eds.) *The Control of Work*, London: Macmillan.

——(1982), *Managing Industrial Relations*, London: McGraw-Hill.

Marsden, D. (1986), *The End of Economic Man?*, Brighton: Harvester.

Marsh, A. (1982), *Employee Relations Policy and Decision Making*, Aldershot: Gower.

Massey, D. (1984), *Spatial Divisions of Labour*, London: Macmillan.

Millward, N., and Stevens, M. (1986), *British Workplace Industrial Relations 1980–1984*, London: Heinemann.

Monopolies and Mergers Commission (1983) *National Coal Board: A Report on the Efficiency and Costs in the Development, Production and Supply of Coal by the NCB*, London: HMSO.

Moore, R. (1975), 'Religion as a Source of Variation in Working Class Images of Society' in M. Bulmer (ed.), *Working Class Images of Society*, London: Routledge & Kegan Paul.

National Board for Prices and Incomes (1968), Report No. 65 (Supplement Payment by Results Systems), London: HMSO.

National Coal Board (1984 to 1986), *Report and Accounts*, London: NCB.

National Union of Mineworkers (1986), 'Memorandum', *House of Commons Energy Committee, Session 1985–1986, The Coal Industry,* London: HMSO.

Nichols, Theo. (1986), *The British Worker Question: A New Look at Workers and Productivity in Manufacturing*, London: Routledge & Kegan Paul.

——and Armstrong, P. (1976) *Workers Divided*, Glasgow: Fontana.

——and Beynon, H. (1977) *Living with Capitalism*, London: Routledge & Kegan Paul.

Nolan, P., and Edwards, P. (1984), 'Homogenise, Divide and Rule', *Cambridge Journal of Economics*, 8.

Offe, C., and Wiesenthal, H. (1985), 'Two Logics of Collective Action' in C. Offe, (ed.), *Disorganised Capitalism*, Cambridge: Polity Press.

Parker, T. (1986), *Red Hill: A Mining Community*, London: Heinemann.

Pettigrew, A. (1973), *The Politics of Organisational Decision-Making*, London: Tavistock.

Pitt, M. (1979), *The World On Our Backs*. London: Lawrence and Wishart.

Pizzorno, A. (1978), 'Political Exchange and Collective Identity in Industrial Conflict' in C. Crouch, and A. Pizzorno, (eds.), *The Resurgence of Class Conflict in Western Europe Since 1968*, London: Macmillan.

Poole, M. (1976), 'A Power Analysis of Workplace Labour Relations', *Industrial Relations Journal*, 7.

Pratten, F. (1976), *Labour Productivity Differentials within International Companies*, Cambridge: Cambridge University Press.

Pryke, R. (1981), *The Nationalised Industries*, Oxford: Martin Robertson.

Purcell, J. (1981), *Good Industrial Relations*, London: Macmillan.

——(1983), 'The Management of Industrial Relations in the Modern Corporation: Agenda for Research', *British Journal of Industrial Relations*, 21/1.

——and Sisson, K. (1983), 'Strategies and Practice in the Management of Industrial Relations', in G. S. Bain, (ed.), *Industrial Relations in Britain*, Oxford: Basil Blackwell.

Ramsay, H. (1977), 'Cycles of Control: Worker Participation in Sociological and Historical Perspective', *Sociology*, 11/3.

——(1980), 'Phantom Participation: Patterns of Power and Conflict', *Industrial Relations Journal*, 11/3.

Rose, M., and Jones, B. (1985), 'Managerial Strategy and Trade Union Responses in Work Reorganisation Schemes at Establishment Level' in D. Knights, D. Collinson, and H. Willmott (eds.), *Job Redesign: Organisation and Control of the Labour Process*, Aldershot: Gower.

Salaman, G. (1974), *Community and Occupation*, Glasgow: Fontana.

Samuel, R., Bloomfield, B., and Boanas, G. (1986), *The Enemy Within: Pit Villages and the Miners' Strike of 1984/5*, London: Routledge.

Scargill, A., and Khan, P. (1980), 'The Myth of Workers' Control', Occasional Papers in Industrial Relations, Universities of Leeds and Nottingham.

Searle-Barnes, R. C. (1969), *Pay and Productivity Bargaining: A Study of National Wage Agreements in the Nottinghamshire Coalfield*, Manchester: Manchester University Press.

Shafto, Tony (1983), 'The Growth of Shop Steward Management Functions' in K. Thurley, and S. Wood, *Industrial Relations and Managerial Strategy*, Cambridge: Cambridge University Press.

Spinrad, W. (1960), 'Correlates of Trade Union Participation: A Summary of the Literature', *American Sociological Review*, 25.

Stagner, R. (1953), 'Dual Loyalty in Modern Society', *Monthly Labour Review*, 76.

Storey, J. (1980), *The Challenge to Management Control*, London: Kogan Page.

Streeck, W. (1987), 'The Uncertainties of Management in the Management of Uncertainty: Employers, Labour Relations and Industrial Adjustment in the 1980s', *Work, Employment and Society*, 1/3.

Strinati, D. (1982), *Capitalism, The State and Industrial Relations*, London: Croom Helm.

Sutherland, I. (1985), 'The Sacked Miners of Scotland; *New Society*, 5 July.

Tagliacozza, D., and Seidman, J. (1966), 'A Typology of Rank and File Union Members', *American Journal of Sociology*, 61.

Taylor, A. (1984), *The Politics of the Yorkshire Miners*, London: Croom Helm.

Terry, M. (1977), 'The Inevitable Growth of Informality', *British Journal of Industrial Relations*, 15/1.

——(1979), 'The Emergence of a Lay Elite?', *Sociologie du Travail*, 31.

(1983a), 'Shop Steward Development and Management Strategies' in G. S. Bain, (ed.) *Industrial Relations in Britain*, Oxford: Basil Blackwell.

(1983b), 'Shop Stewards through Expansion and Recession', *Industrial Relations Journal*, 14/3.

Terry, M. (1986), 'How do We Know if Shop Stewards are Getting Weaker?', *British Journal of Industrial Relations*, 14/2.

Thomas, D. (1983), 'The New Coalminers', *New Society*, 12 May.

Thompson, P., and Bannon, E. (1985) *Working the System, The Shopfloor and New Technology*, London: Pluto Press.

Trist, E. L., and Bamforth, K. W. (1969), 'Technicism: Some Effects of Material Technology on Managerial Methods and on Work Situation and Relationships' in T. Burns, (ed.), *Industrial Man*, Harmondsworth: Penguin.

Turner, H. A., Roberts, G., and Roberts, D. (1977), *Management Characteristics and Labour Conflict*, Cambridge: Cambridge University Press.

Undy, R., and Martin, R. (1984), *Ballots and Trade Union Democracy*, Oxford: Basil Blackwell.

Waller, R. J. (1983), *The Dukeries Transformed: The Social and Political Development of a 20th Century Coalfield*, Oxford: Clarendon Press.

Weber, M. (1947), *The Theory of Social and Economic Organisation*, ed. Talcott Parsons, New York: The Free Press.

White, M. (1981), *Payment Systems in Britain*, Aldershot: Gower.

Wilkinson, B. (1983), *The Shopfloor Politics of New Technology*, London: Heinemann.

Willman, P. (1982), *Fairness, Collective Bargaining and Incomes Policy*, Oxford: Clarendon Press.

Wilsher, P., Macintyre, D., and Jones, M. (eds.) (1985), *Strike: Thatcher, Scargill and the Miners*, London: Coronet Books.

Wilson, D. C., Butler, R. J., Cray, D., Hickson, D. J., and Mallory, G. R. (1982), 'The Limits of Trade Union Power in Organisational Decision Making', *British Journal of Industrial Relations*, 10/3.

Winterton, J. (1985), 'Computerised Coal: New Technology in the Mines', in H. Beynon (ed.), *Digging Deeper: Issues in the Miners' Strike*, London: Verso.

Wright, E. O. (1984), 'Postscript' to L. Perrone, 'Positional Power, Strikes and Wages', *American Sociological Review*, 49/3.

Zald, M. (1962), 'Power Balance and Staff Conflict in Correctional Institutions', *Administrative Science Quarterly*, 7.

Zeitlin, J. (forthcoming), 'Rank and Filism in British Labour History: A Critique', *International Review of Social History*.

Appendix I

The Decision List Used in the Power Measure
(Decision Groups as in Figures 7.1–7.5)

Budgeting   Overtime budget
Manpower budget
Long-term Planning
Short-term planning   Short-term colliery development
Choosing new machinery
Deployment   Selection of face teams
Deployment of EBG and surface workers
Shift organization   Shift starting times
Which shift an individual is on
Promotions   Choosing potential deputies
Appointing managers at under-manager level and above
Welfare amenities   Welfare matters at the pit e.g. pit-head baths, canteen
    facilities
Running the miners' welfare
Discipline   Dismissals
Imposing disciplinary penalties
Safety   The regulation of safety in the mine
Work organization   Allocating jobs between members of the face team
Overtime Allocation   Distribution of overtime
Fixing standards   Deciding what the standard should be
Deciding when a standard should be renegotiated
Deciding whether or not to use an actual method study to aid in fixing the standard
Incentive procedures   What should count as a random interruption
Booking men off an installation so their shift does not count in the calculation of
    bonus
Deciding when an installation is non-measurable and suspending the agreement
Redundancy selection   Which men should take voluntary redundancy
Subcontractors   Whether or not subcontractors should be allowed to work in
    the pit, e.g. on development work
Recruitment

Appendix II

The Interview Schedule Used in the Power Measure

Introduction

I have here a list of some of the major decisions which are made in a colliery, what we want to know is what part you play in making these decisions, how important it is to you to get your own way, and how much influence you feel you actually have over decisions of this kind.

1. Firstly, can you tell me who generally selects the men for face-teams in this colliery?
   - (0) This is decided by the chargeman alone.
   - (1) This is decided by the NUM and the chargeman.
   - (2) This is decided by the union alone.
   - (3) Decided mainly by the union.
   - (4) Decided jointly by the union and management.
   - (5) Decided mainly by the management.
   - (6) Decided by colliery management alone.
   - (7) Decided by management with area management.
   - (8) Area management alone.
   - (NB 'Area management' refers to production manager upwards.)

2. How much influence do you usually have on what actually happens?
   - (5) Get your own way completely.
   - (4) Have a great deal of influence.
   - (3) A moderate amount.
   - (2) Some.
   - (1) Very little.
   - (0) None at all.
   - (2) Varies.
   - If none at all, ask:
3. Have you ever tried to influence decisions of this kind?
   - (0) Yes.
   - (1) No.

4. NB For managers and NUM management
How much influence do the NUM lodge officials usually have on what actually happens?
(5) Get their own way completely.
(4) They have a great deal of influence.
(3) They have a moderate amount of influence.
(2) They have some influence.
(1) They have very little influence.
(0) They have no influence at all.

5. Although you may take the views of the management/union into account, how important is it for you to get your own way on what happens? (Obviously many of the decisions that are made are important but we want you to distinguish between those which are crucially important, those which are very important and those which are just important, quite important or not important at all.)
(4) Crucially important.
(3) Very important.
(2) Important.
(1) Quite important.
(0) Not very, not important.

6. How often do decisions of this kind come up?
(8) Daily.
(7) At least once a week.
(6) At least once a fortnight.
(5) At least once a month.
(4) At least once every three months.
(3) At least once every six months.
(2) At least once a year.
(1) Less than once a year.
(0) Never.

7. When decisions of this kind come up, how often do your objectives differ from those of the manager/union, i.e. how often do you want one thing and the manager/union want another?
(5) Always.
(4) Very often.
(3) Fairly often.
(2) Sometimes.
(1) Rarely.
(0) Never.

8. When your objectives differ what percentage of the time do you get your own way?
   (5) 100%.
   (4) Over 75% of the time.
   (3) Between 50–75% of the time.
   (2) Between 25–49% of the time.
   (1) Under 25% of the time.
   (0) Never.

Notes

1. Administered separately to Colliery Managers and a representative of the NUM branch, usually the branch secretary.
2. The list of decisions used in the interviews are shown in Appendix I.
3. Cards with the range of responses to questions 1–8 were handed to respondents.

INDEX

Adeney, M. 200, 201
Advisory, Conciliation and Arbitration
  Service 25
Allen, V. L. 177, 219
ancillary workers 40, 48
area managers
  and colliery industrial relations 13, 14,
    73, 80, 91, 98, 186, 187, 232
  and Ian MacGregor 15
  and NUM 156, 179
  and productivity 36
Area Method Study Department 77
  see also work study
area monitoring process 7, 74–5, 86–92,
  99, 101, 232, 253
  see also industrial relations managers
Areas (NCB)
  Barnsley 215
  North Derbyshire 47, 49, 55, 98,
    215–16
  North East 98, 129, 134, 182n., 215–16
  North Nottinghamshire 215
  North Yorkshire 98, 215
  Scotland 98, 134, 215, 228
  South Derbyshire 46n., 215, 230
  South Midlands 47, 215–16
  South Nottinghamshire 215
  South Wales 22, 36, 98, 129, 134, 201,
    215–16, 227
  South Yorkshire 56, 98, 176, 189, 208,
    210, 215
  Western 47, 55, 215
Armstrong, P. 148
attendance bonus 26, 49, 224
automation *see* new technology

Baldamus, W. 66, 78
Batstone, E. 63n., 64, 67, 102, 122,
  132–4, 150, 169, 179, 247–50, 255
Barber–Walker colliery company 27
Barnsley Area 215
Beecham, D. 110n., 113
Belgium 176
Benn, Tony 204n.
Beynon, H. 105, 109, 111, 113, 127n.,
  149

Bolsover colliery company 27
Boraston, I. 132, 134, 140
Bradford Group 5, 6, 51–7
branch officials (of NUM)
  accountability of 120–4, 143
  and Area union 139–42, 144
  and branch unity 126–9, 133–5
  and consultation 28, 169
  and consciousness 178–9, 189
  and decision-making 81, 152–70, 172,
    181–5, 192
  and organization 12, 115, 177–8, 190
  relations with management 3, 94, 102,
    116–20, 135–9, 143–4, 179–80,
    185–7, 190–1, 251
  and 1984–5 strike 214, 228
  and workplace bargaining 7, 72, 74, 83,
    88, 97, 98, 100, 168
  see also full-time officials; NUM; union
    power
Braverman, H. 57
briefing groups 2, 27, 55, 192
British Association of Colliery Management
  (BACM) 13, 37
British Leyland 114
British Rail 178, 218, 247, 248, 250
Brough, I. 183
Brown, W. 63, 64, 66, 69, 150
Bullock Report 36
bureaucratization thesis
  description of 105–115, 117, 119,
    126–7
  and mining 9, 120, 124, 135–44, 240
  see also lay elite; trade union
    bureaucracy

Cadeby colliery 222
Central Electricity Generating Board
  (CEGB) 210–11, 212
Central Planning Unit (CPU) 51, 53
chargemen 44–5, 122
Child, J., 23, 52n.
class struggle 107–9, 113, 115, 142–3,
  252
Clegg, H., 62, 140, 147, 168
clerical staff 74